Reading Hilary Mantel

Reading Hilary Mantel

Haunted Decades

Lucy Arnold

BLOOMSBURY ACADEMIC
LONDON • NEW YORK • OXFORD • NEW DELHI • SYDNEY

BLOOMSBURY ACADEMIC
Bloomsbury Publishing Plc
50 Bedford Square, London, WC1B 3DP, UK
1385 Broadway, New York, NY 10018, USA
29 Earlsfort Terrace, Dublin 2, Ireland

BLOOMSBURY, BLOOMSBURY ACADEMIC and the Diana logo are trademarks of Bloomsbury Publishing Plc

First published in Great Britain 2020
This paperback edition published in 2021

Copyright © Lucy Arnold, 2020

Lucy Arnold has asserted her right under the Copyright, Designs and Patents Act, 1988, to be identified as Author of this work.

For legal purposes the Acknowledgements on p. viii constitute an extension of this copyright page.

Cover design: Eleanor Rose
Cover image © Alamy

All rights reserved. No part of this publication may be reproduced or transmitted in any form or by any means, electronic or mechanical, including photocopying, recording, or any information storage or retrieval system, without prior permission in writing from the publishers.

Bloomsbury Publishing Plc does not have any control over, or responsibility for, any third-party websites referred to or in this book. All internet addresses given in this book were correct at the time of going to press. The author and publisher regret any inconvenience caused if addresses have changed or sites have ceased to exist, but can accept no responsibility for any such changes.

A catalogue record for this book is available from the British Library.

A catalog record for this book is available from the Library of Congress.

ISBN: HB: 978-1-3500-7255-8
PB: 978-1-3502-3449-9
ePDF: 978-1-3500-7256-5
eBook: 978-1-3500-7257-2

Typeset by Deanta Global Publishing Services, Chennai, India

To find out more about our authors and books visit www.bloomsbury.com and sign up for our newsletters.

One need not be a Chamber – to be Haunted
One need not be a House –
The Brain has Corridors – surpassing
Material Place –

            Emily Dickinson

For my parents, who told me stories.
For E.T., who listened to mine.

Contents

Acknowledgements	viii
Introduction	1
1 Not *Giving up the Ghost*: Preserving the spectral in Mantel's memoir	13
2 Spectres of Margaret: Thatcherism, care-giving and the gothic in *Every Day is Mother's Day* and *Vacant Possession*	43
3 Spooks and holy ghosts: Spectral politics and the politics of spectrality in *Eight Months on Ghazzah Street*	83
4 The princess and the palimpsest: Skin, screen and spectre in *Beyond Black*	109
5 'If the dead need translators': Heresy, haunting and intertextuality in *Wolf Hall*	145
Afterword	179
Notes	185
Bibliography	217
Index	228

Acknowledgements

This book would not have been possible without the generosity of Hilary Mantel, whose support of the project and key contributions have been invaluable. I would like to thank Nick Ray, a colleague and friend who has seen this project through from its earliest conception to the present day and whose careful and perceptive reading made me a better writer, and whose kindness and intellectual support made me a better thinker. Thank you to my colleagues at the University of Worcester and former colleagues at the University of Leeds who created the special and productive environment in which this project took shape and whose guidance and support, both professional and personal, helped to make this book what it is: Jane Rickard, John McLeod, Julia Reid, Bridget Bennett and Alaric Hall. I would like to thank my students for their energetic engagement with what I brought to the table, energy which drove and shaped this project in innumerable ways.

I am extremely grateful to David Avital at Bloomsbury Academic for contracting the book early on in the process and for his support and enthusiasm for the project. I would also like to thank my assistant editor, Lucy Brown, and her predecessor, Clara Herberg for the patience and kindness with which they have guided me through this process.

I am indebted to the Huntington Library for the generous research fellowship that facilitated the archival research which has shaped this project. I was fortunate to have the opportunity to present material relating to the subject matter of this book which was invaluable in helping me to shape my ideas. For this, I would like to thank Nina Roland and the *Skepsi* team (University of Kent), Danỳ van Dam (University of Amsterdam), and Eileen Pollard and Ginette Carpenter (Manchester Metropolitan University). Earlier versions of this research were published as 'Spooks and holy ghosts: Spectral Politics and the Politics of Spectrality in Hilary Mantel's 'Eight Months on Ghazzah Street', *Critique: Studies in Contemporary Fiction* 57, no. 3 (2016), 294–309 and 'Holy Ghost Writers: Spectrality, Intertextuality and Religion in *Wolf Hall* and *Fludd*' in *Hilary Mantel: Contemporary Critical Perspectives*, ed. by Eileen Pollard and Ginette Carpenter (London: Bloomsbury, 2018), pp. 117–32. My thanks to the editors involved for permission to use that work here. My thanks also to Harvard

University Press and to the Margaret Thatcher Estate for their kind permission to reproduce their material here.

Finally my thanks to my family who have been haunted by this book throughout the long process of its production. Thank you to my sister Alice, and my brother Joe, whose irreverent cheerleading throughout this book's evolution has been unwavering. Thank you to my parents, Karen and Andrew, who taught me the power of stories in the first place and whose tireless belief in my work has been a source of immense strength. And thank you to my partner Edd, without whose love, patience and ferocious belief in me this book wouldn't exist at all. This book is for them.

The third-party copyrighted material displayed in the pages of this book are done so on the basis of 'fair dealing for the purposes of criticism and review' or 'fair use for the purposes of teaching, criticism, scholarship or research' only in accordance with international copyright laws, and is not intended to infringe upon the ownership rights of the original owners.

Introduction

'I think, the ghost has ... become the basic metaphor for me.'

– Hilary Mantel

In a 2005 essay, Hilary Mantel states, 'one of my first ambitions was to write an effective ghost story'[1] and from her earliest writings to her most recent publications, this ambition has been repeatedly achieved. Mantel is a writer who recognizes the power of haunting. The novels which comprise her debut duology – *Every Day is Mother's Day* (1985) and *Vacant Possession* (1986) – deploy a wealth of spectres within a quasi-gothic framework to explore the politics of care-giving in the Thatcherite Britain of the 1970s and 1980s. Her memoir hosts familial ghosts haunting mid-twentieth-century Derbyshire, ghosts who gesture back beyond wartime deprivation and forward to the ambivalent possibilities of the 1960s. *A Place of Greater Safety* (1992), the first novel Mantel produced, is peopled by revolutionary revenants of the 1780s and 1790s while more recently her Booker Prize winning works *Wolf Hall* (2009) and *Bring up the Bodies* (2012) reanimate the Tudor dead; their 'skulls [are] tumbled from their shrouds, and words like stones [are] thrust into their rattling mouths'.[2]

The epigraph for this introduction is taken from an interview I carried out with Mantel in 2015.[3] It provides a useful critical formulation for the essential argument of this book, that is, that spectrality and the motif of the ghost preoccupy Mantel's work, both formally and textually. It is a preoccupation of which we must be mindful if the creative and ethical implications of her writing are to be fully apprehended. I analyse the situation of haunting in Mantel's work not simply in terms of its privileging of the unseen and immaterial but, as Avery F. Gordon puts it, as 'a very particular way of knowing what has happened or is happening'.[4] Mantel herself has asserted that 'ghost stories have to suit the age in which they are written'[5] and I argue that her corpus vividly dramatizes this assertion, accommodating the complexity and contradiction one would expect from a writer who, in her own words, is 'perhaps the only person who has simultaneously been head girl of her convent school and a member of the Young Communist League'.[6]

The trope of the ghost and the situation of haunting form highly plastic and overdetermined figures in Mantel's writing, figures whose inflections and implications are broad ranging and have evolved continually throughout her career in order to offer responses to a series of concerns arising from shifting social, political and cultural contexts. Her use of the ghostly and the spectral is not a self-contained phenomenon which renders a handful of her texts 'ghost stories' in a literal sense, but rather a 'dis-organizing principle' which suffuses the entire body of her work. Mantel recognizes the simultaneously revelatory and disruptive potential of the spectral as a mode of existence and exploits its ability to trouble the status quo and perform disturbing disclosures on multiple levels, disclosures which are as often opaque and enigmatic as they are clarificatory.

In Mantel's memoir *Giving up the Ghost*,[7] while providing one of many accounts of her autobiographical project's purpose, the memoir's speaker states that she is writing 'to locate [herself], if not within a body, then in the narrow space between one letter and the next, between the lines where the ghosts of meaning are' (p. 222). This quotation offers a striking synopsis of the concerns of this work, incubating the chiasmic questions 'where *are* the ghosts of meaning?' and 'what are the meanings of ghosts?' even as it gestures towards a gap accommodating something which is neither present nor absent. Through interrogating those spaces in Mantel's writing which are occupied by that which is not fully manifest, and starting from a position of attempting to locate that which may ultimately resist definitive location, I ask what might become possible in the spaces occupied by such 'ghosts of meaning'. I question how these ghosts might manifest and what work they could be put to, even as their essential evasiveness is acknowledged and maintained. Ultimately, I establish that the spectral provides the intellectual and, crucially, the ethical impetus for Mantel's writing. Before outlining the path this study takes through Mantel's corpus it is necessary to define the terms on which this exploration of her work depends and to understand the distinctive nature of the Mantelian ghost.

The ghost, spectrality, the gothic: these terms underpin the project undertaken in this book, yet all three are inherently shifting and unstable concepts, imbricated yet not, as they are sometimes deployed, synonymous. Running concurrent to a problematic critical blending of these terms (a blending which Mantel herself employs within her writing) is a sense that the ghost has become ubiquitous within contemporary critical terminology following the so-called spectral turn of the 1990s.[8] The 'spectral turn' saw the figure of the ghost taken up as 'an analytical tool that *does* theory'[9] and the language of the spectral adopted widely within the social sciences and the humanities as a critical vocabulary. This adoption has not been unproblematic and has led to what some critics have termed 'rather cyclical, if not overstretched, interpretations of the uses, meanings, and possibilities of haunting'.[10] In unpicking the nature of the instability built into these terms, I seek to clarify how Mantel knowingly exploits the slippages and associations between them while also maintaining a sense of their singularity, a strategy which gives her evolving use of the figure of the ghost and the situation of haunting its power. This clarification leads to an understanding of her statement that the ghost forms 'the basic metaphor' within her writing as populating one side of a metaphorical equation, in which the ghost acts to stand in for myriad phenomena. The diversity of qualities and characteristics possessed by these phenomena renders the results of this 'basic metaphor' necessarily unpredictable and destabilizing, rather than indicative of a flattening ubiquity.

The concept of the ghost resists homogeneity. As Peeren and del Pilar Blanco put it: 'their representational and socio-cultural functions, meanings, and effects [are] at least as manifold as their shapes – or non-shapes as the case may be'.[11] Certainly Mantel's corpus reflects this heterogeneity. While her work often features representations of the ghost as the manifestation of a dead subject returned to the realm of the living, as will be observed in *Beyond Black* and *Wolf Hall*, other works feature more nebulous phantoms, not possessed of subjective identities but nonetheless haunting presences granted a post-mortem existence. This class of ghost is most strikingly found in her debut duology, only partially contained behind the locked door to the spare room of an otherwise unremarkable detached house. Yet the circulation of the physically dead within the world of the living is only one variant of the Mantelian ghost. Mantel's memoir provides a striking explication of how she conceives of the ghost in a way which includes yet exceeds the post-mortem positioning of its traditional manifestations, her enlarged conceptualization of haunting encompassing instead a variety of liminal states. Early on in the text, the memoir's speaker states:

> when you turn and look back down the years, you glimpse the ghosts of other lives you might have led. All your houses are haunted by the person you might have been. The wraiths and phantoms creep under your carpets and between the warp and weft of your curtains, they lurk in wardrobes and lie flat under drawer-liners. You think of the children that you might have had but didn't. When the midwife says 'It's a boy,' where does the girl go? When you think you're pregnant

and you're not, what happens to the child that has already formed in your mind? You keep it filed in the drawer of your consciousness, like a short story that wouldn't work after the opening lines.[12]

As the text draws to a close, the speaker concludes: 'ghosts are the tags and rags of everyday life, information you acquire that you don't know what to do with, knowledge that you can't process; they're cards thrown out of your card index, blots on the page' (p. 233). These rich extracts indicate a series of key aspects of the Mantelian ghost. The first of these is that, for Mantel, ghosts can be generated by potentialities: decisions untaken, lives not lived or cut short. The second, related, aspect is that the realm of the ghost is decidedly not (solely) the realm of the dead, certainly not the realm of the dead human subject. Elsewhere in her writing media technologies, landscapes and objects take on a phantasmal existence or else act as facilitators of spectrality. As will become clear, in Mantel's work a ghost can also be formed by a textual extract; her corpus displays a self-conscious and idiosyncratic approach to intertextuality which renders her intertextual play a mode of haunting in itself. The third key facet of the Mantelian ghost is the way in which it delimits and makes accessible the spaces occupied by the 'blots on the page', the unknowable, the incomprehensible and the unavowable. Finally, one of the most significant variants of the Mantelian ghost is formed not of the dead, nor the inanimate, but of certain living individuals. Psychiatric patients, domestic servants, criminals, prostitutes, the homeless, and those individuals who have simply been erased from the historical record: all are represented within Mantel's work as socially ghosted, crucially denied the status of full subject and living being.

These social phantoms represent a point at which the Mantelian ghost engages with the spectral, a mode of existence predicated not on the division between pre- and post-mortem but between absence and presence, visibility and invisibility. This play with spectrality signals to the attentive reader the key characteristic of the Mantelian ghost, that is, its political nature. As she states, 'ghosts can be someone's decision … ghosts are not necessarily made ghosts by accident or misfortune. You can elect people ghosts by excluding them'.[13] In this statement the status of the Mantelian ghost as a profoundly political matter is confirmed and its ethical implications begin to crystalize. At this point it is necessary to clarify how the terms 'ghost' and 'spectre' are deployed in this study. The distinction between 'ghost' and 'spectre' is not a linguistic differentiation that Mantel makes, indeed, as is evidenced in the above passage, a plethora of terms for 'ghost' are used interchangeably in her work. Nonetheless, I make this critical distinction in order to remain responsive to the evolving and diverse nature of the Mantelian ghost and avoid the homogenizing impulse present in a significant body of post-'spectral-turn' criticism. In the following chapters the term 'ghost' is used to describe a phenomenon created through, or metaphorically invoking, persistence after biological death, though such ghosts in Mantel's work do not necessarily correspond to discrete human subjects (indeed various animals, body parts and objects also possess this kind of existence at certain points in her writing). Where 'spectre' and 'spectrality' are used, they concern a denial or lack of full presence (whether visual, auditory, legal or subjective) which is not predicated on biological death but may be generated by a range of factors including the closing down of historical and individual potentialities, political and social hegemonies or textual practice itself. These categories, while fruitful in terms of mapping the heterogeneity of haunting within Mantel's work, should also be acknowledged as fragile and imbricated, with existence in the mode of spectre having the potential to give way violently to existence in the ghostly mode.

The persistence of the figure of the ghost within Mantel's work has led to a critical debate which has contested the status of the gothic in her writing.[14] This debate is explored in detail in Chapter 2, however, it is pertinent at this point to clarify the position of this study with regard to Mantel and the gothic. Firstly, it is necessary to reiterate that while the literary gothic has, almost since its inception and certainly in its contemporary form, been closely allied with the trope of the ghost and with narratives of haunting, the presence of a ghost does not, in isolation, render a text gothic. More broadly, while the supernatural and the spectral have an affinity with the literary gothic, and often drive its narratives, they are not synonymous with the gothic mode and to use those terms as such robs them of their potency. In short, though Mantel's writing is rife with a host of ghosts and spectres, I reject the notion that her corpus can, or should, be characterized as gothic. This is not to say that the gothic is absent from Mantel's writing but rather that its presence in a selection of her works inflects rather than defines her canon. As the following chapters will make clear, she is a writer who understands the heterogeneity and nuance of the gothic, in particular its potential to generate debates which put at stake the political and ethical status quo, tapping into the gothic's ability to 'mediate between the uncanny and the unjust'.[15] In terms of this study, the Mantelian ghost is not a gothic trope by default. Nonetheless, when it makes an appearance in the context of one of Mantel's knowing deployments of the gothic, it necessarily takes on a different significance and the metaphors it is capable of accommodating subsequently shift.

Critical interventions

Mantel's privileging of the motif of the ghost and the situation of haunting engages with a proliferation of ghosts in works of cultural production since the 1990s. This trend, as is pointed out by Colin Davis, has been accompanied by a preoccupation among contemporary theorists and critics with the dead and the undead.[16] Before examining where Mantel's writing engages with this trend, not simply in terms of works of cultural production generally, but in the work of contemporary women novelists specifically, it is useful to briefly sketch the critical landscape against which Mantel's writing career has unfolded in order to posit the interventions in that landscape made by her work. As Roger Luckhurst puts it, 'a certain strand of cultural theory in France, Britain and America embraced a language of ghosts and the uncanny – or rather of anachronic spectrality and hauntology – following the publication of Jacques Derrida's *Spectres of Marx* in 1993 (translated into English in 1994)'.[17] A wealth of publications emerged in the wake of Derrida's text, and the apparent 'permission' it granted to scholars to 'deal with ghosts'.[18] While a great deal of valuable work is done by these texts,[19] Luckhurst's article is 'suspicious' of this spectral turn and what he terms its 'very generalized economy'.[20] He cites Derrida's exhortation in *Spectres* that 'it is necessary to introduce haunting into the very construction of a concept. Of every concept, beginning with the concepts of being and time. This is what we would be calling here a hauntology',[21] and goes on to argue that Derrida's statement has been read, particularly by literary critics, in a way which has robbed haunting, and the ghosts and spectres that give rise to it, of their political, social and geographical specificity. Ghosts and haunting become powerful, as Martin Jay puts it, 'per se' and 'as such', risking the elision of 'the precise content of *what* is repeated'.[22]

While Avery F. Gordon's 1997 book, *Ghostly Matters: Haunting and The Sociological Imagination*, certainly owes a debt to *Spectres*, Gordon is a theorist who firmly stresses the importance of the particularity of the ghost and its sociopolitical contexts. As she puts it, 'it is not a case of dead or missing persons *sui generis*, but of the ghost as a social figure ... a case of the haunting reminder of the complex social relations in which we live'.[23] In addition to asserting haunting as 'a constituent element of modern social life ... neither pre-modern superstition nor individual psychosis [but] a generalizable social phenomenon of great import',[24] Gordon's text argues for the ghost's ability to make revelatory interventions in the taken-for-granted fabric of everyday life and to make invisible things, however temporarily, visible. As Gordon puts it:

> The ghost is not simply a dead or missing person, but a social figure, and investigating it can lead to that dense site where history and subjectivity make social life. The ghost or apparition is one form by which something lost or barely visible, or seemingly not there to our supposedly well-trained eyes makes itself known or apparent to us.[25]

Crucial for understanding the status of Mantel's corpus as composed of 'ghost' stories is Gordon's insistence that 'that which appears absent can indeed be a seething presence'[26] and, furthermore, that it is from this position that ghost stories, stories about '*permissions and prohibitions, presence and absence,* about *apparitions and hysterical blindness*' are written.[27] Esther Peeren's monograph, *The Spectral Metaphor: Living Ghosts and the Agency of Invisibility* (2014), in many ways builds on and elaborates Gordon's work, positing the ethical and cultural repercussions of the notion that 'the ghost is a metaphor that certain people (are made to) live *as*, the cognitive and conceptual framework through which they are made sense of and come to make sense of themselves'.[28] It is with these psychoanalytically freighted yet sociopolitically conscious theories of the forms, functions and meanings of ghosts in contemporary culture that Mantel's work resonates, sharing with such critical thought an understanding of the ghost and spectre as metaphors for, among other phenomena, a number of marginalized and occluded groups whose status as living subjects has been devastatingly undermined. As such, my reading of Mantel's work as predicated on a plastic and evolving understanding of the ghost and the situation of haunting begins to address not only the critical silence around contemporary narratives of haunting but proposes how such narratives might fruitfully be delineated in a more flexible way.

It is also important to note that Mantel's narratives of haunting form part of a wider trend in contemporary women's writing, in which the 'ghost story', in a variety of forms, has proliferated since the 1980s. Though the beginnings of this proliferation are antecedent to the spectral turn, the growing number of narratives of haunting authored by women anticipates, and runs parallel to, the contemporary critical preoccupation with the ghost. Susan Hill's *The Woman in Black* (1983) is arguably one of the earliest manifestations of this trend, with Clive Bloom describing it as 'Gothic horror revival'.[29] Published four years later, Toni Morrison's *Beloved* is perhaps best known for putting the trope of the ghost to work to communicate the traumatic and enduring legacies of the Atlantic slave trade. The 1990s saw the publication of Alison Lurie's short story collection *Women and Ghosts* (1994), and Margaret Atwood's *Alias Grace* (1996) which blended the crime fiction genre with that of the ghost story.

The turn of the millennium brought a faster growth in examples of the genre, which, like Atwood's book, frequently blended the narrative of haunting with a number of other genres. Prominent examples include Sarah Waters' neo-historical novels *Affinity* (1999) and *The Little Stranger* (2009) and Michelle Paver's Arctic narrative, *Dark Matter* (2010). For the sake of brevity only a handful of examples are given here. Nonetheless, it is clear that Mantel's position as a writer of narratives of haunting connects her work to a cultural trend in which the 'ghost story' is reiterated and reworked to myriad different ends.

Key thinkers

While this study deploys a flexible approach to the use of critical and theoretical voices, seeking always to yield to Mantel's texts rather than force them to adhere to any theoretical framework, the nuance and complexity of her fiction does necessitate a rigorous and thoughtful deployment of theoretical material capable of receiving and maintaining its difficulty and multiplicity. When I questioned Mantel on a possible relationship between her work and psychoanalytic thought, she responded that 'it's not that I read psychoanalytic texts and used them to form my work; it's more that the texts gave form to what I intuited'.[30] It is this 'giving form' that the theory mobilized here seeks to achieve: the provision of a critical vocabulary through which the complexities and implications of Mantel's literary project can begin to be expressed and their nuances captured.

Appropriately given the heterogeneity of Mantel's fiction in terms of her experimentation with both style and genre, this book does not subscribe to a single school of theory or cultural criticism but rather draws upon a range of thinkers whose work, while not united by critical genealogy or disciplinarity, shares an ability to accommodate the diversity and overdetermination present in Mantel's writing. My choice of critical voices is born out of the varied demands made by each of the texts under discussion and the need to establish a critical vocabulary capable of responding to the multiple thematic, political and contextual preoccupations of those texts. Key thinkers whose work shapes the following readings include psychoanalysts Jean Laplanche and Jacques Lacan and philosophers Jacques Rancière, Jacques Derrida and Bernard Stiegler. While these thinkers may in some respects appear disparate, they have been selected for the ability of their thinking to privilege the boundary between the visible and invisible, sensible and insensible traversed by the ghost in movements which make licit its significance, and to think ontological disturbance, uncertainty and ambiguity. Ranciére's 'distribution of the sensible', Lacan's 'Big Other', Derrida's 'secret' and Stiegler's theory of technics are all on some level concerned with boundary phenomena (and, indeed, troubling the possibility of imposing and maintaining boundaries) in a way which makes them invaluable for understanding the heterogeneity and plasticity of the Mantelian ghost.

A host of ghosts: mapping Mantel's haunted canon

This book demonstrates the flexibility of the motif of the ghost and the situation of haunting within Mantel's work, establishing them as being capable of articulating responses to the various concerns emerging from a complex and shifting social and political landscape, a series of which forms the basis of the following five chapters. In Chapter 1 I read Mantel's memoir *Giving up the Ghost* (2003) alongside her collection of short fiction *Learning to Talk*, which was published in the same year. Taking as its catalyst the failure in journalistic and critical responses to Mantel's life-writing either to accommodate its complexity as a creative work or interrogate its relationship with the author's fiction, the chapter argues that *Giving up the Ghost*, far from being a straightforward literary memoir, actively interrogates the unstable and often paradoxical nature of life-writing. I illustrate how this interrogation takes place primarily through Mantel's construction of the text's spectral speaker who understands the work of the memoir as a will-to-presence through writing which is perpetually deferred. The spectrality of *Giving up the Ghost*'s central voice is supplemented by a series of formal and conceptual hauntings, each of which questions the status of the self, fiction, and authenticity in relation to the autobiographical project. I argue that these hauntings are orchestrated through Mantel's use of a specifically self-referential mode of intertextual play as a vehicle for questioning the possibility of a choate narrative of self, particularly with regard to *Learning to Talk* as contested intertext. Such hauntings are also created through the rendering of the physical body as precarious and unpredictable, and through a privileging of the secret and the unknowable within the life-narrative. Through my analysis of these creative gestures I produce a reading of *Giving up the Ghost* which is predicated on preserving rather than exorcising the text's haunting elements. In doing so I demonstrate its demand for an understanding of life-writing not as manifesting an integrated, stable self but as testifying to a story of self which is fabricated, contingent and partial yet nonetheless valuable, a story of self which is, as Mantel puts it, 'complete with the missing bits'.[31]

In Chapter 2 I deal directly with Mantel's fiction, namely her debut duology which traces the lives of two West Midland families over the course of the late 1970s and 1980s. Alongside *Beyond Black*, these novels offer some of Mantel's most overt engagements with the supernatural and, I argue, make knowing use of the tropes of the gothic while nevertheless subverting and exceeding them. Highlighting the anxiety circulating around the regulation of the domestic space and the family unit which is common to both early gothic texts and the political landscape of Britain in the 1970s and 1980s, this chapter argues that Mantel utilizes the gothic in order to articulate how, under Margaret Thatcher's Conservative government, a number of care-giving frameworks were subject to a series of ruptures and collapses. I posit that it is from the site of those failures that the ghosts and spectres which haunt the texts emerge. My examination of familial, medical, psychiatric and social care in both texts reveals care-giving in the duology's fictionalized Thatcherite milieu to be a fragile and contested process. The haunting presences we encounter in these novels, produced by politically and socially generated breakdowns of care, attest to and articulate that fragility and in doing so, communicate the ethical imperatives which adhere to the provision of care, whether by the family or the State.

From an examination of State care as generating various ghosts and spectres, in Chapter 3 I broaden my analysis of the interactions between the political and the spectral through a reading of Mantel's novel *Eight Months on Ghazzah* Street (1988). Based on Mantel's own time living in Jeddah, the novel relates the experiences of Frances Shore as she struggles to adapt to life under Saudi Arabia's conservative Wahhabi regime. Through an engagement with philosopher Jacques Rancière's notion of dissensus and the division of the sensible, I argue that the novel's Saudi Arabian setting allows the complex and often paradoxical relationship between the political and the spectral to be made licit. My analysis of the representation of certain marginalized groups within the text foregrounds how the novel depicts politico-religious regimes as capable, directly and indirectly, of rendering certain living subjects spectral by denying them full political (and in some cases physical) presence. Conversely, I draw out the text's articulation of the relationship between agency and invisibility that grants political authority its potency through a consideration of the government 'spook' whose anonymity and imperceptibility facilitates rather than precludes political participation. With this paradox established, I go on to demonstrate the novel's simultaneous self-reflexivity. I articulate how the gothic is deployed in *Eight Months on Ghazzah Street* to illustrate the conflicts and tensions which arise from attempts to translate one culture into the idiom of another, positing the possibilities that emerge from the use of the gothic and the ghost in a non-Western milieu which accommodates neither.

Having demonstrated the existence in *Eight Months* of a host of spectres whose spectrality is not contingent on any post-mortem positioning, Chapter 4 examines one of Mantel's most striking deployments of the traditional ghost: her 2005 novel *Beyond Black* which centres upon the experiences of Alison Hart, a spiritualist medium working at the turn of the millennium. I argue that *Beyond Black* is concerned with the position of the ghost in a historical moment which is, at least in part, defined by its relationships with tele-technologies. By asking what relationship with the dead is on offer to those in the dormitory towns of England, and which modes of spectrality are made possible or, alternatively, rendered obsolete in this specific historical and geographic context, I demonstrate that the novel questions the very status of the ghost in the contemporary period. I posit that potential answers to these questions can be found in the interactions between the notions of skin, screen and spectre in the novel. Through an interrogation of a multitude of screens, composed of technologies, bodies and language, drawing out the texts inscribed upon them or which they themselves inscribe, it becomes clear that what this text ultimately communicates is the requirement of the ghost and the spectre for a surface upon or against which to manifest.

Progressing from an analysis of *Beyond Black* which dissects the contemporary relationship with history, Chapter 5 is concerned with *Wolf Hall* (2009), Mantel's first Tudor novel. These are texts which have themselves generated multiple conversations about the contemporary subject's relationship to the historical. I argue that *Wolf Hall* has, until now, been subject to a series of reductive reading strategies and reject those strategies in favour of an approach that privileges the novels' position as primarily a literary text whose project is both subtler and more expansive than previous critical viewpoints have allowed. Taking into account two key contextual details arising from the novel's setting within the upheavals of the Protestant Reformation – the explosion of print culture in England and on the continent and the abolition of Purgatory – I make licit the novels' meditation on textual practice, and on the ways in which the acts of reading and writing are subject to acts of haunting. Ultimately, I argue that *Wolf Hall* constitutes a text which displays a 'complex self-consciousness'[32] about writing itself through a dramatization of the linkages between textuality and spectrality.

Speaking of the poetry of Thomas Wyatt in *Bring up the Bodies* Mantel writes: 'his lines fledge feathers, and unfolding this plumage they dive below their meaning and skim above it. ... You close your hand as it flies away. A statute is written to entrap meaning, a poem to escape it.'[33] It is in this space, between entrapment and escape, that this book locates itself, seeking not to capture and constrain the meaning within Mantel's canon but to trace instead its spectral lines of flight. As I will make clear, to discern meaning in Mantel's writing is to encounter ghosts and spectres. It is with Mantel's memoir, where, alongside literary meaning, a host of other, more enigmatic 'phantoms [flap] and [churn] the air' (*Giving up the Ghost*, p. 99), that this exploration begins.

1

Not *Giving up the Ghost*: Preserving the spectral in Mantel's memoir

In exploring the primacy of the ghost and the situation of haunting to the work of Hilary Mantel, it is unsurprising that the critical gaze should be drawn in the first instance to the publication which seems most immediately and overtly to engage with these themes: her memoir *Giving up the Ghost* (2003).[1] However, this instinctive critical focus immediately raises a number of issues, falling as it does upon a text highly unusual in Mantel's oeuvre for its status as life-writing.[2] A self-declared memoir, *Giving up the Ghost* participates in a proliferation of autobiographical writing which has been gathering pace since the turn of the century.[3] Yet, despite a growing raft of subgenres, the terminology that life-writing has produced is far from clear and stable, even with regard to the terms 'memoir' and 'autobiography'. An examination of these instabilities is necessary if the work undertaken in *Giving up the Ghost* is to be properly contextualized.

Ben Yagoda's succinct history of the memoir form refutes the distinction between autobiography and memoir, instead using the terms to mean 'more or less the same thing: a book understood by its author, its publisher, and its readers to be a factual account of the author's life'.[4] Nevertheless, Yagoda traces the evolution of both terms and the historical oscillations between their definitions. To give just one example, Yagoda notes that, while in 1876 Gustave Vapereau asserted that 'autobiography leaves a lot of room for fantasy, and the one who is writing is not at all obliged to be exact about the facts, as in memoirs',[5] Gore Vidal's memoir, *Palimpsest* (1996), overturns Vapereau's definition and understands memoir as 'how one remembers one's own life, while an autobiography is history, requiring research, dates, facts, double-checked'.[6] Furthermore, in recent years the relationship between life-writing, such as memoir, and fictional forms, such as the novel, has been closely interrogated, generating the neologism of 'autobiografiction'. As Max Saunders puts it, 'however truthful or candid an autobiography might be judged, it is nonetheless a narrative, and shares its narrative features with fictional narratives'.[7] Memoir in particular is situated uniquely on the borderland between the fictional and the autobiographical, due to its etymological root in the French *mémoire* or 'memory'. As Yagoda points out:

> Memory is by nature untrustworthy: contaminated not merely by gaps, but by distortions and fabrications that inevitably and blamelessly creep into it. It is itself a creative writer, cobbling together 'actual' memories, beliefs about the world, cues from a variety of sources, and memories of *previous* memories to plausibly imagine what might have been, and then, in one master stroke, packaging this scenario in the mind as the real one.[8]

Thus, on the one hand memoir is positioned as 'a factual account of the author's life', yet on the other inherently resorts to narrative strategies common to fiction and is built upon inevitable fabrications, some conscious, for example, the generation of conversational material that would be impossible to recall verbatim, and some unconscious, undertaken even in the process of forming memories. Mantel herself acknowledges this model of memory, stating:

> When we talk about a memory we are not talking about a fixed entity, but about a process. A memory changes every time we recall it. A memory is a work in progress. It comes to us through our senses and as we perceive we create. And as we remember we re-create.[9]

It is necessary to ask, then, where *Giving up the Ghost* sits within the complex and often contradictory landscape of contemporary life-writing. Initial indications that the text exceeds the conventions of contemporary memoir are found in the way that *Giving up the Ghost* not only acknowledges its status as memoir but explicitly comments on the form. For example, in the first few pages the memoir's speaker states: 'I used to think that autobiography was a form of weakness, and perhaps I still do. But I also think that, if you're weak, it's childish to pretend to be strong' (p. 6). In terms of the speaker's own understanding of the work her memoir is to accomplish, and the book's status within her canon, the text appears initially to adhere to the conventional definition of what such a work seeks to achieve. Early on the speaker says of the text: 'this story can be told only once, and I need to get it right' (p. 5), before going on to describe the work as 'an attempt to seize the copyright in [her]self' (p. 71) and to relate how 'the story of my own childhood is a complicated sentence that I am always trying to finish, to finish and put behind me. It resists finishing, and partly this is because words are not enough' (p. 23). Read together these extracts appear to form a statement of intent, positioning the memoir as an exercise in completion, the generation of a whole and authentic self, claimable only by the speaker. Yet this intention is simultaneously undermined as the memoir acknowledges that such an exercise in completion can only ever be partial due to the insurmountable resistance offered by the insufficiency of language. The speaker goes on to warn that 'some deceptive sights are seen through glass, and the best liars tell lies in plain words' (p. 5), before asking 'is my writing clear: or is it deceptively clear?' (p. 5). This rhetorical question, with its compound destabilization in which the reader is asked to ascertain the presence of a clarity whose very transparency may be paradoxically misleading, is characteristic of the memoir's numerous double gestures.

Despite these provocations on the part of the memoir for reading strategies that exceed generic conventions and accommodate the text's multiple – perhaps undecidable – possibilities, critical responses to *Giving up the Ghost* have, for the most part, attempted to shut down the text's ambiguity and multiplicity. These responses are particularly apparent in readings of the ghostly presences which populate the text. A number of conventional ghosts can be found within the pages of the book, from the ghost of the speaker's stepfather, Jack, descending the stairs on the opening page to the ancestral dead 'peering at their place cards, and shuffling into their chairs' (p. 252) at the memoir's close. Yet to assume that the memoir's titular ghost corresponds with, and is circumscribed by, these traditional phantoms is to refuse the ambiguity of the text. This refusal is only one element of a constellation of naïve readings present in reviews of the memoir, which endeavour both to pin down the class of ghosts which haunt it, and then to exorcise those presences from the narrative or even allege that their exorcism is the project the narrative undertakes.

Early in the memoir the speaker recalls Margaret Atwood's assertion that 'the written word is so much like evidence – like something that can be used against you' (p. 6). This 'evidential' treatment of the memoir is the one that has most often been employed by reviewers of the text, who frequently and problematically conflate the author of the book and its speaker. Kathryn Hughes, writing in the *Guardian*, states that in *Giving up the Ghost* 'Mantel has booted out all of those shadowy presences that have jostled her all her life.'[10] In a review for the *New York Times*, Inga Clendinnen posits the possibility that a traumatic and mysterious encounter involving the young Hilary is simply 'a "realization" of vulgar Catholic teachings intensified by shame at the masked improprieties within her household.'[11] Marianne Brace, writing in the *Telegraph*, cannot resist the urge to begin her review (strikingly titled 'Hilary Mantel: The Exorcist'): 'when Hilary Mantel was seven she met the Devil,'[12] even if she does quickly back away from such a rigid interpretation of the memoir's account of a possibly supernatural encounter. The same cannot be said of the *New Yorker*'s blithe assertion that 'when the English novelist Hilary Mantel was seven years old, she saw the devil standing in the weeds beyond her back fence',[13] while a review in *Publisher's Weekly* insists that the text's 'first and foremost ghost ... is the baby [Mantel] will never have'.[14] This statement attempts to establish a linkage in the memoir between haunting and Mantel's experience of endometriosis and resulting infertility but does so in such a way as to delimit, crassly and reductively, the ghosts within the text. Perhaps understandably, given the impact the illness has had on Mantel, most recently documented in her e-book *Ink in the Blood,* critical writing on *Giving up the Ghost* specifically, and on Mantel more widely, has been preoccupied with the author's experience of endometriosis. The keenness to define and control the ghosts and apparitions in Mantel's memoir evidenced above, to render unambiguous those elements of the text which are most difficult, is paralleled in this preoccupation with her illness.

While reviews of the memoir have proliferated, academic work on the memoir is limited and much of it displays similarly problematic refusals of ambiguity and a susceptibility to unhelpfully reductive or clinically preoccupied readings. Amy Prodromou's chapter 'Writing the Self into Being: Illness and Identity in Inga Clendinnen's *Tiger's Eye* and Hilary Mantel's *Giving up the Ghost*'[15] defines Mantel's memoir as merely an account of illness, an 'autopathography'.[16] Such a definition has the effect of effacing the complexity of the work and allowing illness straightforwardly to dominate interpretation in the same way as it is represented within the text as dominating the speaker's life.[17] Alongside this issue sits a further problem: a lack of nuanced engagement with the relationship between Mantel's life-writing and her fiction. One of the only texts in which this is attempted is Sara Knox's article 'Giving Flesh to the "Wraiths of Violence": Super Realism in the Fiction of Hilary Mantel'.[18] Yet Knox's piece does not focus solely on *Giving up the Ghost*; the memoir is only invoked briefly as a point of origin for a moment in *Beyond Black*.[19] Clearly such a use of autobiography as origin for fiction is dubious, particularly in this case where the apparent reappearance of the moment, 'changed but still recognizable',[20] is uninterrogated and understood merely as evidence that 'the world of Mantel's fiction is not so very far from the world of her life.'[21]

In contrast to these critical responses, I argue that Mantel's memoir has been read naively, not only in terms of its operation within the crowded field of contemporary life-writing, but in terms of how the potentially supernatural elements of the text, including its titular 'ghost', have attracted a stubbornly literal critical approach. While *Giving up the Ghost*'s engagement with haunting at first glance seems glib and slight (exemplified by the humorous colloquialism of the memoir's title), privileging the spectral as a plastic yet principal mode within *Giving up the Ghost* allows the issues present in the critical approaches outlined above to be addressed. In opposition to these reductive reading strategies, this chapter demonstrates that *Giving up the Ghost* must be understood not as a straightforward literary memoir but as a conscious and complex response to the changing status of life-writing within the cultural sphere. The book mischievously references a number of subgenres which have proliferated in the field of life-writing, at various moments evoking the spiritual memoir, the memoir of illness and disability and, in one crucial passage, alluding to but dismissing the tropes of the 'misery memoir'.[22] This playful understanding of genre forms only part of *Giving up the Ghost*'s self-conscious engagement with memoir, however. In addition to telling *a* story of Mantel's life (and indeed a sincere and moving one), *Giving up the Ghost* openly works with the memoir's roots in memory, and the inherent flaws and fictions these roots bring with them, to make available a notion of memory as a 'creative writer', complicating and interrogating the contested boundary between autobiography and fiction.[23]

In addition to exposing the tense relationship between creativity and authenticity upon which memoir is predicated, playing out the 'irresolvable conflict between the capabilities of memory and the demands of narrative',[24] *Giving up the Ghost* is also an elegant exposition of the inextricable connection between the creation of narrative and the creation of self. If Saunders argues that 'autobiography does not transcribe a self that already exists', but rather is an 'act of narration that brings that self into being',[25] *Giving up the Ghost* chronicles a will to presence through writing which is perpetually deferred and disavows the possibility of a full and stable 'transcription' of such a presence. As Linda Anderson, paraphrasing Derrida, has put it, 'autobiography as a demand for unmediated selfhood is, it seems, doomed to reiterate itself endlessly as text.'[26] This deferral and disavowal renders the memoir's speaker a spectre in her own right, and *Giving up the Ghost* a ghost story in more ways than one.

In this chapter I propose an alternative mode of responding to the memoir's multitude of ghosts and spectres which understands the book's speaker as possessing a spectral existence. Furthermore, that spectral voice is augmented by and refracted through a variety of other hauntings, both thematic and contextual, whose disorganizing and destabilizing effects serve to question the status of life-writing as a project in producing a choate narrative while nonetheless emphasizing its ethical possibilities. From an exposition of the spectral status of *Giving up the Ghost*'s 'I' speaker, I interrogate how the memoir's intertextual materials form haunting structures that question the notion of a straightforward and uncontested personal identity. Continuing to think about what the complicated and 'undecidable' elements of *Giving up the Ghost* make possible, finally I look to how the memoir fosters a haunting secrecy that produces readings which are, like the speaker's narrative project, never complete and never stable. Rather than giving them up (whether by exposing, exorcising or debunking them), it is the preservation of ghosts, in all of their forms, that is crucial to this interpretation of Mantel's memoir.

A ghost, writing: the spectral speaker

The 'I' speaker of memoir occupies a slippery and contested place within the field of life-writing in which it makes a claim for authenticity and authority that is frequently problematic and precarious, a precarity which Mantel acknowledges, asking: 'having been so routinely plural, how can you become a mere one? Where is your self located? Where does "I" live?'[27] Working from Virginia Woolf's assertions about the speaker within autobiography, Pollard puts forward an apt conceptualization of the autobiographical 'I', particularly within *Giving up the Ghost*, as an artificial creation,[28] citing Woolf's definition of the 'I' as 'a convenient term for one who has no real being'.[29]

One of the crucial elements of Mantel's memoir that sets it apart from other contemporary literary examples of life-writing is the speaker's seeming acknowledgement of herself as such a one 'who has no real being'. If, as Shari Benstock puts it, (in the Lacanian style) '… autobiography is a fiction that conceals a lack',[30] in the case of *Giving up the Ghost* this lack is what the text on the one hand openly acknowledges and seeks to ameliorate and on the other preserves. On several occasions the speaker frames the work of the memoir as an act of writing herself into being, the crafting of a singular autobiographical narrative posited as an antidote to feelings of fragmentation and dispossession. She describes herself writing the memoir 'in order to take charge of the story of my childhood and my childlessness' (p. 222), seeking to 'seize the copyright in [herself]' to prevent '[her] parents … the child [she] once was, and … [her] own unborn children, stretching out their ghost fingers to grab the pen' (pp. 70–1). The idea of this narrative being the 'author-ized' version of the speaker's life is paired with a notion that writing this account can provide her with a coherent presence in a way that mere physicality has failed to. Speaking of her traumatic medical history, which involved several misdiagnoses, major surgical procedures and numerous drug regimens, Hilary states:

> I have been so mauled by medical procedures, so sabotaged and made over, so thin and so fat, that sometimes I feel that each morning it is necessary to write myself into being – even if that writing is aimless doodling that no one will ever read, or the diary that no one can see till I'm dead. When you have committed enough words to paper you feel you have a spine stiff enough to stand up in the wind. (pp. 222–3)

Yet, at every turn this will to presence through the act of writing is not only thwarted but its very possibility undermined by the speaker herself. The passage above concludes that 'when you stop writing you find that's *all* you are, a spine, a row of rattling vertebrae, dried out like an old quill pen' (p. 223, my italics) and the writing which is intended to perform reparations for the disruptive disintegrations brought about by her medical and familial history is constituted not only by the memoir but by material which goes unread or which, paradoxically, only becomes legible after the speaker's death. Rather than providing a definitive account, the work of the memoir is described as first deferred (as Hilary puts it, 'I have hesitated for such a long time before beginning this narrative' (p. 70)) and then perpetual. The speaker is 'always trying to finish' a work which 'resists finishing ... because words are not enough' (p. 23). Indeed, in its early pages the autobiographical project is described as almost Sisyphean: 'any style [of writing] you pick seems to unpick itself before a paragraph is done' (p. 4). The memoir's attempts to find stability and place among the 'ghost fingers' seeking to possess Hilary's life story, and the unpredictability of her own fluctuating and painful endometriotic body, ultimately locate themselves 'not within a body' but 'in the narrow space between one letter and the next, between the lines where the ghosts of meaning are' (p. 222).

On a number of occasions, the memoir's speaker situates herself not among the living but among ghosts, occupying their spaces and taking on their qualities. The alternative space in which Hilary seeks to manifest through writing ('between the lines', 'between one letter and the next') is in fact a haunted void, which does not communicate but rather accommodates the not-yet-formed and the not-yet-finished. It is also, as will be discussed at the close of this chapter, the place at which the 'ghosts of [her] own sense impressions' 're-emerge ... and shiver' (p. 23). Towards the close of the text Hilary asks, 'what's to be done with the lost, the dead, but write them into being?' (p. 231), implicitly placing herself in their company. Even in the text's less self-reflexive moments Hilary both claims for herself, and has allotted to her, the position of spectre. She tells of how she is cast as a ghost in Noël Coward's *Blithe Spirit* (p. 54), and relates how, after a childhood illness, her 'bullet-like presence, [her] solidity, has vanished. Ambiguity has thinned [her] bones, made [her] light and washed [her] out' (p. 57). Upon attending primary school she distinguishes herself from her peers stating: 'I knew, …, so many people who were old, so many people who were dead; I belonged to their company and lineage, not to this, and I began to want to re-join them' (p. 60). Yet if the work of the memoir places the speaker among a company of ghosts, this placement reverberates through the text. One of these reverberations is found in the memoir's critique of subjective identity, its formation, articulation and cohesion, a critique which is achieved through a series of complex and self-conscious intertextual interventions.

'Show your workings': identity and intertextuality

Giving up the Ghost not only meditates upon the author's experience of subjective identity and personal history as created, contingent and contested but posits that experience as being to some extent universal. Hilary states: 'There are other people who, like me, have had the roots of their personality torn up' (p. 222) and, in a significant passage towards the memoir's close, implicates the reader in the complex process of self-assembly resulting from such ruptures through her use of the second person:

> When you were a child you had to create yourself from whatever was to hand. You had to construct yourself and make yourself into a person, fitting somehow into the niche that in your family has been always vacant, or into a vacancy left by someone dead. Sometimes you looked towards a dead man's shoes, seeing how, in time, you would replace your grandmother, or her elder sister, or someone who no one really remembered but who ought to have been there: someone's miscarriage, someone's dead child. Much of what happened to you, in your early life, was constructed inside your head. … You had to listen at doors for information, or sometimes it was what you overheard; but just as often it was disinformation, or half a tale … How then can you create a narrative of your own life? (p. 223)

In this extract the process of self-formation is understood both as necessarily synthetic and predicated upon a complex series of hauntings in which the subject tries to occupy a space left by the dead but in so doing allows that dead ancestor a ghostly existence rather than claiming an individual identity and solid presence for itself. The hold the familial dead have over their living relatives, and the impossibilities of evading that grip, are fictionalized in Mantel's short story 'Destroyed' in which the narrator's mother insists that 'children should be named for themselves. They shouldn't be named for other people'[31] before nevertheless going on to choose 'George' as her new child's middle name, after her dead brother (p. 30). Significantly, the narrator observes that this middle name is intended as a secret: 'there was something else about the baby's name, something that was going to be hidden' (p. 29). This hiding of the dead in plain sight within the identities of the living is central to *Giving up the Ghost*. Yet the familial ghosts who haunt the memoir's speaker, by turns helping and hindering her struggle to form an account of her life, are paralleled by a series of formal hauntings. At the end of the passage quoted above Hilary invokes fellow writer Janet Frame's comparison of the creation of a life narrative to 'finding a bunch of old rags and trying to make a dress' (p. 223). Such 'rags', as discussed in my introduction, form a crucial element of Mantel's definition of the ghost as 'the tags and rags of everyday life' (p. 233). The memoir offers a self-conscious demonstration of the patchwork nature of a life-narrative through a complex deployment of ghostly intertextual 'rags' which, like the 'hidden' name discussed in 'Destroyed', frequently function if not invisibly then in partial occlusion. In doing so they assure the artificial quality of memoir and formally play out the blending of fiction and non-fiction on which life-writing depends.[32]

Before examining a series of intersections between Mantel's memoir and her fiction, I offer a reading of two intertextual moments within 'King Billy is a Gentleman', the opening story of *Learning to Talk*. An extensive exploration of the importance of intertextuality to Mantel's work and the specifics of her intertextual play can be found in Chapter 5's analysis of *Wolf Hall* and *Fludd*. However, where the intertextual ground in those novels serves to complicate and critique the notion of textual practice itself, the intertextual material present in *Giving up the Ghost* is of a different quality. Here it supplements the memoir's assertion of the ersatz nature of self and the narratives through which that self attempts to become present. Additionally, the memoir's external intertexts set up a resonance between Mantel's life-writing and her fiction and map out an intertextual strategy which is equally applicable to her use of self-quotation.

Prior to embarking on an examination of how *Giving up the Ghost* interacts with the rest of Mantel's canon, it is important to note that the author herself has described a specific relationship between her short fiction in particular and her own life, describing it as 'an attempt to address mysteries' and going on to state that 'a great deal of [the short fiction] is about childhood and puzzles left over from my childhood which I'm trying to work on in fiction.'[33] While this admission should not be taken as evidence for superficial readings of the short fiction as uncomplicated products of Mantel's biography, it is indicative of a need for sensitivity to the resonances which exist between *Giving up the Ghost* and *Learning to Talk* and the implications readings of the memoir might have for readings of the short fiction, and vice versa. This need also necessitates an understanding of the two texts as participating in what Derrida refers to as 'the possibility of literature ... that innocently plays at perverting all of [the] distinctions' between 'testimony ... fiction, simulacra, dissimulation, lie, and perjury'.[34] By attending to the intertextual play within and between these two texts, not only does Mantel's use of intertextuality here emerge as articulating the synthesized nature of the narrative of self, it also facilitates the identification of those moments where her writing troubles the distinctions between fiction and autobiography, 'calls [them] into question or causes them all to tremble'.[35]

Intertextuality in 'King Billy is a gentleman'

The intertextual ground present in Mantel's novels can also be observed in *Learning to Talk*. The collection contains stories published across a sixteen-year span (1987–2002) and all of them, to a greater or lesser extent, contain overt references to other texts. 'King Billy is a Gentleman' is a complex work, concerned in part with Irish nationalism and the narrator, Liam's, experience of living in England but being of Irish descent while simultaneously trying to make sense of a vexed and haunted childhood.[36] The story contains two notable intertextual references. The first is found in the phrase 'urban, squat and packed with guile', a quotation from Rupert Brooke's 'The Old Vicarage at Grantchester'[37] which the narrator uses to describe his mother's attitude towards Mancunians. The other is to W. B. Yeats's poem 'The Lake Isle of Innisfree'[38] whose line 'nine bean rows will I have there, a hive for the honey bee' is quoted in full with reference to the narrator's neighbour's garden. This example of two apparently offhand references (indeed the latter is so peripheral as to appear in parenthesis as a summary gesture intended to encapsulate a desire for a solitary idyll) and the ways in which they complicate the text has profound implications for our treatment of those other intertextual fragments drawn from Mantel's own work, specifically those that have roots within her autobiographical writing.

These implications become apparent when the authors of these intertexts are considered alongside each other.

Brooke is a poet in many ways defined by his Englishness and his Grantchester poem embodies a growing nostalgia for rural England in the early 1900s. A member of the British Navy killed in action in the First World War, Brooke became 'for the elite as well as the popular readership … a kind of receptacle for discourse on patriotism'.[39] As Alisa Miller puts it, 'the myth of Rupert Brooke, the nation's poet soldier, offered a simplified version of an ideal that much of England wanted to see and hear'.[40] Yeats on the other hand was an Irish nationalist and, in the words of Marjorie Howes, 'The Lake Isle of Innisfree' 'offers a speaker whose nostalgia for an idealized Ireland … will remain perpetually deferred'.[41] In his early career Yeats was a prominent member of the Irish Literary Revival and 'The Lake Isle' is an example of the work produced as part of that movement which sought to create poetry that was Irish in origin rather than adhering to English standards and traditions.[42] The embedding of Yeats and Brooke within 'King Billy is a Gentleman' enacts a covert playing out of the sectarian tensions which are explored in microcosm within the narrative and touched upon in *Giving up the Ghost*. Brooke and Yeats are quoted not in the context of an overt discussion of nationalism or nation, however, but incidentally, to facilitate laconic observations or doomed attempts at horticulture. Their political significance permeates the text secondarily, becoming apparent only when these poetic intertexts are closely interrogated. Thus, the voices of Brooke and Yeats perform another function in the story. Just prior to the moment in *Giving up the Ghost* when Hilary admits uncertainly, 'I used to be Irish but I'm not sure now', she states: '[a] question people pose is, How many beans make five?' (p. 36), echoing Yeats's bean rows. This echo indicates that the intertextual voices within the short story may speak to an individually felt tension between Englishness and Irishness, and by extension Protestantism and Catholicism, as much as a national one. Such a reading is supported by a twinning of two folk rhymes, one of which can be found in *Giving up the Ghost*, the other in 'King Billy'. In the memoir Hilary describes skipping with her great aunt and singing an extract from the Irish street ballad 'The Wearing of the Green' (p. 98), a traditionally Republican song. By contrast, the narrator of 'King Billy' endures his English neighbours singing the anti-Catholic, Unionist rhyme 'King Billy is a Gentleman' (p. 13).

The inclusion of Yeats and Brooke within 'King Billy' is not merely a wry intertextual opposition of English and Irish cultural positions. Rather, it plays out the uncertainty which characterizes the phrase 'I used to be Irish but I'm not sure now', a sentiment mirrored in Liam's characterization of himself as 'one of life's Provisionals' (p. 20), which emphasizes a sense of potentiality even as it references the Irish Republican Army. As the story progresses it becomes apparent that its intertexts produce tension rather than resolution. Yeats's own relationship with Irish nationalism was complex and mutable, continually evolving throughout his career.[43] Meanwhile, the section of 'The Wearing of the Green' that is quoted in *Giving up the Ghost* mentions James Napper Tandy, a Protestant who was also a member of the Catholic Republican organization 'The United Irishmen' and was far from an uncomplicated figure within the conflict. Likewise, the extract from 'The Old Vicarage at Grantchester' does not subscribe to a cliché of bucolic Englishness but rather dwells on negative traits, particularly a sly, cunning intelligence. No single conclusion can be drawn from this complex intertextual play. Rather it should be understood as a negotiation around self and identity which is never complete and never straightforward. Moreover, the discussions of Irishness which take place both in *Giving up the Ghost* and *Learning to Talk*, despite the phantasmal quality of their association, nevertheless form a tense intertextual network. The implications of Mantel's intertextual play in 'King Billy' resonate beyond that text to haunt the way Irishness can be read in the memoir, meaningfully recognizing Mantel's own acts of 'working through' and their significance for the work of *Giving up the Ghost*.

Mantel's canon is saturated with intertextual references to a vast range of material. However, in the critical responses to her work, very little comment has been made upon the relationship Mantel's texts might have to each other in terms of their containing acts of self-quotation. The significance of these self-quotations within the context of the literary memoir has been touched upon by Saunders. He sets apart the autobiographies of literary authors as differing in a number of crucial ways from other examples of the genre and understands the most significant of these differences to be the way that such writings have a specific intertextual relationship with the author's works of fiction.[44] He asserts that 'the form of intertextuality constitutive of literary autobiography is the relation between autobiography and the autobiographer's other texts' and as such these autobiographies are capable of 'play[ing] complex games with intertextuality and hybridity'.[45]

The tense and circuitous connections between memoir and fiction forged by Mantel's use of Yeats and Brooke in 'King Billy' are doubly haunting. Not only are the writers in question deceased, the quotations themselves are unmarked and thus their intertextual status spectrally wavers between visibility and invisibility. Bearing this in mind I turn now to analyse several moments in which Mantel uses her own work as spectral intertext. It is useful initially to sketch out the manifestations these textual spectres take, and to state their complex chronological relationship to each other. As with Mantel's approach to intertexts by other authors, it is possible to observe full and partial quotations as well as misquotations of material which bridge the memoir and the fictional texts. For example, in Mantel's 1989 novel *Fludd*, Catholic priest Father Angwin states of his congregation: 'these people are not Christians, they are heathens and Catholics' (*Fludd*, p. 22) and insists that 'the Bible [is] a Protestant book' (*Fludd*, p. 75). This construction re-emerges in *Giving up the Ghost*, though in this instance it is Hilary who recalls how 'my Grandmother thought you didn't want to be reading the Bible, she thought it was a Protestant book' (pp. 204–5) and claims 'I was brought up a Christian, in so far as a Catholic may be called' (p. 204). One of the most striking direct quotations to be found throughout Mantel's corpus concerns the distantly heard slammed door. The motif appears in a number of her novels, but a particularly strong correlation can be observed between *Giving up the Ghost* and *Fludd*:

> Somewhere in the house a door slams. (*Giving up the Ghost*, p. 86)
> Somewhere else in the house, a door slammed. (*Fludd*, p. 8)

Mantel's memoir is predated by all but four of her novels to date. As such, the works have a complex relationship to each other in terms of chronology as incidents in Mantel's early life are rendered in the memoir yet have in many cases already been subject to a fictionalizing transplantation prior to the memoir's publication. Present in these extracts is a disorientating doubling back and forth which gives certain references a predictive quality of which one is rightly suspicious. This doubling back also produces the kind of chronological disturbance associated with the ghost or spectre, whose apparitions bring the past into the present and threaten future return. The pair of quotations given above enact this problematic chronology through the subtle differences in their phrasing, the extract from the memoir remaining in the present tense while the extract from the novel 'relocates' the slamming door physically ('somewhere *else*') and temporally, placing the incident in the past tense. The fact of *Fludd*'s publication prior to *Giving up the Ghost* further disrupts any notion of linear temporality and negates the possibility of finding an 'originary text'. Yet the extracts also prompt a questioning of the effect such a relocation has upon the work an intertext can do within a narrative. Close examination of a number of enigmatic instances of haunting reveal the pressures and reverberations produced by Mantel's use of self-quotation to form a mode of haunting in their own right.

Giving up the Ghost features a compelling description of the apparent haunting of Brosscroft, one of Hilary's childhood homes. The fragmented account of this haunting takes place over sixty pages at the (dead) centre of the novel.[46] The inexplicability of the atmosphere at Brosscroft, and the concurrent search for explanations, is vocalized by Hilary's mother who is overheard apparently rebuking Hilary's stepfather for an unspecified theory regarding the events in the house: "'so? So what do you think it is?" Her voice rises, in an equal blend of challenge, fear and scorn. "What do you think it is? *Ghosts*?'" (p. 96). As is the nature of hauntings, these textual moments do not only appear once. However, unlike other potentially supernatural and ambiguous occurrences in the text, these (re)appearances are to be found in several of Mantel's short stories:

> We lived at the top of the village, in a house which I considered to be haunted. My father had disappeared. Perhaps it was his presence, long and pallid, which slid behind the door in sweeps of draught and raised the heckles on the terrier's neck. ('King Billy is a Gentleman', p. 2)
>
> The puppies had a pretty good life, except at night when the ghosts that lived in our house came out of the stone-floored pantry, and down from the big cupboard to the left of the chimney breast. Depend upon it, they were not dripping or ladies or genteel … These were ghosts with filed teeth. You couldn't see them, but you could sense their presence when you saw the dogs' bristling necks, and saw the shudders run down their backbones. ('Destroyed', pp. 27–8)
>
> I think I see someone turning the corner, down the corridor to the bedroom where my father Henry now sleeps in a single bed. (*Giving up the Ghost*, p. 86)
>
> The dogs, who are no longer puppies, squeal with fear in the night. My mother comes down to them, shivering in her nightdress, and sees their hackles raised, their thin forms shrinking against the dawn light. (*Giving up the Ghost*, p. 96)
>
> I went into the dim pantry with the deep stone shelves. The ghosts rolled under them, sucking their teeth in envy and malice. (*Giving up the Ghost*, p. 120)

The relationships among these extracts, given here in order of publication, are complex and without quoting at unmanageable length the nuance of their interconnection is difficult to convey. Nonetheless, an examination of their particular points of contact demonstrates how the texts refuse the possibility of a straightforward relationship between Mantel's biography and her work. Taking the image of the dogs, terrified by invisible presences, as a starting point, it is clear that these incidents mirror each other in various ways. Yet, just as the differences in tense present in the 'slamming door' quotations enacted the temporal disturbances produced by the complex relationship between Mantel's fiction and her memoir, the transformation from grown dog to puppyhood and back to maturity rejects the notion of an original from which other textual manifestations emerge. Secondly, the resonances on the level of language that are produced when the three passages are read together contribute to a sense of simultaneity. This is particularly apparent in the descriptions of the ghosts and their dwelling places. The emphasis on the teeth of the phantoms is common to both the memoir and the short fiction, as are the descriptions of the stony space of the pantry and the deep recesses from which the ghosts emerge (the 'deep stone shelves' and 'big cupboard' on the sinister 'left' of the chimney breast).[47] From the dogs frightened by supernatural forces to the stony pantry, with the images of the flat stones evoking grave markers, there is an implication that these domestic spooks somehow haunt the same house, are the same ghosts. Yet we should be suspicious of such a reading; material from one text may appear the same when relocated but the effects that material will produce may be radically different.

As Hilary's mother's frightened and indignant questioning makes clear, the presences that trouble the Brosscroft house in *Giving up the Ghost* prompt a desire for definitive interpretation while simultaneously refusing any such gesture. Indeed, even this desire is compromised by a desire *not to know* and *not to speak*, as Hilary reports how she is 'not supposed to overhear' about the fear experienced by a workman in the house (p. 86) and recalls that her mother's attribution of the household disturbances to ghosts 'speaks [her] thoughts: which [she] thought were unspeakable' (p. 96). Hilary speculates that her smallest brother cries in the night owing to the 'shady inhabitants' of their 'new upstairs' whose 'strange shape[s] pass against the curtains and the street lamp' (p. 68) and describes the rooms of her new home as having 'filled silently with unseen, hostile observers' (p. 81). These amorphous 'strange' and 'shady' presences also manifest as uninterpretable scraps and traces, they 'discharge from the burnt walls in puffs, they are scraped into slivers as the old wallpaper peels away, and lie curled on the floors, mocking the bristle brush' (p. 96). To assign these phenomena either the status of supernatural tenants (of the kind which, as will be discussed in Chapter 2, haunt the protagonists of *Every Day is Mother's Day* and *Vacant Possession*), or manifestations of familial trauma, is to prevent them from functioning in the way that the text demands; that is, as unresolvably enigmatic to both the adults and children present. Yet the (re)appearance of these phantoms in 'Destroyed' and 'King Billy is a Gentleman', both fictional tales, simultaneously places them upon a spectrum of literary ghosts. The relationship between the Brosscroft presences and their fictional counterparts demands that the reader broaden their understanding of haunting to accommodate not merely the ghostly presence of the dead returned to life but that which haunts by virtue of its unknowable, undecidable quality.

The secret garden: cultivating enigma

'To let a sad thought or a bad one get into your mind is as dangerous as letting a scarlet fever germ get into your body. If you let it stay there after it has got in you may never get over it as long as you live.'

The Secret Garden, Frances Hodgson Burnett

Thus far this chapter has established *Giving up the Ghost* as being narrated by a spectral voice whose attempts to tell a life narrative, and through that telling be granted secure subjective presence, are supplemented by a variety of hauntings, both familial and intertextual, which serve to make licit the instability and hybridity of narratives of self. Yet, the most critiqued moment of the memoir, the so-called secret garden incident (*Giving up the Ghost*, pp. 105–8), does not rely on supplementation. Rather it centres upon an unnegotiable void which is as haunting as it is destabilizing. An analysis of this incident establishes it not as an anomaly within the series of disorganizing hauntings examined thus far but as a provocation for a reading strategy as perpetual and undecidable as the speaker's project of self-narration. The passage in question relates Hilary's childhood encounter with an apparently malevolent presence which defies description. The encounter has an indelible effect on the memoir's speaker who states that it 'wrapped a strangling hand around [her] life' (p. 106). As demonstrated in the introduction to this chapter, the majority of critical responses to the text crystallize around this moment in a reductive manner, either proffering a lay medical or psychological diagnosis of the incident, or else identifying the presence in the garden as a ghost or devil without attempting to analyse the implications of that identification for how the text might be read. In opposition to these responses I offer a reading which, rather than cloaking the incident with a simplistic supernatural gloss, privileges the moment's defining 'secrecy'.

The centre of this profoundly enigmatic passage is provided by a being which is defined primarily through the ways in which it exceeds physical presence:

I am seven, and I am in the yard at Brosscroft; I am playing near the house, near the back door. Something makes me look up: some shift of the light. My eyes are drawn to a spot beyond the yard, beyond its gate, in the long garden. It is, let us say, some fifty yards away, among coarse grass, weeds and bracken. I can't see anything, not exactly see: except the faintest movement, a ripple, a disturbance of the air. I can sense a spiral, a lazy buzzing swirl, like flies; but it is not flies. There is nothing to see. There is nothing to smell. There is nothing to hear. But its motion, its insolent shift, makes my stomach heave. I can sense – at the periphery, the limit of all my senses – the dimensions of the creature. It is as high as a child of two. Its depth is a foot, fifteen inches. The air stirs around it, invisibly…. I am looking at a space occupied by nothing. It has no edges, no mass, no dimension, no shape except the formless. (pp. 106–7)

In this description of a confrontation which is supernaturally freighted though by no means straightforwardly supernatural, the speaker's vocabulary repeatedly proves inadequate. The enigmatic blank at the centre of the passage defies description and comprehension, both on the part of Hilary and the memoir's reader, forming a moment of ontological excess.

The 'secret garden' incident repeatedly emphasizes the unknowable, indefinable quality of the presence at its heart. Gestures towards description and definition, when they are made, are immediately contradicted. For instance, the presence is initially positioned as measurable, described as being 'as high as a child of two. Its depth is a foot, fifteen inches'. Yet the following sentence insists that 'it has no edges, no mass, no dimension, no shape except the formless' and the tension between the two statements remains unacknowledged. Certainly the 'secret garden' incident describes a confrontation which is experienced as traumatically invasive, both physically and psychologically; Hilary states that 'within *the space of a thought* it is inside me, and has set up a sick resonance within my bones and in all the cavities of my body' (p. 107). In his essay 'Demeure: Fiction and Testimony' Jacques Derrida makes an equation between 'truthful testimony, autobiography in good faith [and] sincere confession' stating that 'in essence, testimony is always autobiographical: it tells, in the first person, the sharable and unsharable secret of what happened to me, to me, to me alone, the absolute secret of what I was in a position to live, see, hear, touch, sense, feel'.[48] This emphasis on testimony's phenomenological component is shared with Hilary's account of her encounter. She speaks of 'the thick taste of blood and sick' in her mouth, the heaviness of her body, the 'sweat running from [her]' (p. 107). Yet what is also common to Derrida's account of autobiographical testimony and the 'secret garden' incident is the notion of the 'sharable and unsharable secret', something Derrida refers to elsewhere as 'unexperienced experience'.[49] For, while the passage is replete with details of Hilary's own bodily reaction, the stimulus she reacts to wilfully exceeds phenomenological description, there is 'nothing' to sense (p. 106), it is 'intangible', 'formless, borderless' (p. 107), even the air it disturbs is 'invisible' (p. 106). The 'secret' at the heart of the experience proves, as Derrida puts it, 'not merely difficult to know …; it is strictly impossible, no doubt not because there is always more to be known but because it is not of the order of knowledge'.[50] Despite the passage's framing as the confession of a profoundly traumatic secret whose telling is an act of will for the speaker, what the extract ultimately conveys is communicated at its outset when Hilary states that 'sometimes you come to a thing you can't write' (p. 105). The 'secret garden' incident is a testimony of encountering the unencounterable, it tells of being *unable to tell* and of the unavowable quality of its secret. Rather than describing the presence at its centre it in fact describes a confrontation with unknowing. As Hilary states: 'I don't know how, or what it was' (p. 106).

Giving up the Ghost, then, is a text in which, as Ginette Michaud describes, 'the secret is kept in the very place of testimony, without being hidden or concealed', its 'particular strength [coming] from the way [it] keep[s] (the) secret, the way [it] set[s] it to work, engendering and letting its effects be felt, the way [it] touch[es] upon it while leaving it intact'.[51] Yet, the 'phantasmaticity' which structures the 'unexperienced experience' at the heart of the passage, which 'exceeds the opposition between real and unreal, actual and virtual, factual and fictional'[52] has been met with various (attempted) critical exorcisms. Previous interpretative gestures have rendered this passage an encounter with the devil or a ghost, the fantasy of a traumatized child or else a migrainous hallucination. However, the text itself anticipates these reductive readings and looking to precisely how they are outmanoeuvred allows us to sidestep the search for origins, definite interpretations and revelations of secrets, maintaining the vital critical suspicion that accommodates the ambiguities of *Giving up the Ghost*.

The first element of the memoir's circumvention of such literalizing readings is found just prior to the opaque unfolding of the secret garden episode. Hilary describes her childhood faith, giving an account of 'carry[ing] a space for God inside me: a jagged space surrounded by light, a waiting space, cut out of my solar plexus' (p. 105). This bodily account of an opening maintained with traumatic results (as Hilary observes directly after this – 'but what came wasn't God at all' (p. 105)) seems to warn against perpetuating such an opening which has the capacity to be experienced as invasive and destabilizing. Yet the filling of that hollow with interpretative gestures results in the denial of the passage's undecidability, as illustrated in the journalistic reviews of *Giving up the Ghost* which attempt to fill the 'space occupied by nothing' with either supernatural or pathological 'somethings'.

This somewhat opaque anticipatory move, designed to stress the importance of the unknowable, insatiable 'gap', is followed and bolstered by a more expansive textual gesture which repeatedly emphasizes the wholly inadmissible quality of the 'secret' at the heart of the passage. If, as Derrida claims, testimony is necessarily autobiographical, 'in order to remain testimony' it must also 'allow itself to be haunted. It must allow itself to be parasitized by precisely what it excludes from its inner depths, the *possibility*, at least, of literature.'[53] This 'haunting' of autobiographical testimony by literature is self-consciously undertaken by Mantel, as evidenced in her use of literary intertexts within the memoir, the most significant of which is Frances Hodgson Burnett's novel *The Secret Garden* (1911) from which the critical episode explored above takes its name. The connection between the autobiographical incident and the famous children's book is a rich one and through its analysis both an understanding of the memoir's central 'secret' as untellable and the interactions of intertextuality with the project of writing the self are made licit.

The Secret Garden centres upon the recovery of two apparently sick children and the actions of incompetent medical professionals. As *Giving up the Ghost* recounts, as a young girl Hilary is often ill, leading her family doctor to give her the derisory nickname 'Little Miss Neverwell' (p. 82), and dismissive and neglectful medical care is a prominent feature of the memoir. Yet it would be a mistake to assume that the parallel between the two texts is so straightforward as to be unworthy of interrogation. Hodgson Burnett was a prominent believer in Christian Science and *The Secret Garden* has frequently been interpreted as espousing its tenets, the garden of the title being the location for processes of healing and recovery. Conversely, the 'secret garden' of *Giving up the Ghost* is the location of a loss of faith and a strangulation of well-being: 'after my bad time in the secret garden, my *mauvais quart d'heure*, I stopped believing in an omnipotent God' (p. 152). While Hodgson Burnett's fictional garden is a place where occluded things are brought to light, traumatic incidents worked through and losses grieved for, the garden at Brosscroft performs the opposite role, forming the location for a moment defined by occlusion and secrecy is not ameliorated but rather reverberates and perpetuates itself. Hilary's garden is a place in which the secret 'remains inviolable even when one thinks one has revealed it'.[54] The connection between text and intertext here cannot be simply defined. Instead, just as the Brooke and Yeats material analysed above articulated the impossibility of a simplistic account of Irish heritage, the relationship between *Giving up the Ghost* and Hodgson Burnett's narrative is composed of frictions and tensions, with certain elements of the texts forming neat parallels while others pull against and complicate each other.

Close attention must be paid both to the presence of this intertext in the memoir, and to the way in which the use of *The Secret Garden* in a direct account of receiving a narrative gives way to a knowing, creative use of the narrative in question. The reference to Hodgson Burnett's novel precedes the encounter in the garden at Brosscroft and the young Hilary's relationship with the story itself is multifaceted. Rather than reading the book, as might be expected (Hilary's reading habits are described in great detail), Hilary encounters *The Secret Garden* in adaptation, through watching it as a BBC television drama:

> Mr and Mrs Aldous have a television set. I go down to watch the children's serial. It is *The Secret Garden*. The curtains are pulled, so the black-and-white picture stands out more; we lie on the rug, chins in our hands, like children in picture books, like illustrations of ourselves. … At the end of many weeks I have saved up the entire story. I go home and announce it to my mother: *The Secret Garden*, here is that story. It spools out and out of my mouth, narrative, dialogue and commentary. (pp. 76–7)

This account of how Hodgson Burnett's story comes to enter Hilary's life is extremely rich. The description of the two children watching the serial 'like children in picture books, like illustrations of [themselves]' is a compound fictionalization as Mantel depicts the Hilary of the memoir understanding herself and her friend to be emulating fictional ideals of themselves. This gesture further spectralizes the 'I' speaker who is depicted as someone else's creation, even as she tries to take ownership of herself through the practice of autobiography. Crucially the account situates *The Secret Garden* in a very particular way with regard to the notion of the secret itself. Initially, *The Secret Garden* possesses no secrecy; the young Hilary 'has' it, possesses it and can reproduce it for her mother in its entirety. Yet the story which is told within *Giving up the Ghost* is not that of *The Secret Garden* but of *encountering The Secret Garden*. There is a gap in the memoir where the novel might be and indeed its plot and characters are never mentioned; only the 'black and white' images on the television screen are indicated. Thus, when the title of the novel is repurposed to provide a shorthand for the otherwise inexpressible incident in the garden a series of tensions arise. For example, unlike Hodgson Burnett's narrative, the 'secret garden' incident is a story which will not 'spool out' neatly and clearly; it is not a story that can be fully told, either to the reader or, at the time, to Hilary's mother whose astonishment remains reserved for her daughter's account of the fictional tale. The story of the 'secret garden' incident 'resists finishing', built as it is around a secret that can never be told. Furthermore, having been adapted from its original context as novel and turned into a television series, Hilary's adoption of the book's title is also a bid to bring to light 'the ghosts of meaning' among which she seeks to locate herself. The shifting emphasis created by her appropriation, which invokes both Hodgson Burnett's garden where plants and people are secretly cultivated and Hilary's garden in which secret or hidden things grow, is a neat demonstration of how Mantel's intertextual play brings to light such ghosts of meaning. The appropriation of the title of Hodgson Burnett's novel, and its use in a number of divergent contexts, serves to warn the memoir's reader not to assume that the story we are being told is the story we expect, or even the one it purports to be. In using *The Secret Garden* in this way Mantel emphasizes how a multiplicity of significatory content is frequently subordinated or rendered excess, gesturing towards the potential of recognizing such spectralized meaning.

'I am disconnecting from my body': precarious embodiment and sensory haunting

Thus far this chapter has demonstrated the need identified in *Giving up the Ghost* to access a means of becoming present and coherent through the act of writing and has explored how that project is necessarily compromised by the presence of intertextual fagments (both familial and literary) and un-disclosable secrets. Crucially this is a project which is explicitly framed as bypassing the bodily. As Hilary puts it, 'I am writing … in order to locate myself … *not within a body*' (p. 222). Indeed, the body, rather than providing an incontestable reference point for subjective identity, is represented in the memoir as an unstable volume whose organs and senses do not behave in predictable ways. In this final section I examine the representation of embodiment in the memoir in order to demonstrate how, by populating *Giving up the Ghost* with corporeal bodies which are frequently on the point of disintegration, and by questioning the incontrovertibility of sensory inputs, the text disavows corporeal integrity as a guarantee of self. Moreover, I demonstrate how these moments of disintegration and disorganization are seized upon as opportunities to question the possibility of a plenary life-narrative which might allow the speaker to become fully manifest.

Before moving to analyse *Giving up the Ghost*'s striking account of synaesthesia, I wish to briefly sketch how the memoir constructs a linkage between the malfunctioning body and the supernatural in a way which renders the body uncanny and prevents it from providing a reliable vantage point from which the work of memoir might conceivably be attempted. The body as fallible object is a central trope of the memoir. Hilary's description of her endometriotic body is couched in the language of the supernatural (as distinct from the spectral). Describing her physical condition on the day she is due to remarry her former husband, Hilary states: 'I felt very ill that morning, queasy and swollen, as if I were pregnant; there was a pain behind my diaphragm, and from time to time something seemed to flip over and claw at me, as if I were a woman in a folk tale, pregnant with a demon' (pp. 11–12). A photograph taken of her following the ceremony shows her 'hollow-eyed, like a turnip lantern' (p. 12), recalling the carved vegetable lanterns created for Halloween. Later, discussing the weight gain experienced as a side effect of certain medication, she describes herself as 'solid, set, grounded, grotesque: perpetually strange to myself, convoluted, mutated, and beyond the pale' (p. 54). As the memoir comes to focus more closely on an initial period of chronic illness, diagnosis and treatment, the descriptions of her bodily discomfort become more dense and extensive: 'I had a pain which I could not explain; it seemed to wander around my body, nibbling here, stabbing there, flitting every time I tried to put my finger on it' (p. 155). Concerned about the level of pain medication she has been taking when her doctor suggests she might be pregnant, Hilary muses: 'I hope not. ... If so, I've overdone it with the aspirin. It'll have fins. Or feathers. Three extra aspirin, three extra heads' (p. 168). The body in the grip of pathology continues to be rendered through supernatural similes until the memoir's close when, still experiencing severe side effects of her medication, she welcomes her move to Saudi Arabia where cultural norms frequently force her to remain inside, 'under artificial light, waxing like some strange fungus' (p. 216).

While the ghost can be grouped among supernatural phenomena, it is important in this case to distinguish it from those figures which Mantel chooses as metaphorical tools to speak about the body. These are predicated not upon distinctions between pre- and post-mortem, or degrees of visibility, as in the case of the ghost or the spectre, but rather on perversions or manipulations of the flesh into something excessive or unpredictable. The witches, demons, chimeras and strange funguses, which are referenced with regard to Hilary's body in the throes of illness, are figures which throw embodiment and the body's possibilities into question. The use of such metaphors to speak about the body, albeit a body – as Hilary puts it – 'enclosing a disease process' (p. 218), posits it as equally unreliable, unpredictable and prone to disordering excess as the memorial material and familial heritage to which the memoir's spectral speaker turns in order to patch together her narrative.

Elsewhere in the memoir the fallibility of the body provides a further mechanism through which the 'ghosts of meaning', whose revelation drives the text, can be made manifest, if only fleetingly. This mechanism is most evident in *Giving up the Ghost*'s treatment of synaesthesia as a kind of haunting, a status which has significant implications for how the use of language in the text can be understood. Synaesthesia is an inherently double concept, both in construction and application. From the Greek *syn*, meaning 'together', and *aisthesis*, meaning 'sensation', the term is predicated on a coupling of phenomena. In a clinical context synaesthesia refers to a neurological situation occurring when 'stimulation of one sensory modality automatically triggers a perception in a second modality, in the absence of any direct stimulation to this second modality'.[55] To this initial definition we should also add that 'cognitive modality' can be substituted for 'sensory modality' when describing the structure of synaesthesia. This specification of sensory *or* cognitive pathways is crucial. In recent years dispute has emerged over whether synaesthesia is an accurate term for the phenomenon, depending as it does on a construction which pairs sensory input with sensory response. Danko Nicolić has argued that, in fact, synaesthesia should 'be understood as an unusual type of "semantic" association whereby, in addition to wiring up different concepts, it wires concepts to sensory activations'. Nicolić suggests that a more accurate term for the phenomenon would be 'ideasthesia'.[56] It is this 'wiring up of different concepts' that is observed in *Giving up the Ghost* – achieved through an account of Hilary's early experience of (and later use of) language as onomatopoeic – rather than the classic model of synaesthesia which refers to a disorganization of specifically sensory modes. It is also worth noting that synaesthesia is not listed in the *Diagnostic and Statistical Manual of Mental Disorders* (DSM); it is not an illness nor is it harmful; it does not 'usually lead to problems in daily living',[57] yet it is a pathology. Medical definitions of synaesthesia insist that the phenomenon 'is distinct from hallucination and metaphor'.[58] Yet synaesthesia is also defined as 'the use of metaphors in which terms relating to one kind of sense-impression are used to describe sense-impressions of other kinds; the production of synaesthetic effect in writing or an instance of this'.[59] Already there is a tension within the term as its various uses pull against each other, one being 'distinct from' metaphor and the other constituting a specific type of metaphor. If 'literary synaesthesia is the exploitation of verbal synaesthesia for specific literary effects',[60] Mantel's memoir plays with this tension and complicates the division between the phenomenon's clinical and creative applications. The majority of medical texts dealing with synaesthesia insist on a clear demarcation between clinical synaesthesia and synaesthesic metaphor, some even going so far as to sort artists of whom diagnoses of synaesthesia have been made into 'true' synaesthetes and those merely using the structure creatively. Yet Richard E. Cytowic and David M. Eagleman assert that such a strict differentiation is impossible and that the two phenomena exist on a continuum which inextricably links perception with language: 'Orderly relationships among the senses imply a cognitive continuum in which perceptual similarities give way to synaesthesic equivalences, which in turn become metaphoric identities, which then merge into the abstraction of language. In other words, the progression looks like this: *perception–synaesthesia–metaphor–language.*'[61]

This play has various implications for how the memoir can be read. Reuven Tsur argues that 'one conspicuous contrast between "genuine" and literary synaesthesia is that the former involves rigidly predictable combinations of sensory modes, whereas the latter requires exceptionally great flexibility in generating and understanding unforeseen combinations and, by the same token, abandoning established combinations'.[62] This formulation is key to understanding the significance of synaesthesia in *Giving up the Ghost*. As we will see, words and concepts within the world of the memoir operate within a synaesthesic logic as the 'ghosts of sense impressions' cause a perceptual and textual disorganization in which words amass phantom duplicates. By writing about and through synaesthesia Mantel demonstrates how the materiality of a word, its graphical inscription and letter sounds, generate associations which exceed conventional linguistic definitions. The following reading of the 'ghosts of [her own] sense impressions', 'shiver[ing] between the lines' (p. 23) in Mantel's work leads to an understanding of her use of synaesthesia as characteristic of the way haunting acts as a 'disorganizing principle' for her work.

The notion of synaesthesia as a mode of spectrality permeates *Giving up the Ghost*. I have already observed how, in the memoir's early pages, when speaking of the difficulty involved in writing about one's childhood, Hilary recognizes the inherent insufficiency of language for the task of narrativizing one's life (*Giving up the Ghost*, p. 23). However, Hilary goes on to attribute this linguistic lack to the fact that 'my early world was synaesthesic, and I am haunted by the ghosts of my own sense impressions' (p. 23). I initially invoked this passage by way of positioning *Giving up the Ghost* as self-consciously undermining the coherence and completion implied by the autobiographical project. I return to it now to examine how, in the same way as the traditional ghost causes the past to erupt into the present and blurs boundaries between absence and presence, these synaesthetic 'ghosts of sense impressions' cause various ontological disorganizations, in this case between the sensory and the conceptual. These disorganizations are repeatedly registered in the second chapter of the memoir, which is concerned with Hilary's early childhood. The young Hilary likes to 'get close to people who are thinking, to glue [herself] to the warm, buzzy, sticky field of their concentration' (p. 39). Kath, the mother of a friend, is considered to have a 'melting name' (p. 42). The nasturtiums in Hilary's garden evoke 'stately and imperial melodies' and 'combine every virtue, the portentous groan of brass, … to the eye, the crushable texture of velvet, but to the fingertip, the bruise of baby skin' (p. 43). This description in particular provides a neat exemplar of literary synaesthesia, the vision of the flowers inducing the sounds of music, the texture of velvet palpable not through touch but sight, the 'bruise of baby skin' not discerned through looking but the touch of a fingertip. Crucially, though, Mantel includes in the description some of the rationale for these linguistic choices, revealing the structures through which literary synaesthesia is produced. The music the flowers are depicted as producing, their status as 'musical instruments' (p. 43), is evoked 'because [the nasturtiums'] shape is like that of gramophone horns' (p. 43). The 'storshions', as Hilary's grandfather calls the flowers, produce distortions of perceptual reality that have a basis in nonlinear associations and unconventional doublings.

The nasturtium passage provides such a clear example of literary synaesthesia because it emphasizes the origin of the descriptions within a creative, imaginative act as the child 'imagine[s] [the flowers] to be musical instruments'. Yet synaesthesia as a neurological phenomenon is not absent from the text and, though its presence is complicated and compromised, it too is articulated through the language of the spectral. The most extensive example of the complication in *Giving up the Ghost* of the dividing line between clinical and literary synaesthesia can also be found in its second chapter. In the passage preceding the paragraph below, the young Hilary has come to believe that she has, in the act of eating a marzipan sweet, ingested or inhaled a housefly: 'The fly was in the room and my mouth was open because I was putting into it a sweet. Then the fly was nowhere to be seen' (p. 31). Having been told that 'flies are universally condemned and said to be laden with filth, crawling with germs' she concludes that 'what more sure way to die than swallow or inhale one?' (p. 31):

> Something is tugging at my attention. Perhaps it is a sense of absurdity. The dry rasping in my throat persists, but now I don't know if it is the original obstruction lodged there, or the memory of it, the imprint, which is not going to fade from my breathing flesh. For many years the word 'marzipan' affects me with its deathly hiss, the buzz in its syllables, a sepulchral fizz. (pp. 32–3)

Though embedded in a highly descriptive and writerly passage, this incident provides a recollection of clinical synaesthesia as the word 'marzipan' comes loose from the object it signifies and instead brings with it a buzzing and hissing, an association both with the fly, and with the sepulchral and deathly. This synaesthesic quality of words for the young Hilary persists, seemingly with the rigid predictability that defines neurological synaesthesia according to Tsur.[63] Two years after the marzipan incident, Hilary questions her mother about the necessity of her attendance at school:

> what if I didn't, I asked, what would occur? She supposed, said my mother, we would be summonsed. I said, is that like sued? I had heard the word 'sued'. It sounded to me like the long, stinking hiss emitted when a tap was turned on the gas cooker, before the match was applied. Sued, gas: the words had a lower hiss than 'marzipan' and long after they were spoken their trail lingered on the air, invisible, pernicious. (p. 62)

Again, in this example the linguistic definition of a word and its materiality, its visual and spoken iterations, are divorced and an association is created between these two disparate concepts which is built upon letter sounds rather than semantic sense. However, the carefully drawn line between what Tsur terms 'genuine' synaesthesia and literary synaesthesia is beginning to break down in this passage as the young Hilary is depicted as experiencing the words as genuinely synaesthesic, while Mantel simultaneously turns this experience into a creative textual gesture through the image of the word sounds persisting as lingering physical presences.[64] The final episode in this account of the disordered sensory world of Hilary's childhood continues to develop this blurring of pathology and textuality and offers at its close an insight into the ultimate significance of such synaesthesic textuality not only to *Giving up the Ghost* but to Mantel's writing as a whole.

The episode occurs on the evening that Hilary and her family move to Brosscroft, the house in whose garden Hilary will experience her '*mauvais quart d'heure*' (p. 152). Her father has gone out to retrieve items left at the old family home:

> My mother goes to the new stove, and then peers into the dark cupboard where the gas meter is kept. The gas is turned off, she says, I will have to – No! I say. I stop her hand. I beg her. No, no, don't do it. Don't turn on the gas before my Daddy comes back. Gas, sue, sue, gas, hiss, hiss bang. I am begging and beseeching. I can't tell her my reason. … She looks at me, a long considering look: 'All right,' she says. I am as astonished as she was when I recited the entire Secret Garden at a stroke. (pp. 78–9)

In time Hilary's father returns: 'man switches on gas. No one sued. No one dead. No mysterious escapes. No invisible presences' (p. 79). Clearly this complex passage contains a powerful account of the potency of the young child's synaesthesic experience, in which words, sounds, concepts and properties become traumatizingly disordered. Yet its construction reproduces the creation of those associations through the repetition of the sibilant 's' sounds at the root of the synaesthesic concomitance. An examination of the passage's central sentence (gas, sue, sue, gas, hiss, hiss, bang) reveals a lack of any connectives or a discernible subject, structurally reproducing the absence of any straightforward linguistic basis for these associations which are instead enabled by the pure phonic materiality of the sounds created in the word's verbal expression.[65] The 'mysterious escapes' and 'invisible presences' threatened by Hilary's synaesthesic experience, combined with the fact that this last instance of synaesthesia takes place in Hilary's apparently haunted home, re-enforces the haunting quality possessed by synaesthesia in the memoir, where the pathological structure is described as allowing the ingress of spectral phenomena whose effects are unpredictable, disruptive and traumatic.

The significance of the passage exceeds this blending of the textual and the pathological. The young Hilary struggles desperately to express the cause of her terror ('I am in the first killing crisis of my life and unable to explain how to avert it' (p. 79)), unable to articulate the linkages which have formed between the words 'gas' and 'sued' and the affective response they produce in her. What we see in this moment of killing panic is that the spoken concept of 'gas' brings with it into Hilary's kitchen phantom words and sounds which contaminate and problematize the original term in a way which is inexpressible. Synaesthesia as utilized by Mantel goes further than making links between pathology and textuality, though it does so usefully and subtly. It also acts to highlight how 'the ghosts of meaning', constituted by the 'mysterious escapes' and 'invisible presences' that the young Hilary desperately tries to avert and dispel, come to haunt the original word and compromise its conventional meaning, agents of a semantic and conceptual disorganization upon which much of Mantel's work relies.[66]

'Other lives you might have led': memoir as ghost story

'All of your houses are haunted by the person you might have been' (*Giving up the Ghost*, p. 20)

At the beginning of this chapter I drew attention to the elision of the difference between *Giving up the Ghost*'s speaker and the author Hilary Mantel, elisions which were accompanied by a naïve approach to illness or else a literalizing approach to spectrality. These elisions have the effect of understanding memoir and autobiography as a unifying force. As Prodromou puts it, 'the autobiographical act – writing the self – challenges postmodern theories of fragmented subjectivity by offering the possibility of the creation of a unified self'.[67] At first glance the memoir may seem to accommodate such a reading. As has been demonstrated, *Giving up the Ghost* is a text insistent upon its function and purpose. It is to be a 'seiz[ing of] copyright' (p. 70), undertaken 'in order to *locate* [the speaker]' (p. 222, my italics). However, these attempts are undermined at every moment in the memoir, their very possibility questioned not only by the spectral quality of the text's speaker, but by the familial hauntings and haunting intertexts she is subject to and author of. Clearly, rather than demonstrating the apparently unifying power of the narrative of the self, *Giving up the Ghost* undertakes a much more slippery and complex enterprise. It produces a narrative of self-as-spectre, a self whose attempts to become fully manifest are perpetually deferred. Yet these attempts have themselves been seized upon by reviewers and critics who ignore the speaker's provocative rhetorical question – 'is my writing clear: or is it deceptively clear?' (p. 5) – in their desire to complete the memoir's project, even as the text's speaker acknowledges such a task to be interminable.

Even as Mantel's account of her life makes claims to be a project in filling lacunae, in digging over the ground of the past and forcing it to 'yield up its dead secrets' (p. 119), it rejects the feasibility of such an endeavour and insists upon the significance of the enigmatic, of the spectral or barely manifest, and of the seemingly empty spaces around which narratives coalesce. Hilary states:

writing about your past is like blundering through your house with the lights fused, a hand flailing for points of reference. You locate the stolid wardrobe, and its door swings open at your touch, opening on the cavern of darkness within. Your hand touches glass, you think it is a mirror, but it is the window. There are obstacles to bump and trip you, but what is more disconcerting is a sudden empty space, where you can't find a handhold and you know that you are stranded in the dark (p. 167).

While initially appearing to subscribe to the idea that 'an autobiography is … a straightforward document', Mantel's memoir ultimately demonstrates that it is 'in reality … a Chinese box of identity where the "I" of the text and the name on the title page are not, and can never be, completely equivalent'.[68] It espouses a model which makes clear that 'the autobiographical self is a fictional construct within the text, which can neither have its origins anterior to the text, nor indeed coalesce with its creator'.[69] When Hilary states 'all your houses are haunted by the person you might have been' (p. 20) she implicitly adds her own spectral voice to that host of potentialities.

Mantel's short story 'A Clean Slate',[70] which closes *Learning to Talk*, eloquently illustrates the impossibility of producing a complete and unified account of family history and, through that history, of self. It does so through an exploration of the relationship between autobiographical fact and fiction. The story centres on a writer's attempts to coax a number of genealogical details from her ageing and evasive mother and is concerned with the point at which the factual fails, what Mantel describes as 'the interface between myth, folk memory and the actual historical record'.[71] The narrator's mother, Veronica, is said to 'lik[e] to make mysteries and imply she has secret knowledge' (p. 124), understanding her history through stories, jokes and 'witty snubs that have come unfastened from their origins' (p. 121). Conversely, the narrator 'distrust[s] anecdote', preferring 'to understand history through figures and percentages of these figures, through knowing the price of coal, the price of corn, and the price of a loaf in Paris on the day the Bastille fell' (p. 121). Yet within the story the factual is continually undermined. The medical documents concerning her mother contain a false age (p. 124) and certain details of her family history told 'AS A FACT' (p. 131) are proven wrong. Even the narrator herself by the end of the story admits – 'I am suspicious of these round figures' (p. 133). Ultimately it is the lacunae that her ancestral narrative encompasses which drive the short story and give it its power. These lacunae are most powerfully registered by the narrator's absent descendants whose lives exist in the state of perpetual potentiality which defines the Mantelian ghost: the only children who 'failed to marry' or 'spent much of [their] life in an asylum' (p. 125), the 'child who died unchristened within minutes of birth. … Not really a person: more like a negative that was never developed' (pp. 122–3). The lessons of 'A Clean Slate' indicate that we are right to maintain our suspicion of Mantel's deceptive clarity in *Giving up the Ghost* and to conclude that when Mantel says of her memoir 'and I begin to construct myself, complete with the missing bits',[72] what is encouraged is an understanding of personal narrative as complete *with* the missing bits, that the secrets, gaps and hollows are a prerequisite for its production. Indeed, such a reading confirms Benstock's assertion that:

> autobiography reveals gaps, and not only gaps in time and space, or between the individual or the social, but also a widening divergence between the manner and matter of its discourse. That is, autobiography reveals the impossibility of its own dream: what begins on the presumption of self-knowledge ends in the creation of a fiction that covers over the premise of its construction.[73]

By maintaining its secrets and preserving rather than relinquishing its ghosts, it is possible to understand Mantel's memoir not as a stable, unified point of origin, nor as a narrative *of* illness, but as an exploration of the dependence of life narratives upon enigmatic hollows, and the ghostly potentialities such hollows produce. *Giving up the Ghost*, with its 'missing bits' and spectral supplements offered by the voices of dead authors and ancestors alike, does not provide a diagnostic or interpretative framework through which to understand Mantel's fiction. Rather it points to a particular mode of reading capable of privileging the secrecy and ambiguity in Mantel's work as a whole.

2

Spectres of Margaret: Thatcherism, care-giving and the gothic in *Every Day is Mother's Day* and *Vacant Possession*

Midway through *Vacant Possession*, protagonist Muriel Axon observes the current inhabitants of her childhood home – No. 2, Buckingham Avenue – as they go about their business, and eagerly anticipates their domestic demise:

> The air was choked with tension and spite, and on the landing all the doors were closed; it was just like Mother's day. The children were locked in their rooms, sniffing glue and crying. ... Suzanne's untended child would wail from the back garden, bleating for the peace of the clouded water from which it came. The evergreens would grow, blocking out the light at the back of the house; foul necessities would incubate in the dark. Soon cracks would appear in the walls, and a green-black mould would grow along the cracks and spread its spores through the kitchen cupboards, through the wardrobes and the bed linen .... Their trivial domestic upsets would turn soon to confusion, abandonment and rage. Acts of violence would occur; there would be bodies. (p. 128)

The gothic inflection given to this anticipated collapse of dormitory-town domesticity is characteristic of Mantel's debut duology, of which *Vacant Possession* forms the second part.[1] The novels' rendering of the lives of two families in an anonymous West Midlands town in the late 1970s and 1980s coalesces around that quintessential gothic trope of the decaying family home which plays host to a series of malevolent ghosts and in which nightmarish events take place. Yet the above passage is not simply and straightforwardly an example of contemporary gothic. The imagined dereliction of 2 Buckingham Avenue takes place on a profoundly quotidian level. Earlier in the passage Muriel imagines dirty milk bottles going uncollected while elsewhere she imagines an accumulation of household waste which brings about not a plague of vermin but a single rat. Crucially, the presences which populate the passage are not phantoms but infants and mothers (p. 128). In this passage it is the wailing and bleating of the 'untended' child which forms the disturbance at the heart of Mantel's gothicized domestic sphere.

Within Mantel's dormitory-gothic environment, Muriel's fantasy of the unattended crying child alone in the garden of 2 Buckingham Avenue encapsulates the focus of *Every Day* and *Vacant Possession*: absent or failed care-giving. In this chapter, I demonstrate that the duology responds to and articulates such failures of care-giving through a nuanced deployment of the gothic mode in which particular emphasis is placed upon the trope of the ghost.[2] I contend that the duology's depiction of these failures and collapses of care undercuts a dominant narrative in which the nuclear family and the familial domestic are understood as inherently nurturing contexts in which the process of parental care-giving plays out functionally. This critique has a profoundly political significance. The novels' fictionalization of Britain during the tenure of Margaret Thatcher's Conservative government, a period in which medical and social care underwent dramatic upheavals, both logistically and rhetorically, invites a reading which recognizes that, through their use of the gothic mode, these texts articulate how society's relationship with care-giving on every level was crucially put at stake during the Thatcher administration.

The identification of a gothic mode at work in Mantel's writing is, however, not an uncontroversial critical gesture. Unlike the voluble journalistic reaction to *Giving up the Ghost* observed in Chapter 1, a critical reticence surrounds the duology. Such a sustained lack of critical engagement is provocative, and its cause is potentially to be found in the ambivalent relationship these two books have with the gothic, simultaneously exploiting and evading it. The gothic as a mode has for some time been a contested site within scholarship on Mantel, in both academic and journalistic contexts. Eileen Pollard suggests that the academic response to the media representation of Mantel's canon as being defined by its indefinability[3] has been to fall back upon the gothic as a unifying element within Mantel's work.[4] While this rejection of the gothic as a homogenizing framework is apposite, this chapter demonstrates that there is a danger here of throwing the baby out with the bathwater. This chapter does not subscribe to Sara L. Knox's assessment of Mantel as 'no writer of the gothic', an assessment which Pollard appears to encourage. Instead it takes as its point of departure Knox's understanding of the gothic as 'too small a handle for Mantel's work'[5] and considers which doors this 'small handle' might open even as the duology exceeds and subverts it.

Having mapped the critical context within which my reading of the duology takes place, it is necessary to establish two disparate yet related points of historical context. The first concerns the appearance of the gothic as a literary mode in the late eighteenth century when a constellation of factors contributed to its emergence. Occurring as it did 'at a time of bourgeois and industrial revolution, a time of Enlightenment philosophy and increasingly secular views',[6] the development of the gothic was 'bound up with shifts from feudal to commercial practices in which notions of property, government and society were undergoing massive transformations'.[7] One of these transformations in particular, and the element which is most significant for the current discussion, concerned the status of the domestic space within cultural, social and economic life. As Kate Ferguson Ellis has argued, the gothic emerged in part as a reaction to the increasing separation between the 'fallen' world of commerce and production, and the domestic sphere. This separation left the space of the home a site of idealization and thus 'attendant anxiety'[8] arising from the difficulty of maintaining the 'constitution of the home as a "place of peace" into which evil never came'.[9] Moreover, if the gothic mode developed partly as a reaction to the idealization of the domestic sphere, it is also particularly preoccupied with the figure traditionally placed at the centre of that sphere: the mother. Multiple critics have posited that at the heart of the female gothic in particular is a confrontation with motherhood and mothering.[10]

These concerns and confrontations were in circulation once again in Britain in the latter part of the twentieth century as Margaret Thatcher's Conservative government placed the space of the home and the status of the nuclear family, indeed motherhood and parenting in general, at the forefront of much of their rhetoric. This placement is evident in the language used by the New Right to articulate their view of the role of government. The British New Right, the political movement from which Thatcherism emerged, expressed a desire for policy decisions to emulate, as Rodney Lowe puts it, the actions of 'responsible parents ... who strive for the independence of those temporarily dependent upon them' and compared a government's economic decisions to '[those] of a housewife balancing her budget',[11] while Thatcher herself described the State as 'that ... imaginary mother figure for our age'.[12] Outside of her overtly party-political speeches, the prime minister repeatedly used newspaper and broadcast interviews to reiterate the centrality of the family and the home to the nation's success. In addition to giving numerous accounts of her own childhood in which her mother's prowess as a housewife and homemaker was foregrounded,[13] Thatcher's media appearances continually reified the familial domestic and insisted that Thatcherite Britain was a country in which 'family life is rightly treasured'.[14] In a speech to the Conservative Women's Conference she insisted that 'the family is the building block of society. It is a nursery, a school, a hospital, a leisure place, a place of refuge and a place of rest. It encompasses the whole of society. It fashions our beliefs. It is the preparation for the rest of our life'.[15] The space of the privately owned family home (understood by Thatcher as 'more than ownership of bricks and mortar' and instead 'something to hand on to the next generation'[16]) was similarly idealized and inextricably linked with successful and responsible parenting. As Thatcher put it in her speech to the Conservative Party Conference in 1981:

> the family is the basic unit of our society and it is in the family that the next generation is nurtured. Our concern is to create a property-owning democracy and it is therefore a very human concern. It is a natural desire of Conservatives that every family should have a stake in society and that the privilege of a family home should not be restricted to the few.[17]

This manipulation of the language of the familial domestic went beyond rhetoric, as is apparent in policy decisions around social care in this period, which took place against the backdrop of an ideological project concerned with the regulation of the domestic space and the family unit. In 1988 Thatcher insisted that the family must be strengthened, issuing the dire warning that 'unless we do so, we will be faced with heart-rending social problems which no Government could possibly cure – or even hope to cope with'.[18] Accordingly, the family and the familial domestic were repositioned as the only truly appropriate environment for care-giving (whether for children, the elderly, the disabled, or the mentally ill): 'Conservatives were convinced ... that the proper agency for personal individual care was not the State. Rather, it was the family.'[19]

Beginning with an examination of the domestic space within *Every Day* and *Vacant Possession* in the context of Thatcherite reification of that environment for its care-giving potential, in the initial section of this chapter I analyse the significance of 2 Buckingham Avenue's status as a 'haunted house', reading the various ghosts that populate that home as remnants of dysfunctional and abusive care-giving relationships. I then go on to examine how the hospital as a quintessential care-giving environment is presented as compromised and collapsing. Focusing on the account of mental health care provision in the duology, this section demonstrates the spectralizing potential of psychiatric care in this period. Finally, I analyse how *Every Day* and *Vacant Possession* use the gothic mode to critique Thatcherite social care policy with particular reference to the 'care in the community' movement and establish how the duology depicts these initiatives, and welfare services in the Thatcher era more broadly, as rendering their recipients social ghosts. Via an exploration of care-giving on these three concentric levels (domestic, medical and societal) I identify and analyse the multitude of ghosts and spectres that emerge from, and populate the scene of, care-giving in Mantel's imagined Thatcherite Britain. More broadly my reading of *Every Day* and *Vacant Possession* demonstrates how, from the earliest moments of her writing career, Mantel is interrogating the ethical and political implications of the figure of the ghost, tapping into the gothic's ability to 'mediate between the uncanny and the unjust',[20] in order to recognize that, as Avery Gordon puts it, 'the ghost is not simply a dead or missing person, but a social figure, and investigating it can lead to that dense site where history and subjectivity make social life'.[21]

Haunted Houses, Monstrous Mothers and the Scene of Domestic Care-Giving

In her 1979 'Renewal of Britain' speech Margaret Thatcher asserted that 'there is no adequate substitute for genuine caring for one another on the part of families, friends and neighbours'.[22] Her statement is typical of the Thatcherite position outlined above; that it was the family unit who were best placed to undertake caring responsibilities and the space of the privately owned home[23] was the appropriate environment for that care. Indeed, during Thatcher's tenure as prime minister, Conservative policy on social care and welfare was predicated on the rolling back of 'the boundaries of State activity in terms of social provision' and a concurrent promotion of the 'traditional family unit as an institution'.[24] Mantel's representation of the maternal relationship between Evelyn and Muriel speaks back to the figure of the ideal mother which was returning to prominence in the 1980s,[25] serving to complicate models of mothering in which the figure of the mother is either unimpeachable or unequivocally abusive. It is apt, then, to begin this analysis with an exploration of the domestic spaces to be found within *Every Day* and *Vacant Possession* and the acts of care-giving their inhabitants undertake and/or receive.

Housing and Care-Giving in Thatcher's Britain

Throughout the duology Mantel presents her readers with a range of domestic spaces, each of which, through its dereliction and disorder, undermines the

Conservative idealization of the familial domestic and its ability to provide a care-giving environment. However, the domestic landscape she presents is not merely a fictional device. It is also reflective of the historical reality of the state of housing stock in England during Thatcher's premiership. Writing in the *Guardian* in 1984, Peter Jenkins remarked on the ubiquity in Britain of 'urban dilapidation and squalor, a rotting housing stock and rusting transport facilities; shabby-looking people in filthy streets'.[26] The English House Conditions Survey, carried out between 1986 and 1987, 'found about 900,000 homes in England, nearly 5 percent of the total, which were unfit to live in'.[27]

Mantel references this dereliction of the domestic sphere through the multitude of slums, squats and dilapidated residences described in the texts. One of these spaces is home to Colin Sidney's daughter, Suzanne, who ends up living in an 'unfit' residence following the birth of her daughter: 'the flat – two rooms really – was dirty and neglected, a near slum. There was a scrap of fraying carpet, then bare boards; windows were cracked and crisscrossed with tape. There were mattresses strewn over the floor' (*Vacant Possession*, pp. 225–6). Muriel herself ends up living in another of the homes deemed unfit to be occupied. The house where she rents a room has been 'condemned long ago, put on a schedule for demolition, but it seemed likely that before its turn came it would demolish itself, quietly crumbling and rotting away, with its wet rot and dry rot and its collection of parasites and moulds' (*Vacant Possession*, p. 69). Even the Sidneys, a nuclear family in the ideal Conservative mould, complete with stay-at-home mother, initially live in a house in which everything 'had been rickety, leaky or shoddy' and which was 'a triumph of jerry-building' (*Vacant Possession*, p. 22). Clearly the space of the home within these narratives is far from the idealized environment described in Thatcherite rhetoric. Rather, these domestic spaces allow Mantel to articulate a sense of homes of all kinds (not only the rented flat but the privately owned home) as being riddled with flaws that are pernicious and endemic yet difficult to locate, exemplified by the various kinds of rot that affect the house where Muriel lives, undermining the structure imperceptibly until the moment of its collapse.

Every Day and *Vacant Possession* present the family home as a space that is at best not fit for purpose and at worst on the verge of physical collapse, explicitly undermining the notion of such spaces as havens for care-giving. While such a representation is an acknowledgement of the profound problems with housing stock in Britain in the 1980s it is also important to acknowledge that the significance of these degraded spaces goes beyond an inscription of historical reality. In order to fully understand how the domestic architecture of the duology comments on care-giving relationships it is necessary to analyse the relationship Mantel builds between these homes and the care-giving relationships that take place within them. In doing so it is possible to demonstrate that, rather than the gothic providing a smokescreen behind which the horrifying realities of perverse and failed care are obscured, the use of this mode allows Mantel to emphasize that, in contrast to the safe havens of Conservative ideology, homes, even in the middle-class and leafy neighbourhood of Buckingham Avenue, 'are very unsafe spaces to linger'.[28]

In the early pages of *Vacant Possession* Muriel recalls being pregnant: 'she felt a movement inside her, very strange. Mother said "you're occupied"' (p. 38). Evelyn Axon's description of her daughter invokes what Marinovich terms the 'House–Body equation',[29] an analogue between the figure of the mother and the space of the home which has wide reaching implications for the present study. In the passage that opened this chapter, Muriel's musings upon the degradation of 2 Buckingham Avenue are not restricted to architecture and furnishings. Instead, as the house is imagined to collapse, Sylvia Sidney, matriarch of the household, is fantasized growing morbidly obese, 'waddl[ing] and roll[ing] about the house, and hid[ing] when the doorbell rang' (p. 128). In *Vacant Possession* Isabel Field, Muriel and Evelyn's former social worker, newly returned to the area and in the early stages of pregnancy, describes herself as disorganized and unstable, 'always … bursting into tears, and falling over, and losing things' (p. 21). Correspondingly Isabel's reintroduction to the narrative takes place among sealed packing crates and damaged household objects in her new home (p. 21). 'Very cold' (p. 211) and sparsely described within the narrative, Isabel's house mirrors her antipathy towards a maternal role; when her husband suggests they adopt his lover's baby Isabel replies that she would 'rather drown it' (p. 179). Later in the same conversation, she reveals her own pregnancy to her husband who insists that she stop drinking, fearing damage to the baby to which Isabel replies 'you never know … who'll be most damaged in the end' (p. 179). Clearly, then, these disordered and dilapidated homes, are not merely historical details or parodic nods to the derelict ancestral homes of early gothic narratives, but form analogues with the putative carers who inhabit them. Yet, it is not simply physical decay and degradation that besets the family home in the duology. While 2 Buckingham Avenue, home initially to Evelyn and Muriel, then, following Evelyn's death, the Sidney family, is in a poor state of repair structurally,[30] it is set apart from the other domestic spaces in the duology by virtue of the fact that it is profoundly haunted. This quality prompts questions about the nature and significance of the ghosts of 2 Buckingham Avenue within the context of Mantel's critique of care-giving.

'The spectre of ambivalence'[31]: haunting and mothering

From the outset of *Every Day* it is clear that 2 Buckingham Avenue is a home populated as much by the dead as the living. Structurally compromised by the ghosts embedded within its architecture, the house is 'a three-bed two-reception property on a large corner plot, all jostled and crammed with the teeth-baring dead, stranded souls whistling in the cavity walls, half animated corpses under the flagstones outside' (*Vacant Possession*, p. 37). Sara Knox describes the Axons' home as 'a house so in possession of itself that it has no truck with its occupants'.[32] Certainly, the phantoms that occupy Evelyn and Muriel's home 're-signify the terms under which it might be occupied',[33] placing a variety of permanent and semi-permanent embargoes on entry to various rooms. The kitchen is subject to periodical ghostly occupation; early on in the novel Evelyn receives a note stating 'GO NOT TO THE KITCHIN TODAY [sic]' and observes that 'the days when they forbade her the kitchen were becoming more frequent, they were driving her increasingly to the front parlour with its hard chairs where she had seen the dead' (*Every Day*, p. 20). Likewise, the Axons' spare room is occupied by what Evelyn terms 'the less substantial tenants' (*Every Day*, p. 88) and the door is kept locked in an attempt to contain the malevolent impulses of the presences within. Yet, while the ghosts of 2 Buckingham Avenue provide one of the most striking and idiosyncratic elements of the duology, it is essential to recognize how Mantel, from the opening pages of *Every Day*, creates a link between the situation of haunting and the provision of care. Extracts from Muriel's social work case file are bookended by the account of Evelyn's performance of a séance at the request of her neighbour, the elder Mrs Sidney (p. 10), and various disturbing descriptions of the spectral activity that has recently taken place in the Axon household (pp. 17–21). The vexed and complicated relationship between Evelyn and her daughter provides the central focus for the narrative of *Every Day* and an analysis of this relationship provides the key for understanding the origins, functions and meanings of the ghosts that populate the Axons' home.

In the wake of what Evelyn takes to be an act of ghostly vandalism she attempts to explain to her daughter the nature and activity of the numerous phantoms within the house. As Evelyn puts it:

> there is more than one set of persecutors. There are the tenants with their constant jibes, their petty destructiveness .... It is possible to see them, quite possible, but they are very quick. ... But the other inhabitants, their effect is more – she presses her hand to her ribcage. In the soul, she wants to say (*Every Day*, p. 27–8).

Yet, despite Evelyn's insistence that there are 'two sets of persecutors', the ghosts that haunt the Axons' house do not act in accordance with any strict division or definition, as much as Evelyn may wish to impose one and exert some semblance of control over their potency. These ghosts are overdetermined, possessing various interlinked significances and making available a number of simultaneous interpretations of their activities. This overdetermination is crucial in that it renders the phantom 'tenants' and 'inhabitants' of 2 Buckingham Avenue capable of accommodating the complexity of the parent-child relationship and the multitude of factors that shape and potentially contaminate and incapacitate it. Both the multiplicity of the Buckingham Avenue ghosts and the way in which they are united by their emergence from a scene of compromised care-giving speak to the presence of overwhelming maternal ambivalence.

An unhappy medium: The séance as care-giving situation

While, as will be made clear, the ghosts haunting 2 Buckingham Avenue constitute the 'rags and tags' of a care-giving process hopelessly marred by a maternal ambivalence produced by, and producing, trauma, abuse and depletion, the maternal relationship is not the only situation in which ambivalence in a caring context, and its haunting consequences, are demonstrated. At least some of Evelyn's persecutors make their entrance into the Axon household via the situation of the séance. Advising an acquaintance against using a Ouija board, Evelyn warns that 'people get in … things get in … the house gets overcrowded' (*Every Day*, p. 135) while Muriel recalls how Evelyn 'regretted her séances' and observes that 'the house was full of what she had conjured up' (*Vacant Possession*, p. 37). Though not at first glance a self-evident example of a situation in which care-giving takes place, Mantel's treatment of the séance, both within the duology and elsewhere in her writing, allows the relationships between medium and client, and medium and ghost, to be read as involving a variety of kinds of care, even if the provision of such care is by no means inevitable.

Evelyn is not the only medium to appear within Mantel's novels. *Beyond Black* (2005)[34] tells the story of Alison Hart, a spiritualist making her living from her mediumistic practice at the turn of the millennium. Alison understands her profession to be based on the provision of comfort and consolation to her living clients, ameliorating unbearable truths about death and the nature of the dead. Faced with an audience member who has lost her pet dog and her husband, Alison implies that the pair will be reunited in death: 'Let her think it, that dog and master are together now; let her take comfort, since comfort's what she's paid for. Let her assume that Tiddles and his boss are together in the Beyond' (*Beyond Black*, p. 23). On another occasion Alison makes contact with an audience member's son, who was delivered stillborn. In addition to passing on the messages apparently given by the boy's ghost Alison carefully manages the parent's grief and distress:

> 'I'm sure those nurses and doctors were doing their best, and they didn't mean to hurt you, but the fact is, you weren't given a chance to grieve.'
> The woman hunched forward. Tears sprang out of her eyes. ...
> 'What I want you to know is this.' Al's voice was calm, unhurried, without the touch of tenderness that would overwhelm the woman entirely; dignified and precise, she might have been querying a grocery bill. 'That little boy of yours is a fine young man now. He knows you never held him. He knows that's not your fault. ... He understands what happened. He's opening his arms to you, and he's holding you now.' (p. 39)

These acts of comforting render the séance situation one in which care-giving ought to be taking place. Indeed, it is implied that there is a high price for failing or refusing to undertake such care. When Alison is questioned by Colette, her assistant, on why she insists upon managing and sanitizing the information she gives to her clients, Alison replies that if she didn't do so: 'They'd run a mile ... It'd kill them' (p. 32).

Evelyn's attitude to her trade is radically different from Alison's. As has been noted, *Every Day* opens with Evelyn giving a séance for her recently bereaved neighbour. Yet Evelyn's mediumistic practice is devoid of any actions that might provide comfort or moderate grief, fear or distress. When brusquely prompted by Evelyn to speak about her late husband, Mrs Sidney's response is one of unadulterated grief:

> Mrs Sidney crumpled, as if she had been dealt a blow, her bag slid from her knees to the floor, her shoulders sagged, great gouts of grief came dropping from her mouth. ... her face seemed to be slipping in and out of some grotesque and ludicrous mask. ... As she talked she gasped and retched at the memories, but in the end she calmed *herself*. (p. 11–12, my italics)

As this passage makes clear, despite her overwhelming distress, Mrs Sidney is left to calm and comfort herself as Evelyn fails to intervene. Evelyn's own description of her contact with the dead dispenses with any traditional consolatory fictions of the afterlife. She states: 'it appears that they tell some people that all is very beautiful on the ninth plane and that there are flowers and organ music, but they never said that to me, and if they do say it I think they must be confusing it with the funeral' (p. 12). When she finally appears to make contact with Mrs Sidney's husband her account of his whereabouts is as uncompromising as it is catastrophic for Evelyn's client, as Evelyn reports that Arthur Sidney 'is roasting in some unspeakable hell' (p. 13). It is only much later in the novel that the effects of Evelyn's mediumistic practice upon Mrs Sidney are revealed through a conversation between her adult children, Florence and Colin Sidney:

> 'We talk about her as if she were dead.'
> 'I sometimes wish she were ... I think and think ... that morning when I went over to Cousin Eileen's, and I came back, she'd been out, there was her bag in the hall, four months after Father's death – whatever happened, Colin? She was normal in the morning.'
> 'They said her brain was damaged.' (p. 93)

Colin goes on to recollect how, following this nebulous 'damage' to Mrs Sidney's brain, she is admitted to hospital where her doctor reports that she is suffering from 'delusions of nihilism' in which she believes 'she no longer exists' (p. 94). These extracts confirm the shattering effect upon Mrs Sidney of Evelyn's failure to practise her mediumship in a way that provides care. Her terror and grief ignored and dismissed, then compounded by Evelyn's assertion of Arthur Sidney's horrifying fate, Mrs Sidney is traumatized to the point of putative non-existence, her subjective integrity utterly compromised. As Mantel puts it in the preparatory notes for *Vacant Possession*: 'since she attended a séance at the Axon house, the elder Mrs Sidney has never been herself; indeed she has been no-one at all'.[35] Clearly, then, Evelyn's mediumistic practice, devoid of any of the care-giving elements observed in Alison's spiritualist work, has a disintegrating effect upon those who encounter it. The consequences of Evelyn's séances are not only felt by her clients. Her inability to meaningfully mediate between the living and the dead also allows into her home a number of ghosts who manifest as frightening fragments: 'as [Evelyn] moved to the foot of the stairs something grazed her sleeve and she pulled away. Go, go, she thought savagely; I did not invite you here. A bloody handprint stained the cream emulsion, the leprous skull grinned behind glass. Mr Sidney's twisted mouth, in another place' (p. 17). It is not merely Evelyn's mediumistic work that gives rise to a host of persecutory phantoms, however. Her role as a mother is similarly compromised. Having broken the news of her husband's spirit's whereabouts Evelyn hurries Mrs Sidney from the house, following which she worries not about the well-being of her client but about her own health and the effect the séance has had on her, crucially stating: 'I shall give this up ... because it is making me ill; if one day I took some sort of fit and were laid up, what would happen, who would look after Muriel?' (p. 14). Building on the earlier analysis of the analogue Mantel constructs between care-giving figures and the environments of care, I now address the question of by whom, and in what ways, Muriel is 'looked after', and the phantoms that the ambivalent care-giving gives rise to in the duology.

Put simply, maternal ambivalence refers to a mother's simultaneous possession of feelings of love and hatred towards her child.[36] The phenomenon has been recognized by a number of child psychotherapists and psychoanalysts, most notably D. W. Winnicott, who stated in his paper 'Hate in Countertransference', 'the mother ... hates her infant from the word go'.[37] This description resonates powerfully with Evelyn's memory of Muriel's birth in which her daughter is both 'like someone horribly executed' and 'a lovely daughter' whom Evelyn views with 'pity turning at once to exasperation' (p. 102). In her book *Torn in Two: The Experience of Maternal Ambivalence* Roszika Parker asserts that while 'maternal ambivalence is not a static state but a dynamic experience of conflict ... ambivalence itself is emphatically not the problem; the issue is how a mother manages the guilt and anxiety ambivalence provokes'.[38] Parker goes on to posit the existence of manageable maternal ambivalence, in which the 'safety catch' of maternal love prevents full rein being given to feelings of hatred and destructiveness, in opposition to unmanageable maternal ambivalence, in which this 'safety catch' fails[39] and the urge 'to destroy the child, to feed off its life, to turn it to stone, drive it mad, abuse or abandon it'[40] – always present in the mothering experience – gains the upper hand. The unmanageable quality of Evelyn's ambivalence towards her daughter is inscribed throughout *Every Day*. 'Mother always said that she would haunt,' recalls Muriel as she is being admitted to Fulmers Moor psychiatric hospital (*Vacant Possession*, p. 45), and while Evelyn's threats of post-mortem return are never explicitly realized, the relationship between mother and child is, from Muriel's birth onwards, nonetheless deeply dysfunctional. The reader is provided with an extensive if not exhaustive account of Evelyn's attitude towards her daughter in the early pages of the novel in the form of excerpts from Muriel's social services file, documents whose recognizable official format gives the lie to the Conservative notion that the family unit holds the key to healthy and adequate care-provision. These passages not only place Evelyn and Muriel's relationship within a constellation of care-giving that includes both the family unit and the agents of State-sponsored care but also give an early indication that this ostensibly care-giving relationship is deeply flawed. As Muriel's first social worker puts it: '[Mrs Axon's] attitude to

[Muriel] seems to be one of basic contempt and that the client does not have ordinary feelings ... she seems to have a negative attitude to client's mental and emotional development' (*Every Day*, p. 15). As the novel progresses a picture emerges of Evelyn as unable to relate to Muriel as fully human. Having already speculated as to whether Muriel possesses a soul (p. 28), Evelyn goes on to recall how 'her first years were spent in cleaning Muriel, in reconciling herself to her existence' (p. 44), understanding and treating Muriel as an object, an object that is, moreover, malevolent and frightening: 'at first [Muriel] had said, "Mother, Mother," and Evelyn thought that it was "Murder" she had called out in the dark' (p. 44).

If the ambivalence present in Evelyn's relationship with Muriel is played out practically, it is also echoed and amplified in her interactions with the ghosts which haunt her home. When Evelyn recalls Muriel's early life it is made clear that at least some of the ghosts who persecute her begin to arrive following Muriel's birth. With reference to Muriel's early years the text states that 'Evelyn wanted to be alone in the house; the house filled up, more than she dreaded' (*Every Day*, p. 44). The actions of those phantoms with free run of 2 Buckingham Avenue have a profoundly infantile quality and include pushing and pinching, undertaking acts of petty vandalism and tugging at Evelyn's clothing in a parody of a child seeking attention from an adult. In one episode Evelyn is subjected to an entire morning of 'rappings and bangings at the front door. The screams and laughter of spiteful children [ring] in [her] ears' (*Every Day*, p. 182), an episode which places Evelyn 'at the mercy of manipulative, malevolent, withholding beings'.[41]

Perhaps the most striking element of Muriel and Evelyn's relationship is a pathological lack of differentiation, which echoes Estella Weldon's characterisation of the 'perverse maternal attitude' as one that 'manifests as a desire to engulf, to de-humanise, to invade, to take control of and merge with the [child]'.[42] Mantel describes Evelyn as reading Muriel's mind, 'thinking in her brain' (*Every Day*, p. 29) and, most disconcertingly, depicts Muriel physically transforming into her mother: 'Muriel's shoulders droop. Her knees stiffen, her hand quivers for support on the banister. At each tread she feels pain, she grimaces, she gasps a little. All her resources for today are played out. She is becoming Evelyn, for the night' (*Every Day*, p. 26). The most interesting instance of this 'mind reading' occurs with reference to Muriel's physical hunger. This episode merges a discussion of feeding, a process whereby something is taken inside oneself, and an instance of violent and depleting invasion of the self by the other. The facilities for the provision of food in the Axon household have already been significantly skewed by the ghostly embargo on entrance to the kitchen and Evelyn and Muriel have been driven into the parlour where they are reduced to eating food out of cans stored in a sideboard: '[Muriel] wants one of the tins of meat; all evening she cherishes her longings and her hunger, the feelings she has that Evelyn does not know about. At eight o'clock Evelyn says: "We could have a tin of meat." Inside, Muriel squirms in pain. Her thought has been read again. Dragged, filleted, out of her living head' (*Every Day*, p. 25).

Mantel's description here queasily collapses the differentiation between psychic and biological sustenance while simultaneously collapsing intersubjective boundaries. Muriel's physical hunger is inextricably linked to her thoughts and feelings around it. This moment of 'mind-reading' is given a particular potency through the way in which it perverts a conventional parent-child interaction in which the parent intuits the hunger of their child and provides appropriate sustenance in a timely manner. Here this parental intuition is rendered not as comforting or satiating but as traumatic and invasive, extracting something of the child's essence in a display of cannibalistic maternity.

This image of the devouring care-giver is registered on a metaphorical level in the duology through recurrent references to the eating of eggs, themselves symbols of reproduction and new life which implicate the mother figure. In *Vacant Possession* Sylvia tries to deny her husband eggs on the ground that he is on a diet while Colin's attempts to cook an egg for himself are unsuccessful and troubling: 'Colin stood over the cooker and looked down at his egg, bobbing dizzily in a mass of leaking white. As if alive it flew about and tapped itself against the side of the pan' (p. 12). This idea of the egg still being alive as it is cooked is alarming in itself but when read alongside Colin's later comparison of 2 Buckingham Avenue to the house of Atreus (p. 203), renowned for its association with the parental cannibalization of children, it gains a further sinister significance, undermining Colin's status as a hapless but harmless father figure. Muriel's treatment of eggs in the duology carries a similar metaphorical weight. In *Every Day* she displays a preference for raw eggs, at one point placing her breakfast egg on her palm and allowing it to roll off and smash on the kitchen floor (p. 80), while *Vacant Possession* features the recurring image of Muriel sucking the yolk out of hard-boiled eggs. The unsettling quality of Muriel's egg-eating habits is commented upon by one of the Sidneys' children: '"Daddy," Claire said, "You should see the way [Muriel] eats eggs, it's really disgusting. She cuts a piece off the end and then she sucks it out – like this"' (*Vacant Possession*, p. 154). Mantel's description of the painstaking way in which Muriel breaks into her egg before eating it, shattering the shell which contains the egg's contents and maintains its structural integrity, peeling away the skin beneath to suck out the centre and leave a hollow behind, operates as an extended metaphor for the chronic lack of definition, not only between Muriel and the 'mind-reading' Evelyn, but between carers and the recipients of care of all types within these texts.

Seeking Whom They May Devour: Feeding and Eating in *Every Day is Mother's Day*

As has been indicated above, scenes of feeding and eating in the Axon household are notably maladjusted. Descriptions of the food and drink available in the house are universally unappealing, the foodstuffs stale, raw or otherwise inappropriate and Muriel's relationship with food is thoroughly dysfunctional, a dysfunction which is inextricable from her maternal relationship. The following passage describes the consequences of Muriel's disobedience as imposed by Evelyn:

> As punishment, [Muriel] was being deprived of food. It annoyed Evelyn that she wasn't more affected by this. If you put food in front of her, she ate it; if not, she didn't miss it. By herself she would starve, Evelyn thought, or make herself very sick. She would bring a raw egg to the table, and set it down with every appearance of satisfaction; choose what was raw or half cooked or stale, in preference to the good food her mother provided for her. (*Every Day*, p. 67)

Mantel's emphasis here on Muriel's choice of 'what was raw, half cooked or stale' is telling, confirming Muriel's possession of 'an indiscriminate appetite ("a craving to take in everything that offers itself, together with an inability to distinguish between what's valuable and what's worthless")'[43] and a vexed relationship with what should be kept out and what should be taken in. Clearly the scenes of feeding and eating within the duology provide an index for the quality and character of the care-giving relationships in which they take place.

It is useful to note here the generalized disordering of scenes of feeding and eating present in *Every Day is Mother's Day* and *Vacant Possession*, a disordering which forms a trope that allows a reader to confirm when a moment of care-giving is, or should be but is not, taking place. For example, a series of disastrous Christmas meals are staged both inside and outside 2 Buckingham Avenue. Florence Sidney's Christmas visit to the Axons bearing a plate of warm home-made mince pies ends with several of the pies pitched to the floor and Florence having a large glass of neat scotch forced upon her at half past eleven in the morning. Meanwhile, at the Sidneys' house, the remains of Christmas dinner congeal or else are trodden into the carpet while the assembled company are described as 'nauseous', 'gross and sated' (*Every Day*, p. 119). Crucially, during the Sidneys' residence at 2 Buckingham Avenue, milk brought into the house goes off with alarming speed, referencing the chaotic treatment of the formula milk that Evelyn brings home for Muriel's newborn baby. The text relates how, only two days after the birth of the baby, 'there was no more milk. Muriel had spilled a lot, wasted it, even drunk some of it herself' (*Every Day*, p. 190). This focus on milk as spoiled, wasted and insufficient articulates the notion that the first feeding relationship between mother and infant forms a blueprint for subsequent feeding relationships but by no means is the positive quality of that relationship taken for granted.

In one overt example Mantel juxtaposes Evelyn Axon's contemplation of feeding her daughter to the ravenous spectres of 2 Buckingham Avenue with a detailed description of the meal that Sylvia Sidney had prepared for her family that evening:

> [Evelyn] always plans that if they get too close she will put her hand on Muriel's chest and push her slithering down to them, fat bait, something to lick their lips over.
>
> Sunday: Sylvia cooked roast beef (she does it brown, a full twenty-five minutes per pound plus twenty minutes), roast potatoes, carrots, frozen peas: rhubarb crumble, at which she is a dab hand, and custard. (*Every Day*, p. 59)

This stark disparity sets up an uncomfortable contrast between two very different maternal approaches to the provision of nutrition.

As Evelyn's fantasy of feeding Muriel to the ghosts of 2 Buckingham Avenue attests, it is not only the house's living inhabitants whose approach to food and feeding is disturbed and disturbing. The phantom tenants haunting the house are understood to be possessed of a sadistic hunger and this urge to devour is remarked upon by both Muriel and Evelyn:

> Evelyn sat on the bottom step, and rocked herself back and forth like a child. Such appetites, she thought, such vile appetites for raw and bloody meat. Were their jaws at work, behind the spare-room door? And if she went up there would she hear them, salivating and sucking, smacking unpicturable lips? Baby flesh would tear like butter. (*Every Day*, p. 136)

Bearing in mind the use of feeding relationships within the duology to reflect and critique parental and maternal relationships, a question is posed by the destructive hunger associated with these ghosts, namely, what significance they have for Mantel's exploration of domestic care-giving. The horror inspired in Evelyn by the appetites of 2 Buckingham Avenue's ghosts is a manifestation of the maternal ambivalence already demonstrated in her relationship to Muriel, and communicates a terror of being cannibalized and overwhelmed by infantile demands, a feeling eloquently expressed by one of the mothers interviewed for Parker's *Torn in Two*: 'I can't bear the endless demands, …, the impression of a bottomless pit. I feel that I am going to be devoured; that there will be absolutely nothing left of me.'[44]

Thus far the persecutory ghosts of 2 Buckingham Avenue have been identified not as a homogenous mass with a single effect and meaning, but as emerging from a séance situation in which Evelyn's inability to effectively mediate between the living and the dead permitted unreconstituted fear, horror and grief to enter and populate the Axon household. It has also been demonstrated that these phantoms, products of failed care-giving, simultaneously make manifest the consequences of the unmanageable ambivalence Evelyn demonstrates towards her daughter. Yet if Evelyn suffers the consequences of her haunting ambivalence towards her daughter, in the form of the persecutory and devouring infantile spectres who frighten and humiliate her, Muriel too possesses her own mode of spectrality born of receiving such compromised and ambivalent care.

Muriel Axon: a ghost carrying a ghost

A deliberate concomitance is created between Muriel and the house's 'less substantial tenants' from the opening pages of *Every Day* which, as has been noted, twins an account of a séance with extracts from Muriel's own social services case file. Muriel imitates the malevolent poltergeist activity, stealing and moving household items (p. 17), committing acts of self-harm which she insinuates are the work of the ghosts (pp. 29–30) and leaving (it is implied) threatening notes which Evelyn takes to be of supernatural origin (pp. 24, 32). Muriel's resemblance to the ghostly inhabitants of the Axons' home goes further than a conscious aping of their persecutory activities. Evelyn experiences her as somehow phantasmal and not fully present, feeling 'more and more, when [she] was in a room with her daughter … as if no one was there' (*Every Day*, p. 32), and describing the pregnant Muriel as 'a ghost carrying a ghost' (*Every Day*, p. 79). Muriel's indiscriminate appetite echoes the 'vile appetites' of the household ghosts and Evelyn's recollection of Muriel as a young child possessing 'a powerful urge to bite, to tear with her teeth' (*Every Day*, p. 44) further reinforces

Muriel's correspondence with the inhabitants of the spare room with their 'unpicturable' jaws (*Every Day*, p. 136). Psychoanalyst Leonard Shengold has asserted that 'a result of chronic early overstimulation or deprivation' in children is a retreat into a state of 'hypnotic living-deadness, a state of existing "as if" [they] were there'.[45] Muriel's manner of relating to her mother closely resembles such a state, reinforcing her status as ghost within the Axon household:

> when Evelyn spoke to her, she became like an empty cavern. Muriel Alexandra's body stands irreproachable like a guardsman on parade, while her own thoughts slip off to gambol and strut, enjoying their own existence. (p. 24)

Shengold goes on to recall Sàndor Ferenczi's assertion that an abused child 'changes into an obedient automaton' adding that 'the automaton has murder within' and indeed the reader finds Evelyn's suspicions of Muriel's murderous intentions to be proved correct:

> [Muriel] thought certain thoughts, like: I will kill you. Then many times a day Muriel would think thoughts, rejoicing in the deception. I will trip you down the stairs and break your neck. Mother mother mother. (p. 24)

That the spectres which populate 2 Buckingham Avenue make manifest the various consequences of a series of care-giving relationships malfunctioning beneath the weight of unmanageable ambivalence is clear. Yet, if, as Winnicott suggests, 'mothers who do not have it in them to provide good enough care cannot be made good enough by mere instruction … there are those who can hold an infant and those who cannot',[46] Mantel's duology asks where that lack or inability originates. *Every Day* and *Vacant Possession* possess a textual landscape in which no positive representation of familial care-giving is to be found and in which caring relationships are characterized at best by distance and apathy.[47] Nowhere is this underlined more clearly than with reference to the story of Evelyn's own profoundly traumatic childhood, a story that includes the death of both parents, one to a progressive and distressing unnamed illness, the loss of her family home, the stigma of her father's extramarital affairs, emotional neglect and her contemplation of suicide (pp. 116–18). Throughout this passage Evelyn is represented as neglected, cold and inadequately clothed and located outside of the sphere of parental attention. As an adolescent Evelyn periodically visits her ill mother who is confined to a nursing home and described as 'smelling of urine' and 'scream[ing] if she was touched' (pp. 117–18). When we consider Roszika Parker's assertion that 'mothering is a multigenerational process'[48] (and indeed Margaret Thatcher's own assertion that 'the family is not only mother and father and children – it is grandparents, aunts'[49]) it becomes clear that Evelyn's inability to mediate unbearable emotional excitation, as in the case of Mrs Sidney's séance, or to connect with her daughter as fully human, is attributed in the novel to Evelyn's own lacking and traumatic experience of parenting. These multigenerational failures of mothering affirm child psychologist Bruno Bettleheim's assertion that 'the key to good enough childcare is empathy, stimulated by the parent's capacity to recall their own childhood emotions and experiences'.[50] Evelyn's childhood, which seems to her 'to have taken place in another century' (p. 118), is a wasteland of loss, neglect and trauma which, in her interactions with Muriel, is handed down to her daughter.

Ghosts from the nursery: abuse, trauma and haunting

While the ancestral spectres of Evelyn's own emotionally deprived childhood haunt the narrative only through Evelyn's reminiscences, her deceased abusive husband does so explicitly, a phantom who makes manifest the persistence of trauma and its impact upon maternal capability. Shortly after her mother's death, when Evelyn is seventeen, she is abruptly married off to Clifford Axon, one of her uncle's work colleagues who is suspected 'of indulging in sexual deviations' (*Every Day*, p. 118). Despite his sudden death when Muriel is six, Clifford malevolently persists in the narrative, appearing first in ominous anecdotes, then as an inscription in his old overcoat which Muriel discovers and brings into the house, implying to Evelyn that 'Clifford had come back, and hung his coat on the hallstand' (p. 86). However, it is only as *Every Day* is coming to its close that Evelyn's uncle's suspicions are revealed to be true:

> Perhaps we should have more children, [Evelyn] thought ... but after Muriel, Clifford had not wanted to risk repetition. He said he would amuse himself. He would go down to the shed and she must turn a blind eye. A blind eye to whatever he kept in there and whatever comings and goings there were. That was what she had always done, until one day she had seen the child from next door heading down the path. When Clifford came in for his tea ... she asked him, 'Do you take children down there?' ... Clifford's face then: 'A blind eye, Evelyn, a blind eye'; the threats in his voice, the promise of a week of bruises and Muriel tossed into her bedroom, unfed and screaming. (*Every Day*, p. 174)

The image of Muriel's mistreatment combined with the confirmation of the perpetration by an adult of the systematic abuse of small children stands in stark contrast to the gothicized events of the narrative preceding it owing to the deliberate rooting of the revelation within the quotidian domestic. The full-length passage details Evelyn's nervous spilling of milk and sugar on the table as she confronts Clifford and includes mundane details of the day and time of the scene ('three thirty – it was a Sunday'). The eruption of such physical violence into a text that has previously been preoccupied with the paranormal and supernatural produces a shift in the work the gothic has been doing in the novel up to this point. To fully understand the nature of that shift, it is necessary to turn to an anecdote told to Colin by Isabel, the Axons' social worker.[51]

Isabel recounts to Colin the story of a Jewish couple in hiding from the Nazis during the Second World War. The couple's hiding place is a small 'hole under a trapdoor inside [a] farmhouse. The floor of the farmhouse was made of earth' (*Every Day*, p. 129). The environment is claustrophobic and suffocating. During the course of the war, the woman gets pregnant and gives birth to a baby girl, all the while underground. In order to maintain silence and not give away their position, whenever the baby cried 'they put their hands over her mouth. For a year and a half' (p. 131). The couple survive the war but the toll on their child when they emerge from hiding is terrible. As Isabel puts it, 'she was like a wild animal. When she was brought out of the hole she screamed and clawed and attacked people. At other times she was completely mute. As if they still had their hands over her face' (p. 131). This disturbing story, in which parental care is horribly perverted by terrible circumstances appears at first to have little in common with the horrors and abuses perpetrated in the Axon household. Yet certain details tie the two narratives together in such a way as to put them on a spectrum of collapsed, failing or otherwise perverse parental relationships. The description of the young Muriel's 'urge to bite, to tear with her teeth' echoes the animalistic behaviour of the traumatized child in Isabel's story, but a more striking commonality emerges in Muriel's apparent reaction to this urge which is 'to keep her mouth covered with her hand' (*Every Day*, p. 44). This resonance between the two images of a hand over a child's mouth is accompanied by a further textual echo. Following the revelation of Clifford's abuse the passage continues: 'years passed like this, the nameable fears giving way to the unnameable, the familiar dread of evening muffled under a pall of fog, of blackness, of earth; all the days lived as if underground, and Muriel, [Evelyn] thought, if I could have mourned myself, if I could have drawn breath, I might have pitied you' (p. 174). This description of Evelyn and Muriel's life at 2 Buckingham Avenue during Clifford's lifetime powerfully echoes the description of the deeply traumatized family unit living beneath the earth, in fear for their lives.

While, clearly, these two narratives of warped and dysfunctional parental relationships are not analogous, their inclusion in *Every Day* and the points of resemblance and of tension between them gesture to a specific ethical position regarding how and why care-giving fails. As Bettleheim, and countless caring professionals after him have repeatedly emphasized, the key to successful care-giving relationships, particularly maternal relationships is the care-giver's capacity for empathy. Evelyn's comment that if she could have 'mourned' herself she might have pitied her daughter poignantly illustrates how that capacity for empathy can be snuffed out by parental trauma. Yet it is not only maternal care-givers whose empathic potential is compromised in these texts. Isabel too complains that in qualifying as a social worker attempts have been made to 'educate [her] out of feeling' (*Every Day*, p. 74).

This refusal or inability to empathize suffuses the novel, reaching beyond those who perform a care-giving role, to encompass public attitudes towards familial care and the abuse that can be perpetrated under its auspices. When Colin complains that Isabel's story is a 'terrible one', stating that he doesn't 'like to think about stories like that', Isabel counters that 'none of us likes to think of other people's hells. We avoid it if we can' (p. 130). The treatment of Evelyn and Muriel's narrative by the other characters within the duology demonstrates a similarly avoidant attitude to their dysfunctional care-giving relationship. This is exemplified when the Axons' social services file is lost by Isabel and then stolen by one of Colin's work colleagues, Frank O'Dwyer. Ignorant of who the individuals involved are, Frank plans to use the case notes as the basis of a novel. Speaking of the file, one of his friends states that 'Frank could never … have invented such grotesquerie by himself' while Frank goes on to suggest that he 'might turn it into a sort of allegory, you see, about the state of our society' (p. 159). When Colin informs Isabel of this turn of events she protests: 'But it's not a story, it's just what people do. It's just a record of what they do' (p. 164), articulating the contested status of this narrative of compromised care, and by extension, the duology itself.

While O'Dwyer's plans for a 'state of the nation' novel based on Evelyn and Muriel's case file self-consciously parodies what Mantel herself is undertaking within the duology, they also make a complex statement about the relationship the novels have to non-fictional accounts of abuse, neglect and deprivation undertaken within the privacy and notional safety of the family home. The gothic tropes around which the Axon household is constructed, the poltergeists and persecutory phantoms, the dilapidated family home with its forbidden rooms and arcane objects and documents, serve to distance and misdirect readerly attention, obscuring, almost until the novel's close, the profoundly human origins of the terror and trauma in Evelyn and Muriel's lives. Through Frank's planned novel, the Axons' 'real' suffering forms the basis for a work of fiction, and in so doing, real-life equivalents for Evelyn and Muriel are also implied. Mantel's own experiences of social work are pertinent here, specifically her essay 'The Woman in the Hall'.[52] The triad of the duology, O'Dwyer's planned novel and the 'factual' account of her professional experiences which Isabel attempts to produce, combine to communicate a self-conscious awareness of the ethical responsibility inherent in turning real suffering into fiction. This self-reflexiveness is compounded by the way in which the suggestion of real world 'women in the hall' refuses to allow the reader the chance to participate in an avoidance of 'other people's hells'. It is this refusal that changes the stakes of Mantel's use of the gothic mode in *Every Day*, demanding that the reader recognize how both the interpersonal and professional structures which could facilitate the empathic connection upon which healthy care-giving depends are so frequently inadequate or absent.

'This homely home-from-home': Medical Care-Giving

The domestic environment is far from the only care-giving environment to feature within the duology. Mantel's critique of care-giving within the milieu of the 1970s and 1980s also takes in various clinical settings, the most compelling of which is Fulmers Moor, the psychiatric hospital to which Muriel is removed following her mother's death. In representing the space of the psychiatric hospital Mantel contributes to an extensive literary tradition,[53] although, in terms of historical and geographic contexts, Mantel's treatment of the psychiatric ward environment differs significantly from the majority of canonical novels on the subject. *Vacant Possession*'s treatment of in-patient psychiatric care concerns a specific moment in the history of mental health policy in the United Kingdom, representing the beginning of what Andrew Scull has termed 'decarceration' – that is, the closure of psychiatric wards housed in former Victorian asylums and discharge of their former patients into the community – a context which, as is demonstrated below, is strikingly inflected through Mantel's use of the gothic mode.

Situated outside of the dormitory towns in which *Every Day* took place, Fulmers Moor is initially described in such a way as to give an impression of a deracinated and ahistorical location, its 'crumbling grey core' (p. 44), deprived of any architectural features which might situate it within a particular historical moment, supplemented by the prefabricated and temporary structures of 'Nissen huts' (p. 44) and 'new buildings made of metal and varnished wood and plate glass' (p. 44). Muriel's admission to the deracinated space of Fulmers Moor is itself presented as a thorough process of depersonalization as she is inculcated into the routines and spaces of the hospital: 'this is your locker, this is your orange bedspread, this is your bedside mat, this is where you will live. ... The nurse took away her dress. She took away her knickers. She gave her a thin cotton gown' (p. 45). This deindividuation is not merely gestural but is inscribed linguistically. The nurses use the pronouns 'us' and 'we' to refer to patients when defining what kind of behaviour is acceptable from the patients and what is not as the following exchange demonstrates:

> The nurse smiled. 'We don't want to droop, do we?'
>
> 'I don't know what we're talking about,' Muriel said, 'Our head hurts.'
>
> 'We mustn't be cheeky. We'll learn that soon enough, dear.' (*Vacant Possession*, p. 45)

The seeming gesture of friendliness and inclusivity in this exchange is undercut by an aggressive exertion of control and the implication that punitive consequences are attached to a failure to learn the spoken and unspoken rules of the hospital. This exchange provides an illustration of Goffman's statement with regard to the entry of a patient into a psychiatric hospital or similar residential institution that 'staff often feel that a recruit's readiness to be appropriately deferential in his initial face-to-face encounters with them is a sign that he will take the role of the routinely pliant inmate. The occasion on which staff members first tell the inmate of his deference obligations may be structured to challenge the inmate to balk or to hold his peace forever'.[54] The apparent muddying of the division between nurse and patient is commented on by another patient, Sholto Marx: '"The patients for the shifts," he remarked, "or the shifts for the patients?"' (*Vacant Possession*, p. 53). His remark calls into question precisely who is at the service of whom in the in-patient setting. The border crossing from the outside world into the world of the hospital, and being subject to the hospitality offered by that setting, begins a process of spectralization that is compounded by nursing practice. Mantel's choice of narrative voice when relating the experiences of the patients at Fulmers Moor attests to an erasure of individual identity, collapsing as it does any discrete subjective voice and implying a blending together of individual experience:

> My mother died ... I had this accident ... I worried all night because I hadn't done my homework ... I should never have gotten married ... I had no idea there was such filth in the world ... At this point there was no food left in the house ...

> I knew he had got a knife ... I knew that if I allowed myself to go to sleep I should die during the night. Each night in the six o'clock news there is a special message for me. People stare at me whenever I set foot in the street. Someone had broken my glasses/started a fire/informed on me ... Marilyn Monroe stole my giro. I went to the café till my money ran out. (*Vacant Possession*, p. 47)

Only when exiting the space of the institution are subjects treated as individuals and the significance of this border crossing from institutional space to societal place and back is inscribed materially in a passage that relates how Muriel and her fellow patients are given 'special clothes' for an excursion into the community:

> She had special clothes for the outing, given her out of a cardboard box kept in the nurses' room: a blue frock with six buttons and a mackintosh that was only a bit small. Back on Greyshott she got given her old smock again. A nurse stood over her waiting to take the outside clothes away. (p. 51)

In Mantel's representation the hospital forms an atopia within the novel where the patients' attempts to create place and community through their interactions (for example patient Emmanuel Crisp's impromptu parodic sermons and communal hymn singing (p. 50)) are inevitably thwarted by the routines of the hospital or the patients' own illnesses and where the strictures and routines of the hospital environment continually reinforce a paradoxically isolating de-individuation.

The patients of Fulmers Moor are forced to carry out their entire existence within an environment which, by its nature, denies them individual identity and autonomy, a state which frequently becomes unbearable. In one incident Effie, another of Muriel's fellow patients, runs 'screaming and cursing down Greyshott Ward and out into the corridor' where she protests that: 'I don't need getting up at six thirty every day, Christmas day, birthday, Queen's official birthday and every bleeding Sunday. I need to get up when I want and make myself a little cup of tea' (p. 53). Following this outburst Effie is 'dragged' back to her ward and 'dumped' on her bed after which she 'subside[s] ... her chest heaving with the shock and horror of her outburst' (p. 53). As the orderlies' response to Effie's attempts to break free of hospital routine demonstrates, violent and direct outbursts are ineffectual in counteracting the deathly depersonalization of existence at Fulmers Moor. Unable to countermand the 'instructions for use' that determine the patients' existence (provided not only by the signposts mentioned above but by the implicit threats and physical restraints used by the hospital staff) the slippage of subjective identity created within the psychiatric hospital forces upon the patients of Fulmers Moor a deeply spectral existence. The patients seemingly oscillate between presence and absence. This occurs literally in terms of the removal of certain patients from the hospital into the community only for them to return again. However, it is also manifested metaphorically, via the effects of certain drug treatments upon their recipients as this passage detailing another of Effie's manic episodes demonstrates:

> From time to time a ripple of emotion made [Effie's] face quiver. She would put a hand up to stop it, and then she would leap up in a frenzied pursuit of the nearest nurse. 'I want my Largactil,' she would bleat, 'I want my Modecate, I want my nice Fentazin syrup.' Tranquillised, she would lean against the wall, her face serene again; only the blink of an eye, only a minute Parkinsonian quiver of the extremities, to show that she was alive at all. (*Vacant Possession*, pp. 51–2)

Effie's uncanny 'undead' quality, produced by her movement between tranquillized absence and agitated presence, is reproduced in the varying modes of liminality occupied by her fellow patients. These characters occupy a threshold between coherence and incoherence, delusion and clarity, subject and object. This last oscillation registers itself most potently in Muriel's fellow patient, Phillip, who suffers from a delusion that he is a machine: 'I am a tractor. I am a Centurion tank … I am the internal combustion engine' (*Vacant Possession*, pp. 53–4).

It is important to remember that the 'insane asylum' only assumed its modern form in the eighteenth century and formed part of the landscape of many early gothic texts.[55] Ellis describes it as an institution 'whose antipathy to domestic life is perceived as intrinsic'[56] and certainly, in the late 1970s and early 1980s, the psychiatric hospitals based in the original Victorian 'mad houses' constituted houses only in that they 'warehoused' the mentally ill, enclosing them structurally and preventing their circulation in wider society. By utilizing once again the psychiatric hospital within the gothic mode,[57] Mantel underscores how the long-stay in-patient wards of the 1970s and 1980s exist on a continuum with their Victorian predecessors and questions whether, even in the absence of the gross abuses of psychiatric patients in that era, significant correlations might not still exist. The reading above permits an understanding of the psychiatric hospital as a gothic no-place, whose gothic nature stems from its inescapable quality and whose capacity for providing meaningful care for the mentally ill is provocatively questioned since the environment inherently exacerbates the kinds of fragmentation of subjective identity which result from mental illness itself. As Effie's episode makes poignantly clear, *Vacant Possession* depicts the disintegrative effects of mental illness which combine with drug treatment and nursing practice to result in a spectralized individual, fluctuating between multiple binary states.

Homing Instinct: Community Care-Giving in Theory and Practice

If this kind of in-patient care leads in Mantel's duology to a spectralization of the mentally ill, in 1985 the Thatcher government began to reform care in such a way that these particular ghosts were exorcized from the institutions of the state, notionally to go and 'haunt' the houses of their families as part of the 'care in the community' movement. These individuals form societal ghosts within Mantel's narrative, haunting their former communities in a multitude of ways. Following the 1983 Audit Commission report 'Making a Reality of Community Care' a model was adopted whereby patients were discharged from long-stay hospital wards into the care of their families or, where this was not possible, rented accommodation outside of a clinical setting. If in the eighteenth century 'the mental hospital replaced the family and the community as the epicentre of care and control',[58] the 1980s saw a reversal of this position. The decade 'between 1972 and 1982 saw the closure of 40 of the larger psychiatric hospitals in England' and between 1954 and 1982 the number of psychiatric beds in English hospitals was slashed by 55 per cent.[59]

It has already been observed that the Conservative government sought to establish the family, as well as religious and charitable organizations, as the appropriate agencies for the provision of care. Mantel weaves a series of Thatcherite tenets throughout the narrative, placing them into the mouths of her characters. Colin parrots the famous Thatcherite maxim of the time, 'there is no alternative',[60] and upon confronting the married banker who is the father of his daughter's child states: 'this is 1984. Victorian Values' (*Vacant Possession*, p. 164).[61] The doctor who attends Colin's mother following her discharge from hospital responds to protestations that the family can't cope with their caring responsibilities by glibly stating 'charity begins at home' (*Vacant Possession*, p. 178). Even Mantel's choice of name for Francis, the Sidneys' local vicar, references Margaret Thatcher's paraphrasing of the prayer of St. Francis upon her arrival at Downing Street as prime minister.[62] These ventriloquial repetitions render Conservative rhetoric a further spectre circulating within the narrative. The public discord surrounding the widespread introduction of care in the community is voiced in the following extract by Sylvia Sidney and Francis. Both characters act as symbols for what the Conservative government of the day deemed the most appropriate agencies for care:

> 'It's a con trick, all this about discharging people into the community. They're doing it to save money.'

'Quite true,' Francis said ... Community care properly carried through is a most expensive option. Done shabbily, it's cheap. The social workers, God bless them, have been urging it for years. Now they've fallen right into the budgeter's trap.' (*Vacant Possession*, p. 154)

This exchange neatly highlights the discrepancy between what theorist Richard Titmuss termed the 'sense of warmth and human comforting' evoked by the concept of care in the community and its reality. Titmuss states that 'a situation was being created in which "the care of the mentally ill [was transferred] from trained staff to untrained or ill equipped staff or no staff at all"'.[63] This situation is described in the narrative by Sholto who confirms that 'what [the authorities] claim ... is an ongoing bean feast, flats, nurses, jobs, day centres. But if you want to avoid all that you'll have no trouble at all. There aren't enough to go around' (*Vacant Possession*, p. 57). Sholto's comment voices the crucial problem at the heart of the care in the community initiative in the 1980s, that is, a critical discrepancy between demand and resourcing. As Ben Nelson put it in the *Times*, in response to the 1988 Griffiths report on community care, 'there appeared to be a grave mismatch of resources to need. About 90 per cent of expenditure on the mental health services was spent on hospital services and 10 per cent on community care. But the demand was almost exactly the other way round, with 90 per cent of people requiring help in the community and 10 per cent in hospital'.[64]

This lack of resources was not limited to psychiatric medicine. Care for the elderly was subject to the same enthusiasm for a move to community-based care, an enthusiasm which repeatedly led to disastrous breakdowns of the caring situation as family members struggled to cope with the demands of providing medical and personal care to elderly relatives who were often frail and confused. Writing in the *Guardian* in 1988, Jane Brotchie recorded the feelings of claustrophobia and isolation brought about by the sudden imposition of caring responsibilities upon ill-equipped individuals, stating that:

> lack of freedom of choice aggravates the strain and makes carers vulnerable to depression. As physical exhaustion takes its toll, feelings of inadequacy, failure, and hopelessness emerge. Carers often criticise themselves for being irritable and short-tempered with the people they look after. One spoke of her despair and of her desire to kill herself: she felt increasingly unable to continue nursing her incontinent and physically abusive mother. The doctor prescribed anti-depressants.[65]

This account of one female care-giver being 'strong-armed' into taking on caring responsibilities previously shouldered by the State,[66] and her subsequent inability to cope, is sharply reflected in Mantel's text as Colin and Florence's mother, Mrs Sidney, (who is doubly incontinent and suffering from a delusion that she is May of Teck, a deceased member of the British royal family), is discharged from a geriatric ward into her daughter's care after many years as an in-patient. The staff nurse on Mrs Sidney's ward points out to Colin and his wife that 'they want to close this place down, and anybody they can get out, they will get out' (*Vacant Possession*, p. 94). In short order Mrs Sidney is returned to her daughter's home and uncaremoniously abandoned: '"all yours!" [the ambulance crew] cried as they sped off down the path' (*Vacant Possession*, p. 161). After only a short period of attempting to care for her mother at home, Florence becomes overwhelmed, as she tries to explain to her mother's doctor during one of his visits:

> Florence had run downstairs after him and followed him into the street. 'I can't go on,' she wailed. 'Dr Rudge, listen to me.'
> Dr Rudge stopped in surprise, bouncing his car keys on his palm. 'But you've got the district nurse, Miss Sidney. Be thankful for small mercies.'
> 'But I can't manage! The smell! And the way she wakes up and thinks she's at Marlborough House! It frightens me!'
> ...
> '... I can't go on.' Florence's voice rose into the damp afternoon. 'Don't you understand? We can't take anymore, any of us.'
> ...
> Dr Rudge cursed under his breath, and felt in his overcoat pockets for his prescription pad. He scribbled on it and ripped the page off.
> 'Try this to calm you down, Miss Sidney.' (*Vacant Possession*, pp. 183–4)

Florence's experience of being forcibly repositioned as the most appropriate caregiver for her elderly mother clearly taps into contemporary accounts of how the move to a care-in-the-community model often put unbearable pressure not only on the patients who were made subject to it but the relatives and neighbours who were intended to deliver it. Yet, this depiction of an unmanageable, suffocating caring relationship does not feature in the duology merely as a historical detail. Rather, it is given a gothic gloss.

As soon as Mrs Sidney takes up residence in her daughter's home eerie domestic malfunctions of the kind more usual in the adjacent 2 Buckingham Avenue begin to occur; the clocks stop telling the right time, pictures keep falling off the walls, the house-plants begin to die and broken glass appears on the kitchen floor, seemingly from nowhere (*Vacant Possession*, p. 169). Mrs Sidney herself is described as a revenant: 'nothing but a nightgown of yellow winceyette held in the old lady's bones, but her face had become animated, lips twitching, eyes opening wide' (*Vacant Possession*, p. 97).[67] Her delusion that she is May of Teck, the deceased Queen Mother, lends a further spectral aspect to her presence in the house. Mantel continues to render this instance of community care through the lens of a parodic gothic, as Mrs Sidney simultaneously occupies the role of gothic tyrant and sequestered heroine. When Mrs Sidney is eventually murdered by Muriel, who provides her with an overdose of sleeping pills, suspicion immediately falls upon the harassed and overwhelmed Florence. Despite her vehement protestations, Colin and Sylvia and the ineffectual Dr Rudge insist upon Florence's guilt while also conspiring to conceal it from the outside world. In creating this familial secrecy around a secret which in fact does not exist Mantel parodies the gothic convention of the family secret, the revelation of which drives the narrative, while simultaneously constructing a situation in which medical, social and familial care-giving structures catastrophically rupture. The secret which the gothic mode ultimately reveals here is the open secret of the inadequacies of Thatcherite social care policy and the phantoms created through those inadequacies. Mrs Sidney is not the only character to die as a result of their discharge into the community. Effie's ability to cope in the world outside of Fulmers Moor is questioned by Sholto explicitly when he remarks 'you might [pass], Muriel. I might pass, if I don't fall down and foam. Crisp will pass. But Effie – never' (*Vacant Possession*, p. 56). Sholto's suspicions prove correct; Effie's expulsion from Fulmers Moor directly results in her death; she becomes homeless and, having been brought into hospital 'frozen and raving', dies of pneumonia (*Vacant Possession*, p. 159). Effie, like Phillip who hangs himself in the anonymity of his council flat,[68] becomes a ghost in the traditional mode, her presence lingering in the text even after her death in the narrative. However, Effie's fate is not shared by all of Muriel's fellow patients. Some survive their discharge only to find themselves living not as literal ghosts but as social spectres in their former communities, as is the case for Sholto.

Following his discharge Sholto is depicted in the gloom of a pawn shop, among a multiplicity of obsolete objects such as the keys for unknown locks and a phrenologist's head, a relic of a long-debunked clinical discipline. He is described leaping out of the dark brandishing a sabre and blowing a 'clarion call' on a bugle. The text asserts that 'it would have been no surprise to hear him claim that now was the winter of his discontent' (*Vacant Possession*, p. 76). Within this setting Sholto forms a further anachronistic relic, human remains of a care system that has become or been deemed defunct. The use of the opening lines of *Richard III* linguistically registers this anachronism while simultaneously pulling into circulation another. Sholto's imagined claim also invokes the winter of 1978–9 during which widespread strikes were undertaken by a number of public sector trade unions, including those representing grave diggers and refuse collectors. The period came to be referred to in the press as the 'winter of discontent' and was a significant factor in the election of Margaret Thatcher in June 1979. By claiming for Sholto the Thatcher era as his 'winter of discontent' the text posits Sholto's disenfranchisement as permanent;[69] he is isolated, unaffiliated with a 'union' of any kind that could represent him to the State structures that abandon him upon his discharge from hospital. It also undercuts the narrative put forward in Thatcher's speech upon being elected prime minister in which, paraphrasing St Francis of Assisi, she stated that her government would bring faith, harmony, truth and hope where before there had been doubt, discord, error and despair.[70] The combination of the Shakespearean text the passage alludes to and the reference to a period in British history during which bodies went unburied and rubbish piled up in the streets proposes that, for Sholto and those like him, the advent of Thatcherism, far from ending the winter of discontent, was the start of its stubborn chill.

Through the character of Sholto, Mantel addresses a specific issue surrounding state care-giving in the 1970s and 80s, namely the problem of those patients who are returned to their former communities only to find that they have been dissolved or rendered obsolete in the meantime. In a powerful passage Mantel describes how Sholto returns to his community only to discover a wasteland in its place:[71]

> When he turned off Adelaide Street a terrible sight met his eyes. The whole district had been razed. Osborne Street was down, Spring Gardens had been flattened. The Primitive Methodist Chapel was boarded up and all the gravestones had been taken away. He tramped through the meadow of blight where the bones of Primitive Methodists had once rested; the ground strewn with glass and broken pots. He squatted down, turning over the shards. The weather was damp; his holdall was smeared with yellow clay. From where he knelt he looked up and read a sign: MOTORWAY LINK BEGINS MAY 1983. (*Vacant Possession*, p. 59)

This passage locates the abandoned and rejected Sholto within a landscape defined by an absence of containing structures and the presence of broken and defunct objects. The broken pots he finds are indicative of a shattering of formerly containing objects and the literal human remains associated with this landscape, the 'bodies of the primitive Methodists', are rendered anonymous and liminal, their gravestones removed and the bodies themselves indeterminately located. The architectural structures in this landscape, the houses and chapel that had the potential to provide a containing, sheltering environment have all either been rendered one dimensional, 'flattened' or 'razed', or have had their openings onto the world boarded up, turning them from potential shelter to actual crypt. Mantel's transformation of the graveyard into a 'meadow of blight' is significant too. Blight, a term for a plant disease but also conventionally applied to areas of urban decay, is the only thing that will grow in this degraded environment alongside rosebay willow herb, a weed which thrives on turned up earth and which proliferated in the bomb craters left following the Second World War. The cumulative effect of the damp mud, twisted scrap metal and the 'swastika spray-gunned on a wall' is to position this wasteland as a symbolic conflict zone, as Sholto recognizes, stating 'I thought the war was over' (p. 59).

Sholto's fate is not the only aspect of state care-giving to be critiqued within the duology. While 'care in the community' formed one of the most distinctive elements of Conservative health and welfare policy during the Thatcher decade, *Every Day* and *Vacant Possession* also address the provision of State care in a broader sense, providing a provocative representation of the activities of the Department of Health and Social Security (DHSS). As has been discussed, the care-giving landscapes within the duology, whether familial or societal, form sites where providers of care frequently come to dominate, invade and deplete those they are ostensibly caring for, sites upon which a kind of care-giving that spectralizes the recipient takes place. This has been demonstrated in the case of Muriel, who operates as a kind of fleshly spectre within 2 Buckingham Avenue, and in the case of the psychiatric patients admitted to Fulmers Moor, their physical and subjective presence powerfully compromised by drug treatments and mental illness. However, this spectralization can also be observed on a social level through the character of Miss Anaemia.

Social Care – DHSS and the Evil Eye of Welfare Provision

Muriel's fellow tenant in the house on Napier Street, Miss Anaemia is a benefit claimant and as such comes into regular contact with the DHSS. The character provides a vehicle for an exploration of the psychological impact of this particular aspect of social care, an exploration which is coloured by a powerful element of irony, as is signalled by Mantel's description of Miss Anaemia's joblessness and experience of claiming benefit as a 'full-time occupation' (*Vacant Possession*, p. 112). Miss Anaemia is referred to in the text predominantly by the nickname which obscures her true identity, reducing her to her unmarried status ('Miss') and a medical condition defined by lack or depletion. Her adoption of multiple identities in an effort to claim her benefit payments is similarly indicative of a fracturing of identity resulting from an attempt to access state care. She tells Muriel:

> 'I'm a claimant. I make up different names. Primrose Hill's one I go under, Penny Black.' She whispered to herself. 'Black Maria, Bad Penny, Faint Hope, Square Peg.'
> 'Is it frightening?'
> 'It's terrifying,' Miss Anaemia said. 'It makes your palms sweat' (*Vacant Possession*, p. 81)

If we accept Julian Wolfreys' assertion that 'names, conventionally applied, fix the limits of identity'[72] then the use of a nickname here, bestowed on the character by Muriel but shared only with the reader, indicates an erasure of those limits. In a significant passage Miss Anaemia reflects upon the detrimental effect that her contact with the DHSS has had on her sense of self:

> She never thought much about anybody else; claiming benefit was a full-time occupation. Her mind was getting narrowed down somehow; certain phrases like 'means' and 'rebate' seemed to have taken on an overriding significance, layers and layers of portent, which only peeled away for a split second, just as she was waking or falling asleep. When she saw a queue, she had an urge to join it. A hundred forms she must have filled in, two hundred; all this information spinning away from her, out of her head and off into space. The process was extracting something from her, filing away at her essence. She was no more than the virgin white space between two black lines, no more than a blur behind a sheet of toughened glass. (*Vacant Possession*, p. 112)

This passage, concerned with the process of claiming social security payments, implies that the external systems through which the State provides financial support are internalized entirely by their recipients. Not only behaviourally ('if she saw a queue she had an urge to join it') but linguistically, the structures of State care-giving infiltrate and eventually obliterate individual subjectivity as the work of the DHSS increasingly dominates Miss Anaemia's internal world. Mantel represents the work of the DHSS as ideologically situated in such a way as to perform an erasure of subjective integrity and individual identity that turns Miss Anaemia into a social ghost. This status as a phantom is underlined in her physicality: she possesses an extreme pallor, a thin and insubstantial figure and 'translucent' skin. Even her touch is 'ice-cold and clammy' (*Vacant Possession*, p. 80-1). These physical attributes combine with Miss Anaemia's sudden appearance at the top of staircases and from darkened doorways in the condemned structure of the house on Napier Street (*Vacant Possession*, p. 80) to invoke gothic convention in a way which reinforces Mantel's sociological assertions.

The presence of the DHSS within the duology is carefully constructed to create an atmosphere of paranoia and a sense of constant surveillance. A case of mistaken identity leads Miss Anaemia to believe that she is being watched by DHSS employees. While in reality this is not always true, the unstable quality of Mantel's narrative voice and the paranoid outlook she grants to her characters render it impossible to identify the 'watcher' being spoken about at any one time. The fact that these ostensible agents of State care provision are represented primarily as forces of surveillance becomes particularly significant in the context of the concept of the 'Evil Eye'. Lucidly articulated by Stephen Frosh, the notion of the 'Evil Eye' is dependent upon the notion that 'looking involves appropriation; conversely being looked at means to risk having something taken away'.[73] This is particularly suggestive when read alongside Miss Anaemia's sensation of depletion, her feeling that 'the process [of securing financial support] was extracting something from her, filing away at her essence' (p. 112). That the watchful presence of the DHSS staff is responsible both for the depletion of Miss Anaemia's 'essence', her 'sense of self', and the insertion into her psyche of the linguistic and symbolic structures associated with the claiming of benefit, is also supported by Frosh's description of the 'Evil Eye' which understands the phenomenon as 'an example of destructiveness operating at a distance. No contact is necessary … just a devouring glance, that inserts something in the other and consequently poisons it from within, drying up its liquid, sucking out its inside'.[74] This description recollects the discomforting images of egg eating discussed earlier with reference to parental care-giving and serves as a reminder that State care of the kind described in *Vacant Possession* can have an equally invasive and depleting effect upon its recipients. Indeed, all of the duology's characters struggle to separate themselves from their carers, physically and psychically, to achieve a defined subjective existence and to avoid being cannibalized or hopelessly hollowed out by the attentions of their ostensible care-givers. For Miss Anaemia this depletion is figured partially in her experience that something is 'filing away her essence', an experience that puts a suggestively bureaucratic slant on this manifestation of the evil eye; instead of being drained away or devoured in a cannibalistic sense, Miss Anaemia's essence is reduced to 'files', red tape and paperwork.

Confessions of a Social Worker: Isabel Field as Gothic Heroine

'Help? She needs an exorcism' (*Vacant Possession*, p. 166).

The above observation by social worker Isabel's husband illuminates the final facet of Mantel's representations of the interactions between haunting and care-giving in the Thatcher decade; that is, the consideration of whether to provide care is to open oneself up to the possibility of haunting. As such, it remains to ask what it means to be haunted by attempts to provide care rather than as a result of receiving care and, more specifically, how does Mantel characterize such a carer, the figure of the social worker, within this deployment of the gothic. Informed by the time Mantel spent as a social work assistant in 1974,[75] the character of Isabel provides an embodiment of the intersection between the personal and politico-social faces of care-giving. During the late 1970s and 1980s the social worker was a figure treated with profound suspicion by the Conservative government. As Lowe puts it, 'Conservative ministers, like many members of the public doubted the competence, and were highly suspicious, of the underlying motivations of social workers. Was their principal purpose to encourage their problem clients to conform to or challenge conventional norms [sic]. The fundamental Conservative instinct was that clearly it should be the former but in practice it was the latter.'[76] I argue that this suspicion arises from the way that the social worker's role leads them to bridge the gap between the public and private spheres, to infiltrate the space of the home as agents of State care. The duology recognizes in the social worker a figure possessed of a powerful congruence with the concerns of the gothic. Concerned primarily with those 'locked in and locked out' of the caring structure of the home,[77] the social worker's societal preoccupations mimic the textual preoccupations of the gothic, as they seek to expose family secrets, bring to light scenes of domestic violence and of enforced captivity. Isabel penetrates the threshold between public and private and on both visits to the Axon household provokes the kinds of 'confrontation with motherhood' frequently orchestrated as part of the gothic mode. Isabel's initial visit to 2 Buckingham Avenue allows Mantel to orientate her representations of maternal and social care alongside one another but Isabel's second visit, in which Evelyn tricks her into entering the spare room and locks her in, provokes rather a different confrontation. The relationship between nutritional processes such as feeding, eating and digesting, and their intrapsychic equivalents, has been established in this chapter and it is a relationship that psychoanalyst Wilfred Bion also appreciated. He asserted that 'the mind needed the nourishment of "getting to know a person" in much the same way as the body needs food and that terrible stuntings and bluntings occurred if the mind was starved of it'.[78] In this context the hunger of the ravenous infantile spectres in the spare room becomes more sharply defined, as does Isabel's traumatized response to encountering them. While the ghosts of the spare-room figure rejected infant distress, hunger and fear, their power to terrorize comes in evoking the terror of being overwhelmed by the demands of an other, of an attempt to provide care that consumes the care-giver, that eats them alive. It is this to which Muriel refers when she relates to Sholto that 'in my mother's day ... we used to have a special room in our house. In that room, my mother said, were things that would pick the flesh from your bones' (*Vacant Possession*, p. 180).

Isabel's struggle is indicative of a wider difficulty with regard to social care during the 1980s. She states 'I didn't have anything left over from my work to give to anybody' (*Vacant Possession*, p. 86) and this lack of internal resources, her inability to cope with the anxiety and distress that her work brings her into contact with, is also indicative of the lack of physical and financial resources being offered to social workers during this period and speaks to the profound difficulty of providing state care in the face of heavy caseloads and 'generic' social workers, as Isabel's rationale for writing up and publishing her experiences of social work confirms:

> then everyone would know how social workers operate and why things go so badly wrong. How you get given cases you can't handle, and how clients conspire against you, and circumstances seem to conspire too. How it messes up your personal life. How you live with yourself afterwards; when disaster has occurred. (*Vacant Possession*, p. 21)[79]

Textually, Isabel performs the role of a gothic heroine. Alternately locked out of and then into the domestic space she seeks to infiltrate, her quest for knowledge of Muriel's existence which she is denied (both in terms of access to 2 Buckingham Avenue and through the lost and incomplete documentation associated with the Axon case) and her eventual incarceration in the spectrally occupied 'spare room' aligns her with the heroines of the original gothic texts.[80] As she tries to provide a framework for her gothic narrative of social care she trails off: 'WHILE I WAS IN THE BEDROOM –' (*Vacant Possession*, p. 85). The lacuna at the end of the sentence implies the threat of sexual violence that forms the undercurrent of all gothic narratives and which is explicitly articulated in *Every Day*.[81] Through Isabel, Mantel depicts social work as an endless and unachievable task whose very impossibility comes to haunt the individuals who undertake it.

Isabel's attempts to write her 'confessions', as she calls them, see Mantel invoking the gothic trope of the story so unspeakable it struggles to be told.[82] Throughout the narrative the motif of the illegible document recurs: Muriel's case file for example, which introduces her to the reader in *Every Day*, is riddled with lacunae caused by lost documents and is lost in its entirety, then stolen not once but twice during the course of the narrative. Isabel first struggles to find the physical materials necessary to begin to write her narrative, eventually using fragments of paper which compound her already fragmented narrative. Her difficulty in binding together these written fragments and posting them in order to get them published in the Sunday papers denotes a generalized denial of the truth of the deficiencies and failures of State care: 'the exposé had turned out quite bulky. She couldn't get it in an envelope. Strange that failure should take up so much space; that foolishness and ineptitude should need so many stamps' (*Vacant Possession*, p. 221). Isabel's testimony proves too large even to be contained by the postal service. Her narrative of attempts at and failures of care is rejected by a society for whom social workers were seen as interfering where no interference was warranted (for example in the 'Cleveland Scandal'[83] in which a number of parents were wrongly accused of child abuse) or failing to act when the family unit proves toxic, as in the case of Jasmine Beckford.[84]

Foregone conclusions: subjective disintegration and failures of care

What, then, are the results of these failures of care-giving, of the circulation of spectres in care-giving relationships? Mantel states of Muriel that 'what she lacks is a theory of mind'.[85] It is possible to perceive in this remark the true repercussions of the failure of care-giving in these narratives, that is, the slippage of subjective identity. The absence of a caring figure and, conversely, overly close, spectrally possessive caring relationships that Mantel depicts result in a textual landscape in which subjectivity is radically destabilized. This instability was established with regard to Muriel's fellow patients in Fulmers Moor but is not limited to them. Characters such as Effie and Mrs Sidney suffer from delusions about their own identities, believing themselves to be members of the royal family or supernatural beings, as demonstrated in Muriel's own assertion that she is a changeling. Others have such a tenuous hold on their own identities that they risk being erased all together as in the case of Miss Anaemia, or having their identities appropriated as in the case of Muriel's colleague 'Poor Mrs Wilmot', whose name and life story Muriel usurps. Mantel's nebulous use of narrative voice which slides between free indirect discourse, and numerous different first-person narratives contributes formally to this sense of a fragility of subjectivity in the face of a collapse of care-giving. However, her use of the trope of the changeling provides an encapsulation to the devastating effect of inadequate care-giving on subjective integrity.

Soon after Muriel gives birth, Evelyn becomes convinced that her grandchild is not a human being at all but a changeling. By invoking the figure of the changeling Mantel taps into a specific discourse regarding motherhood and the supernatural, but also invokes a figure whose subjectivity is profoundly flawed. In folk belief a changeling is the replacement left when fairies or elves steal a human child while its mother is absent or distracted. In and of itself, then, the figure of the changeling is representative of a failure of maternal attention and Mantel's conceptualization of it reaffirms this:

> If it is a changeling, you ought to give some thought to getting the real one back. The ones they take lead miserable lives. They look in at people's windows. Their growth's stunted. They're always cold. (*Every Day*, p. 189)
>
> A changeling is a filthy thing. It's got no imagination. ... A changeling's a cruel thing. It likes its own company. It likes its own kind. (*Vacant Possession*, p. 145)

The statement 'it's got no imagination' confirms the changeling's status as an object which replaces a subject and its treatment in the narrative supports this interpretation. This notion of the changeling is continued in Mantel's depiction of Colin Sidney's son Alistair who is described as having stunted growth and is depicted in *Vacant Possession* wearing a 'jersey all-in-one' reminiscent of the romper suits worn by newborns. Significantly Alistair has his bedroom in what the Axons used to term 'the spare room' and it is strongly implied that the previous occupants haven't given up their tenancy.

The disintegrative force of the collapse of care-giving frameworks is registered in the pathological attitude Muriel possesses towards the formation of identity. She copies others, producing duplicates to be used at the opportune moment:

> By watching people, by stealing their expressions and practising them she was adding to her repertoire. I was no one when I came here she thought; but after a few years of this there's no telling how many people I'll be. (*Vacant Possession*, p. 51)

> It was easy to assume the abject form of Mrs Wilmot, but the imitation of Edna's vitality seemed to deplete her own inner resources to the point of near-extinction. She could not risk a situation where Edna and Mrs Wilmot wiped out Muriel entirely (*Vacant Possession*, p. 73)

This approach to identity is accompanied by an attendant preoccupation with physical dismemberment, the literal disintegration of bodies. The bone Muriel steals from a neighbourhood dog at the outset of *Every Day* (pp. 23–4) forms the first of a plethora of disintegrations. Muriel comes across boxes of false eyelashes in a chemist's window and describes her interest at the news that her mother underwent a post-mortem after her death (*Vacant Possession*, p. 73). Mrs Wilmot's false teeth are stolen and discovered in the lawn of 2 Buckingham Avenue, grinning up ominously at Colin Sidney (*Vacant Possession*, p. 134). The phrenologist's head, first produced by Sholto and an icon of dismemberment in itself, symbolizes the dissection of the human psyche into its component parts. These bodily disintegrations are accompanied by a series of exhumations. Throughout the narrative physical corpses emerge at an alarming rate. The body of a murdered woman is found in a lake where it had been inadequately submerged (*Vacant Possession*, p. 216), 'an Iron Age corpse' is found preserved in a bog and plans are made for the remains to go on show at the British Museum (*Vacant Possession*, p. 156), and the bones of what is implied to be Muriel's baby ('I think I read somewhere that babies' corpses often mummify and turn up years later, uncannily preserved' *Every Day*, p. 87) are fished out of the canal in which Muriel and Evelyn drowned it years earlier. Such a prevalence of body parts and remains emerging within the pages of a duology set in the dormitory towns of the West Midlands points to an understanding of the dead and the mutilated as stubbornly persistent.

By choosing the gothic mode Mantel gains access to a multiplicity of registers from the psychological to the sociopolitical to express widely circulating anxieties about breakdowns of care in the 1970s and 1980s. These ghost stories perform an uncomfortable dissection of the potential for the family unit, far from providing the ideal environment for the provision of care, to incubate its opposites, neglect and abuse. It is impossible to read *Every Day* and *Vacant Possession* without recognizing that what Mantel puts in question in these narratives is society's relationship with care on every level, from the individual psyche to the sociopolitical sphere. Mantel herself advocates that fiction 'has a moral dimension'[86] and her novels demand that the reader be 'hospitable' to the experiences of the other: 'much wickedness stems from our failure to imagine other people as fully human, and as our equals'.[87] Through treating the ghost story as 'a crucible for political mediation and historical memory'[88] and by situating her representation of Margaret Thatcher's Britain within a contemporary gothic framework, Mantel articulates the potential for haunting that always attends scenes of care-giving and in doing so sets up an oscillation between the injustices that she perceives in the society around her and the 'spectres of Margaret' resident within and without the home.

3

Spooks and holy ghosts: Spectral politics and the politics of spectrality in *Eight Months on Ghazzah Street*

On the first page of her memoir, Hilary Mantel sees a ghost and makes an admission. She describes seeing a movement, 'a flickering', on the staircase of her Norfolk home and states: 'I know it is my stepfather's ghost coming down.'[1] This distinctive way of seeing and the problematic status of the knowledge it leads to, are familiar to Mantel. 'I am used,' she says 'to "seeing" things that are not there. Or – to put it in a way that is more acceptable to me – I am used to seeing things that "aren't there."'[2] This sensitivity to the apparently insensible, and in particular to the figure of the ghost and the operation of the spectral, is not limited to Mantel's biographical experiences. Later in the same chapter she exhorts herself to tell her readers how she came to 'sell a house with a ghost in it,'[3] a phrase which could just as accurately describe her writing career. Yet, upon initial reading, Mantel's third novel, *Eight Months on Ghazzah Street*,[4] based upon the author's time living in Saudi Arabia, appears as an anomaly within this trend. The dead do not return in this narrative. Indeed, they are represented as irrevocably lost, and no 'literal' ghosts haunt the novel's protagonists, Frances Shore and her husband, Andrew. Certainly, *Eight Months* is not a book about ghosts. Rather, I argue, *Eight Months* is a text concerned with the hinterland between the sensible and the insensible occupied by the spectre. It is a text driven by the need to articulate the politically charged nature of that liminal space wherein individuals and events can be rendered spectral, rooting questions about the politics of invisibility in an interrogation of the politico-religious system operating in Saudi Arabia, where Wahhabi Islam forms the basis of political governance and where 'there is no division between the secular and sacred or between church and state.'[5] If, as has been discussed, *Every Day* and *Vacant Possession* are texts predicated upon an articulation of the various phantoms occupying a haunted

Thatcherite milieu, in which the practice of care-giving has become hopelessly compromised, *Eight Months* can be understood as continuing this project of contemplating the connections between haunting and the political. Constituting the kind of reworking of autobiographical material discussed in Chapter 1, *Eight Months* interrogates how the political operates according to spectral structures.

If *Eight Months* is not a book about ghosts but about spectres – things or persons whose presence is crucially compromised – the quality of spectrality itself must be understood as something related to but distinct from 'ghostliness'. In her memoir Mantel recalls playing the role of a 'ghost' in Noël Coward's *Blithe Spirit* but rather than emphasizing the post-mortem positioning associated with the ghost she characterizes her role as 'a phantom of air and smoke' (*Giving up the Ghost*, p. 54). This description of a non-subject, composed of an emptiness permeated by smoky traces which evoke the process of burning and of dematerialization, exemplifies precisely the play between absence and presence, visibility and invisibility, sensibility and insensibility that defines spectrality. It is specifically this liminal positioning which typifies the workings of political and religious systems[6] and that allows the state to operate invisibly but indisputably in homes and minds, permitting those apparatus to walk through the walls erected between public and private. Louis Althusser argues that it is possible for political and religious ideology to breach the private domestic domain precisely because it functions primarily invisibly through imaginary relations to the real conditions of existence.[7] This ambiguous straddling of presence and absence which is undertaken by the apparatus of the state, and which gives its function a spectral quality, is lucidly described by Althusser when he asserts that political or religious ideology possesses a material existence but, crucially, that this existence 'does not have the same modality as the material existence of a paving stone or a rifle'.[8] It is present and yet that presence is partial and idiosyncratic. This 'spectral politics' is precisely what is experienced by Frances and Andrew in *Eight Months* as they are, to quote Mantel, 'bounced from the extreme of domesticity to the extreme of politics'.[9] Yet, Mantel's rendering legible of these moments of political haunting is mirrored by a preoccupation with the political significance of *being* spectralized, of being rendered a 'phantom of air and smoke' who can never be fully seen and fully heard. By identifying the significance of the invisibility associated both with the operation of politico-religious regimes and the subjects they spectralize, it becomes possible to map the complex interactions between the political and the spectral in *Eight Months*.

Diverging from the well-trodden critical path that looks to Jacques Derrida to facilitate discussions of the spectral and the political, I turn instead to the work of Jacques Rancière regarding what he terms 'the distribution of the sensible' in order to establish that, while haunting and spectrality are undeniably central components of the gothic project, in the context of *Eight Months* they are the key to recognizing this text as a profoundly political novel. This is not the first occasion upon which Rancière has been put to work in reading Mantel. Esther Peeren's analysis of mediumship in *Beyond Black* also turns to his definition of the political and the distribution of the sensible.[10] By deploying Rancière's thought in the context of *Eight Months*, I couple the potential for political insight and intervention he finds in the idea of 'visiting as a foreigner'[11] with Mantel's own narrative of travel and 'foreignness' in order to expose the potency of the political gestures made by *Eight Months*.

By reading Jacques Rancière alongside Jacques Lacan's notion of the big Other, I map out the complex and sometimes paradoxical relationships between agency, invisibility, spectrality and power present in the text. However, Robert Irwin's review of the novel for *Time Out* provides a suggestion that this spectralized Saudi Arabia may be problematic from a critical perspective. Irwin describes the novel as 'a Middle Eastern *Turn of the Screw*'[12] and while this reference to Henry James's infamous ghost story rightly recognizes the gothic atmosphere and profound ambiguity of Mantel's text, acknowledging the novel's status as a ghost story of sorts, the presence of the gothic and the use of the spectral in *Eight Months* pose a problem that changes the critical stakes of what Mantel is attempting in this text.[13]

The text critiques the politico-religious regime in Saudi Arabia using a carefully crafted spectral metaphor, yet within the Islamic faith the concept of the ghost is wholly absent. This being the case, Mantel's spectralization of Saudi Arabia could be viewed negatively as an attempt to think about a politico-religious system in terms that do not apply to it or, worse, as an ethnocentric imposition. As such, having established the significance of spectrality to the novel, it is necessary to address this clash between subject matter and mode of representation. In closing, I demonstrate that the discord between the overarching metaphor of the text and the theological assertions and cultural practices to which the text refers is intentionally created, that the imposition constituted by Mantel's invocation of the gothic is a deliberate one. Following a discussion with her Muslim neighbour Yasmin, Frances concludes that 'of course [Yasmin] can't break out of her culture …. No more can I break out of mine. No more would I want to; no more does she' (p. 121). I argue that this impasse is what is principally highlighted by the presence of the spectral in *Eight Months*. By creating in Frances a quasi-gothic heroine who is only able to relate to the text's fictionalized Saudi Arabia through the decidedly Western, Protestant lens of the ghostly, and by crafting a narrative whose events are profoundly ambiguous, both to the novel's protagonist and to the reader, Mantel is able to articulate how attempts to translate the cultural and politico-religious milieu of Saudi Arabia into the terms of another culture can only result in stubbornly enigmatic remains which register affectively as well as textually. Just as Frances is thwarted in her attempts to gain an explanation for the mysterious events taking place in her home, to make visible and audible that which has been veiled and muffled, so too is the reader frustrated, left with a text populated by apparitions that refuse to fully appear, a narrative that refuses, ultimately, to tell. Mantel's spectral strategy also enables her to call into question previously taken-for-granted definitions of politics and political action, rendering the act of attempting to see 'beyond appearances ... to another reality',[14] the reality spectralized by mainstream political agents, the most deeply political of gestures.

The ladies vanish: Agency, invisibility and the writing of Jacques Rancière

As it seems to me the first right a person has is the right to be seen. And that is denied to women by the veil. But you really have to have lived there to know it, to know what a gang of women under the veil look like when they move through a public place. It is as if they are not there.[15]

It is a delimitation of ... the visible and the invisible, of speech and noise that simultaneously determines the place and stakes of politics as a form of experience. Politics revolves around what is seen and what can be said about it, around who has the ability to see and the power to speak.[16]

Eight Months draws heavily upon Mantel's personal experience of living in Saudi Arabia during the 1980s. In a piece written for the *Guardian* she describes how, on arriving in Jeddah airport, her first experience was a lack of acknowledgement, stating 'no one met my eyes', and recounts how, in response to her sympathetic glance, the gaze of a male fellow passenger 'jerked away'.[17] This encounter with what Mantel describes as the 'avoidant gaze'[18] characterizes the experience of Frances as she attempts to negotiate her new life in Jeddah. Early in the novel Frances attempts to purchase painkillers from a male shop assistant while out with her husband. Instead of speaking to Frances the assistant looks past her, addressing his questions about the transaction to Andrew 'as if [Frances] were a ventriloquist's doll' (p. 112), causing her to ask 'am I visible?' (p. 112). This exchange, with its central question of visibility, has impact far beyond articulating the experience of a female Western incomer to a conservative Muslim society. More broadly the incident illustrates lucidly the thinking of Jacques Rancière with regard to how political systems operate. It is important to note that for Rancière 'politics' has a very specific meaning that differs from an understanding of the political as 'the practice of power or the embodiment of collective wills and interests and the enactment of collective ideas',[19] the policymaking and enforcing of governmental bodies etc. Rather, Rancière defines politics as being 'before all else ... an intervention in the visible and sayable'[20] and understands a political action to be one that disturbs the distribution of the sensible, that is, the apparently 'natural logic' of the 'distribution of the visible and invisible, of speech and noise [which] pins bodies to their places and allocates the private and the public to distinct "parts"'.[21] As such, participation in the political system is necessarily predicated upon what Rancière terms the division or 'partition of the sensible', a division between what and, more importantly, who 'is visible or not in a common space'.[22] By bringing the two quotations that opened this section into conversation with each other it is possible to see that what Mantel defines as the denial of a basic right has profound political implications; to be deemed invisible, set outside the realm of the sensible, is automatically to be excluded not only from political enfranchisement as manifested in participation in the day-to-day processes of democracy but also from 'the community of citizens'[23] as a whole, to be denied the status of those who 'partake'.[24] Crucially, the correspondence between Mantel's assertions and those of Rancière make it clear that *Eight Months* constitutes a political gesture in its own right, a gesture which places the ability to be seen and heard at the centre of political subjectivity and narrativizes the difficulties and dangers of contesting the partition of the sensible.

As Frances's experience in the pharmacy demonstrates, the difficulty of being seen that Mantel encountered upon her own entry into Jeddah is transposed into the Saudi Arabia of *Eight Months*. This preoccupation with visibility and invisibility exceeds Frances's individual experience, finding its most potent articulation in the novel's representation of veiling.[25] Shortly after her arrival in Jeddah, Frances encounters a group of veiled Saudi women in a supermarket:

> Around her, women plucked tins from shelves; women trussed up in their modesty like funereal laundry, women with layers of thick black cloth where their faces should be. ... 'I didn't know the veil was like this,' she whispered. 'I thought you would see their eyes.' (pp. 57–8)

The disappointment of Frances's expectation that the full veil frequently worn in Saudi Arabia would not prevent eye contact emphasizes how the veil not only negates visual identification, due to the 'cloth where their faces should be', but also prevents a more profound identification by precluding eye contact and rendering imperceptible the female viewpoint, literally the point from which these women see the world. The use of the verbs 'pluck' and 'truss' in the passage is linked through their association with the preparation of poultry and thus the same linguistic field is applied to the foodstuffs on the shelves and to the women purchasing them. Such an association has the effect of communicating the shift that full veiling in this context appears to produce – that from subject to object. This articulation of the ultimate consequence of invisibility being an acute difficulty in being recognized as a subject rather than an object is significant and resonates with another semantic trend in the novel concerning apparent confusions between subjects and objects. There are frequent moments in the text in which veiling, invisibility and lack of agency come to be associated with death or spectrality, associating living female subjects with the object of the post-mortem body. The 'funereal laundry' of the previous passage is the first indication of a link being created between death and the veiled women that Frances encounters, an image which is compounded by an earlier description of a 'mill of petitioners', attempting in vain to attract the attention of a Saudi politician, as 'a basket of laundry animated by a poltergeist' (p. 40). Later in the novel this association is given a further spectral inflection as, from the back seat of a car, Frances observes a veiled group crossing a busy road:

> In front of them, a collection of black-veiled shapes had drifted into the road. They hovered for a moment, in the middle of the great highway, looking with their blind muffled faces into the car; then slowly, they began to bob across to the opposite kerb. (p. 92)

The uncertain quality of the women's movements, hovering, drifting and bobbing, combined with their reduction to an indefinite physical 'shape', gives them a phantasmal quality and through invoking the crude image of the 'ghost in a sheet' of popular culture Mantel is also able to posit these women as being subject to a social ghosting in which they are 'muffled' and blinded, denied the ability to be, as Rancière puts it, among those 'who [have] the ability to see and the talent to speak'.[26] Elsewhere in the text veiled women 'glide' in a silent 'deep-below world' that recalls the underworld domain of the dead, a recollection made more potent when, in the following paragraph, Frances visits a souk where she handles some traditional beaded face-masks, intended to serve the same purpose as the veil and whose owners are conjectured to be either 'emancipated or deceased' (p. 210). Veiling provides a striking figurative representation of the way in which the politico-religious system in Saudi Arabia obscures or negates female presences in public spaces, the shared 'common' spaces in which Rancière argues participation in the political system must take place. However, this is not the only instance in the novel where certain subjects are depicted as possessing a mode of non-present presence. The representation of the domestic servants who quietly populate the text of *Eight Months* provides a crucial insight into how the Wahhabi regime actively produces social ghosts. In his book *Dissensus: On Politics and Aesthetics* Rancière discusses how certain categories of individuals, for example women and workers, have been excluded from the social by virtue of an insistence upon their association with the sphere of the domestic.[27] The consequence of this occlusion of certain groups due to the spaces they occupy renders them unable to claim the position of political subject, of a 'person' fully occupying the realm of the sensible. This denial of personhood is strikingly demonstrated in the opening chapter of *Eight Months* as Frances discusses with an air steward the possibility of her taking a taxi when she lands in Jeddah:

> 'It's bad news, a man picking up a strange woman in a car. They can gaol you for it.'
> 'But he's a taxi driver,' [Frances] said. 'That's his job, picking up strange people.'
> 'But you're a woman,' the steward said. 'You're a woman, aren't you? You're not a person anymore.' (p. 29)

This exchange posits an alarming impending transformation in which womanhood and personhood move from being two mutually compatible categories to a situation in which one category negates the other. The representation of veiling in *Eight Months* makes it apparent that the text is articulating the position occupied by the women of Jeddah as being profoundly compromised; in public and thus in the eye, and I use that word advisedly, of the law they are non-present presences. Situated outside of the realm of the sensible, unable to be fully seen, for their voices to be wholly audible and comprehensible as speech rather than as noise, the veiled women Frances observes occupy an uncomfortably liminal position between visibility and invisibility, subject and object. They are unable to be meaningfully and individually acknowledged due to their status as surplus to the sensible order as it applies to the public sphere in Saudi Arabia. Correspondingly, the ghost as phenomenon can in part be defined by its refusal of discrete ontological categories and its troubling of the notions of the sensible, occupying as it does a liminal space between sensibility and insensibility, straddling the boundary between the visible and the invisible. This placement is one shared by the domestic servants depicted in *Eight Months* and its impact is profound, rendering them non-persons, a group whose members cannot be addressed individually, not because they defy definition but because they have not been granted any subjective identity. Throughout the novel the names of domestic staff prove slippery and ungraspable to their employers and rather than attempting to master the difficult syllables, Frances's friends try to perform dominating acts of renaming:[28]

> 'What is your maid's name?' Frances asked.
> Samira told her. But she was none the wiser. It sounded like 'Sarasparilla'. But that was not possible. In answer to her questioning look, Samira merely shrugged. 'I did try to call her something simpler,' she said. 'But she won't answer to it.'
> ...
> Frances tried to catch the maid's eye; perhaps she might, just with a look, express her concern? But she failed. The girl slid out of the room, seeming to melt into the shadows of the heavy furniture. (pp. 124–5)

Mantel's description of Sarasparilla's apparent immateriality, her 'sliding' from the room and 'melting' into the shadows, signals a systematic placement of those in domestic service in Saudi Arabia as less 'present' in some crucial way than their employers. This lack of presence, which is in fact a lack of acknowledgement, a failure to be fully admitted to the realm of the sensible that Frances is also subject to, is symptomatic of a spectral existence. Indeed, Frances's first discussion with Yasmin about the lives of domestic servants in Jeddah prompts Yasmin to state that 'the poor things are trying to commit suicide …. They throw themselves off balconies' (p. 68), a generalized description which creates an image of the maids as perpetually between life and death, 'trying' to commit suicide rather than 'committing' it, always in the act of falling between the domestic space and a post-mortem existence. While literary depictions of servants frequently draw upon the spectral metaphor,[29] the mode of ghosting the servants in *Eight Months* are subject to has a religiously freighted specificity. Yasmin mentions the fact that many of those in service have been forced by economic necessity to leave their children behind and emphasizes their perceived lack of morality: 'these young girls come to the Kingdom as housemaids, and then they cause trouble. … They get unhappy … because they have left children behind them at home. Also, the Saudi men, you know, they find that these girls are not very moral' (p. 68). Shortly after her conversation with Yasmin regarding her maid Frances reads the correspondence column in a newspaper in which one correspondent asserts that 'the Kingdom's social and cultural heritage does not allow women to mix with men either in life activities or in work. The right place for a woman is to look after her husband and children' (p. 73). In having to leave behind their family units to take up paid work in households which will unavoidably bring them into contact with men to whom they are not related, either by birth or marriage, the female domestic servants of Saudi Arabia are depicted as necessarily situated outside of the purview of religion and the law; in order to carry out their jobs they must be considered to be non-persons or else be in perpetual violation of the laws of the Kingdom. Possessed of an existence and yet denied personhood, denied their own names and spaces,[30] the domestic servants of *Eight Months* are depicted as having no option but to live as social spectres.

Clearly, *Eight Months* is a text that engages compellingly with Rancière's suggestion that a lack of visibility frequently equates to a lack of agency and enfranchisement. Yet if Rancière insists that visibility is what guarantees participation in the political and legal system, he neglects to address the fact that the very invisibility that is imposed in order to disenfranchise and exclude certain groups mirrors the invisibility possessed by those organizations responsible for reinforcing the apparently 'natural logic'[31] of the partition of the sensible, a logic that is in fact wholly artificial and as such can be unsettled. However, the act of intervening to disrupt the distribution of the sensible is by no means without risk as an examination of two similar incidents from the novel makes strikingly clear. The presence of a group of veiled women who stray in front of the car carrying Frances and her neighbour almost results in a traffic accident: 'they screeched to a halt. Hasan had stabbed his foot on the brake; they were flung forward against the front seat' (p. 92). Yet when Frances ventures out of her house without wearing the full veil and attempts to cross a main road, a motorist deliberately tries to run her down: 'a boy in a Mercedes pulled up, waved her in front of him. As she stepped out from the kerb, he revved his engine, the car sprang forward, and she had to leap from under its wheels. She heard the brakes applied; caught herself up, heart racing, and looked back at the driver of the car; understood that it had not been an accident' (p. 238). Frances's very visibility compromises her presence within the common space of the street. Indeed the relationship between physical visibility and the recognition of someone as a subject with the ability to occupy public spaces is foreshadowed at the end of the first passage when, following their near miss, Frances asks her neighbour, 'would the drivers stop for me?', to which her neighbour replies, 'I don't know. It might depend on how you were dressed' (p. 93). The spatial aspect of these two instances of road crossing is important. For Rancière, the degree to which a subject is deemed to belong to the realm of the sensible is predicated upon 'what they do and the time and space in which this particular activity is performed'.[32] The Jeddah of *Eight Months* is no exception to this formulation; the occupations open to women are tightly circumscribed, restricted to roles accommodated by the domestic sphere, and these roles are precisely situated outside of a common space. The movements that can be made by the women of Saudi Arabia are tightly controlled and the design of Jeddah's pavements emblematizes this politico-social circumscription as Frances finds out:

> Every few yards it was necessary to step down from the eighteen-inch kerb and into the gutter; the municipality had planted saplings, etiolated and ill-doing plants inside concrete rectangles, and it did not seem to have occurred to anyone that the saplings would block the pavements, and pavements are for walking on. But clearly they are not for walking on, she thought. Men drive cars; women stay at home. Pavements are a buffer zone, to prevent the cars running into the buildings. (pp. 74–5)

This passage articulates clearly how the conspicuous yet anonymous restriction of certain people's movements to certain spaces and times is a major preoccupation, not just in this passage but in Mantel's Saudi Arabia generally. Early on in the novel Frances and Andrew find themselves unable to move due to evening prayers: '"There is no God but Allah and Muhammed is his Prophet," Andrew muttered. Grilles crashed down over the shop windows, doors were barred. ... "We timed this trip badly. But people are always getting caught out like this. There's only a couple of hours between sunset and night prayers"' (p. 59). However, it is the anonymity and nebulous quality of the agency that insists upon these regulations which is perhaps the most striking element of the above passage, and its powerfully present absence provides evidence of a paradox within Rancière's thought. This paradox can be resolved, however, by returning, through Althusser, to Lacan and his concept of the big Other.

Spectral surveillance and the Gaze: Rancière with Lacan

'You can almost think of nothing else in Saudi except for the business of looking and being looked at.'

– Hilary Mantel[33]

When Althusser describes the process of interpellation which 'recruits subjects from individuals'[34] he states that for this interpellation to take place 'a unique and Other Subject, i.e. God' is necessary, a 'Subject with a capital S to distinguish it from ordinary subjects with a small s'.[35] Graphically and conceptually this 'Other Subject' calls to mind another figure, one central to Lacan's conception of the Symbolic order: that of the big Other. In Lacanian thought the big Other comes to constitute the figure to whom we attribute the functioning of the Symbolic order, 'the locus of speech and (potentially) the locus of truth'[36] around which our social interactions are notionally structured. As Žižek lucidly points out, for Lacan 'the absolute "big Other" [is] God Himself'.[37] The narrator of *Eight Months* observes that the unyielding, repeating geometry of a rug in Frances's neighbour's home recalls 'the unfathomable nature and eternal vigilance of Allah himself' (p. 84). This description of Allah articulates perfectly the Lacanian big Other's unapprehensible nature and, crucially, its omniscient scrutiny. It is this scrutiny that is made manifest in Lacan's conception of the gaze. The gaze here should be understood as the sense that one is observed, seen by something that one cannot see observing. It is a gaze 'that circumscribes us, and which in the first instance makes us beings who are looked at … not a seen gaze but a gaze imagined by me in the field of the Other'.[38] As we will see shortly, the gaze of the big Other renders legible the invisibility of the ultimate arbiters of politico-religious systems. However, this gaze also needs to be understood in the context of *Eight Months* as being involved in the same nexus of invisibility, spectrality and agency observed above with reference to the figure of the veiled woman, to be acknowledged as a spectre in its own right.

The Lacanian gaze can be described as 'a point of failure in the visual field … a point where perception breaks down';[39] it is unapprehensible.[40] If we consider for a moment the location of the spectre within the visual field, the point it occupies can be defined as 'the space in which representation is fragmented'[41] by virtue of the resistance of the spectre to the act of representation itself. The spectre is by its nature never fully apprehensible and thus cannot be fully accommodated by conventional modes of representation or perception. Likewise, both spectre and gaze can be understood as that which resists being perceived and can only be acknowledged 'at the limit of comprehension'.[42] The ghostly quality of the gaze is established in *Eight Months* from its opening chapters. On her first morning in Jeddah Frances is left at home alone by her husband. In his absence she takes a tour of her new home. She draws back her curtains to reveal wooden blinds. These in turn are raised to give a view onto a brick wall. The glass in her kitchen door is frosted, as is that in her bathroom window which slides open to reveal yet another wall (p. 45). Frances cannot see out and nor can anybody see in. Yet when she retires to her sitting room she is overcome with self-consciousness, feeling 'as though someone were watching [her]' (p. 47). Even as she is cloistered from the world by her opaque windows and locked doors, shielded from any human stare, the gaze, apparently emanating from a disembodied 'someone', continues to exert pressure on Frances who '[does] not feel at all in possession of the ground' (p. 46) of her flat. Her constant movements – switching on lights, changing positions, abandoning her attempts to read, itself an activity which combines the visual quality of the word 'see' with its alternate meaning of 'to understand', in favour of unpacking – provide an illustration of the ways in which an awareness of the gaze causes the subject to 'tr[y] to adapt himself to it'.[43] The surveying presence Frances experiences so profoundly renders her incapable of establishing her flat on Ghazzah Street as her home. It thoroughly displaces her in a movement which recalls Julian Wolfreys' assertion that the ghost displaces us where we ought to feel most secure: within the domestic scene.[44] In the world of *Eight Months* such security is precluded from the start by this spectral surveillance.

As the novel progresses Frances feels herself haunted by this disembodied gaze both inside and outside of her home. Even when putative watchers are identified, these figures constitute only placeholders for the haunting and persecutory gaze of the big Other. These misrecognitions, in which the power of observation is attributed to an object which has eyes but does not 'see', can be found in the fish served to Frances at supper which 'look[s] up at her with a small, dead, prehistoric eye' (p. 223) and the tiles that decorate Frances's hallway which seem to resemble 'small faces, each with its splash of scarlet, its swirl of black' and leave Frances feeling 'as if she were being watched by bloodied eyes; by the victims of some Koranic punishment' (p. 202). It is in this final sentence that the potential source, if not identity, of the surveying presence is posited. The 'Koranic punishment' that Frances imagines implicates the political and legal authority constituted by Islam in Saudi Arabia in this process of observation and neatly encapsulates the 'confusion' between Althusser's 'law which interpellates individuals' and 'religious subjection'[45] that is perpetually taking place in Saudi Arabia where no difference is drawn between the religious and the legal. This surveying religious and legal presence is embodied earlier in the novel when Frances and Andrew visit the site of the building he is helping to construct in Jeddah. Already anxious about committing any inadvertent indiscretion, Frances observes that she and her husband are being watched: '"Andrew –" she swivelled a glance over her shoulder, uneasy – "there's a policeman across the road, he's staring at us"' (p. 101).

To fully understand the significance of the presence of the police officer in the passage it is useful to return to Rancière and examine his conceptualization of the police. Rather than constituting just one of the multiple apparatus which exist as 'social function[s]'[46] 'in relation to the requirements of legal practice',[47] Rancière defines the police as 'the symbolic constitution of the social' stating that 'the essence of the police lies neither in repression nor even in control over the living: its essence lies in a certain way of dividing up the sensible'.[48] The authoritative stare of the police officer which discomforts Frances initially appears to constitute the voyeuristic gaze of an individual subject. However, just as the 'eyes' in the above passage were misidentified as the true source of surveillance, this understanding of the police officer's stare is also not entirely accurate; it is not an individual that looks through the eyes of the police officer. Rather, his gaze is possessed by the discarnate presence of legal and religious authority: behind the individual police officer, Mantel positions the Rancièrian police.

In a rhetorical move that darkly satirizes the use of retaliatory punishments or *qisas* in Saudi Arabia, and the related aphorism 'an eye for an eye will make the whole world blind', the omniscient and haunting stare of the religious authorities depicted in *Eight Months* is paralleled by a focus on Frances's own specific mode of blindness which takes both deliberate and involuntary forms. The frustration she feels at the novel's outset when she struggles to gain a view onto the outside world from her flat is reprised at the midpoint of the text when she is forced to leave her blinds closed all day, ostensibly to facilitate some repair work to her apartment. She complains that she has been 'blinkered' (p. 99) and speaks of her desire for 'a third eye ... one that would see more deeply than the other two' (p. 99). This latter statement contains the double meaning of the word 'see', implicating not only the idea of visual apprehension but also intellectual understanding, and as the novel gathers pace the dangers of such 'insights' are repeatedly reiterated to Frances, whose interrogation of and confrontations with the secrecy and occlusions that characterize life in Jeddah are a source of anxiety to those around her. Yet the gaze is only one element of the ways in which the phantasmal big Other functions in this text. Shortly after Frances's encounter with the police officer she reads an article in a local newspaper about capital punishments carried out that week. The article states that 'while giving out details of the offence and punishment, the Interior Ministry made it clear that the government would vigorously implement the Sharia laws to maintain the security of the land and to deter criminals … The executions were carried out after Friday prayers' (p. 105). As the final sentence confirms, the invasive power of political and religious authority can, in an instant, move from the visual register to the material, from looking to touching. Avery F. Gordon lucidly sums up this spectrum of expressions of power: 'power can be invisible …. It can be obvious, it can reach you through the baton of the police, it can speak the language of your thoughts and desires. It can feel like remote control, it can exhilarate like liberation, it can travel through time, and it can drown you in the present. It is dense and superficial, it can cause you bodily injury and it can harm you without seeming ever to touch you.'[49]

Political poltergeists

This shift from looking to touching is clearly inscribed in an incident that takes place as the novel draws to a close, an incident which constitutes the culmination of a determination by Frances to undertake her own 'redistribution of the sensible'. From the outset of the novel Frances's combined curiosity and apprehension regarding the purpose of the flat that sits, ostensibly empty, above her own gathers momentum. She hears someone moving beyond the door of the 'empty' flat (p. 214). Later, while out on the roof of her apartment building, she sees that a large crate has been inexplicably erected on the vacant apartment's balcony, a crate which then appears to have been moved by the struggling of someone or something enclosed within it (p. 221). Having caught her neighbour's maid about to enter the vacant flat with a meagre portion of food, and been met with frightened dissembling when she asked for an explanation, Frances concludes that 'I have been told lies. I have been lied to all along, or rather I have been in error as to what I chose to believe' (p. 220). Despite warnings from multiple individuals Frances continues her attempts to reveal the truth as to the nature of the 'empty' property, demanding answers from Andrew's boss, Eric Parsons, whose response is chilling:

> You know, you were told, about the empty flat. And you were told to be careful. … if you involve yourself – if you are thought, Frances, to be making a nuisance of yourself, to have come into possession of any information that you shouldn't have – then it will be Andrew who bears the brunt of any indiscretion. … I am first in the firing line, my dear, and there are some things that I cannot afford to know. Once past a certain point, you see, you become an undesirable person, and then who knows what happens? Because there comes a certain point where

they don't want you here, and if you see what I mean, they don't want you to leave either. (pp. 240–1)

What takes place here is clearly a rebuttal of Frances's attempt to disturb the partition of the sensible by breaking the silence imposed around the 'empty' flat on Ghazzah Street. Parsons' response to Frances constitutes nothing more than a reaffirmation of the 'taken for granted configuration of perception and meaning that ... defines the conditions in which arguments can be made, recognized as such and engaged'.[50] Indeed, when Frances asks Parsons 'Won't you even listen to me?' he responds with a categorical 'no' (p. 241), shutting down any possibility of an argument taking place. This exchange vividly inscribes a confrontation between police and politics in which it is demonstrated that 'political struggle is not a matter of rational debate between multiple interests [but rather] a struggle to have one's voice heard and oneself recognised as a legitimate partner in debate'.[51] Furthermore, Parsons' refusal to recognize Frances as 'a legitimate partner in debate' serves to support the current partition of the sensible. By placing the mystery of the empty flat outside of those phenomena that can be acknowledged, let alone debated, he adheres to the 'principle' of the police – 'the absence of void and of supplement'.[52] Meanwhile, Frances's insistence upon gaining access to the flat's concealed truth is an attempt to perform a profound act of dissensus, the political action constituted by the 'demonstration (manifestation) of a gap in the sensible itself ... mak[ing] visible that which has no reason to be seen'[53] from the perspective of the established sensible order.

It is following this exchange that Frances and Andrew return to their apartment from a shopping trip to discover that they have apparently been burgled: 'The wardrobe gaped open; some of their clothes had been dragged from the hangers, flung about the room. Drawers were pulled out' (p. 244). Yet as Frances and Andrew progress through the house they discover that their 'housekeeping money', a significant sum, has not been taken. Indeed, the only thing of monetary value to have been stolen is the Shores' camera, an object capable of capturing the visible, of holding it to account and providing evidence. As such the theft of the camera signals an intention by the invading presence to regulate the gaze and restrict its deployment. As the passage continues, the burglars' point of entry into the Shores' flat becomes a point of contention:

It was obvious how the burglars had got in. They had come through the big window with its sliding panel; the length of wood that should have blocked the track lay on the carpet. It had been removed from the inside. 'You forgot to put it back,' Andrew said. He saw her face. 'I'm not blaming you. I know you want a breath of air sometimes. ...'

'If I want air I go to the roof. I didn't take the wood out.'

'You must have. Who else could it have been?'

'No one.' (p. 244)

This 'no one', who opens up the Shores' home 'from the inside' and leaves 'no greasy fingerprints ... no smudges' (p. 249), identifies this instance of home invasion rather as a scene of haunting in which the items that are damaged and stolen possess a symbolic value within a matrix of acts of vandalism and disruption designed to displace and disturb. Frances observes that 'they've taken the Thagama candle sticks. Some food has gone, out of the fridge' (p. 245). She later discovers that the intruders have 'mauled and despoiled [her] summer frocks' and that 'her soapstone tortoise [is] gone from the bedside table' (p. 246). With the theft of the candle sticks, structures for supporting illumination, the visual field is metaphorically thrown into darkness and uncertainty and it becomes more difficult to 'see' clearly. The destruction of Frances's 'summer dresses', items of clothing which she cannot publicly wear in the Kingdom, and theft of her soapstone tortoise (an object which breaks the Islamic prohibition on the figural representation of humans or animals) indicates the incursion of religious and legal restrictions into the private sphere of the home. The dispossession of the Shores within their own home, the removal of 'the small valueless things that [they] cannot bear to lose' (p. 246) along with food items which are symbolic of the Shores' ability to sustain themselves within their domestic space, constitutes a wholesale 'destabilization of the domestic scene',[54] a destabilization that, as has been demonstrated, was in play in the flat on Ghazzah Street from the moment Frances arrived. The 'someone' Frances senses watching her on that first morning has, through the burglary, been given flesh, removing any possibility that the Shores' flat could constitute 'home' as Julian Wolfreys has defined it.[55]

The scene, framed as a burglary in the first instance, a criminal act, quickly takes on the sensation of poltergeist activity, the actions of a persecutory ghost who seeks to displace living tenants from their homes.[56] Having come to terms with their material losses, and decided not to involve the Saudi police in the matter, Andrew and Frances seek to settle their nerves with a drink. Alcohol being prohibited in Saudi Arabia, the bottle of Scotch they received as a present is secreted under their kitchen sink and their home-brewed wine stowed in the bathroom:

> Andrew glowered over the remains of the bottle of Scotch; smashed, it lay on the draining board. ... [He] turned quickly and made for the little bathroom where they kept their wine supplies. As soon as he opened the door a ripe

heady odour from the upturned jerry cans rolled past them. Almost tangible, it billowed down the passageway, and washed through the flat. ... There had been twenty-four bottles, in a cardboard box; even the box was ripped to shreds, and its remnants bobbed on the frothy tide from the jerry cans, a scum of yeast and water and half-fermented fruit. (p. 247)

The methodical destruction of the Shores' alcohol, the existence of which is a direct contravention of the law in Saudi Arabia, positions the invasion of the flat as spectral law enforcement, a disembodied yet potent force which is registered through the emphasis upon smell in the passage, causing the presence of the anonymous intruder to linger phantasmally after the corporeal perpetrators have departed. The presence that has occupied and vandalized the flat is 'almost tangible', pervading the entire property and yet immaterial. Present yet incomprehensible, the 'ripe, heady, odour' causes the Shores to reassess the status of their domestic space in relation to the Saudi authorities, of whom it had been previously stated that '[they] do not enter private homes on a whim. They'll come if you attract attention to yourself' (p. 63), and to acknowledge that the 'stench of fermentation' is more properly 'the smell of violence' (p. 248). That this passage figures a religiously motivated act is explicitly stated:

> 'I think,' Frances said, 'that we have been left a message.'
> 'Message? Rip off the *khawwadjis* and save them from sin, is that what you mean?' (p. 248)

In the wake of this spectral incursion, Andrew angrily repeats that he '[is] not going to be frightened off by the bloody vagaries of [his] imagination' (p. 248).[57] His assertion underlines the potency with which the State's potential for persecutory action operates predominantly through the individual subject's imagination. In so doing, it underlines the concomitance between the State as represented in *Eight Months* and the figure of the ghost, a figure whose power is similarly 'mostly exercised through the imagination'.[58] Andrew's statement anticipates the persistence of the ghostly home invasion, if only in his mind where the possibilities for its repetition have the potential to be endlessly rehearsed, returning and returning again as revenant par excellence. Andrew's statement makes apparent that this is law enforcement carried out by the most intimate of 'interior ministries', who can not only watch and act without being seen but whose offices are internalized, whose presence 'is experienced, in the unconscious economy of the subject, as a traumatic, senseless injunction'[59] and whose actions are as potent and persecutory as those carried out by their embodied representatives.

'Who knows what's under the veil?': Quasi-gothic and cultural blindness

Throughout *Eight Months* confrontations arise between the novel's Western protagonists and their conservative Islamic environment. Perhaps the most powerful of these can be located as the novel draws to its close when, returning home from a trip to the doctor, Frances discovers a veiled stranger in the stairwell of her apartment building:

> Someone was in the hall ... a veiled figure, going upstairs. I no longer believe in the veiled lady, she thought; I know she is a fiction, a lie. ... The figure moves, not at a visitor's pace, but headlong: not furtive, decisive: and the momentary glimpse she caught seemed to contradict some observation she had once made.
>
> ...
>
> The visitor stopped dead. An outline of features beneath black cloth .... The visitor was tall; a strapping lass. Frances raised her hand. The visitor pulled back but she had made contact. She tugged at the concealing *abaya*, felt it part, felt something cold, metallic under her hand. She reached up, with her other hand, and clawed at the veil. But a veil is not something that you can pull off ... because the black cloth is wound around the head. The head strains back; and then she is pushed away with all of the visitor's ungirlish strength, sent flying against the wall.
>
> ...
>
> Frances stood up shakily. Surprisingly she felt no pain; no evidence of the encounter, except the chilly bar of flesh in the palm of her hand, where she had touched the metal of the gun's barrel. (pp. 234–5)

This passage is powerful not least because it at first appears to adhere to the structures of haunting that permeate the novel before violently undermining those structures. The events that lead up to this confrontation all contribute to this passage manifesting initially as an instance of haunting.[60] As discussed above, from Frances's very first morning in her flat the presence of something or someone in the flat above her own comes to typify a feeling of occulted figures and forces in operation in her new country. As in a conventional ghost story, footsteps and voices are overheard in supposedly unoccupied rooms, objects, whose purpose is unclear, appear, move and disappear impossibly. The apartment building becomes a haunted house, the empty flat a forbidden enclave embedded within the narrative, whose spectral inhabitants can neither be identified nor fully repudiated.[61] Frances herself comes to act within the narrative as a quasi-gothic heroine and nowhere is this positioning more apparent than in her final confrontation with the veiled intruder she discovers in the stairwell. Only a few lines prior to the encounter she has returned from a futile medical appointment, the result of which she suspects will be 'a little bottle of tranquilizing pills', conjecturing further that she will be required to make a self-diagnosis of a 'neurotic imagination' (p. 234). It is possible to read the passage as a failed exorcism, an attempt to 'debunk' the phantom that has been haunting the apartment by bringing its identity fully into the realm of the sensible. Yet to do so would be to miss the crucial significance of the passage.

Early on in the novel Frances learns of a rumour that the 'empty' flat is used by a couple having an adulterous affair, an explanation which attributes the haunted quality of the flat to the necessity of occulting certain activities from the spectral surveillance of the religious authorities. This rumour at first appears to be symbolically supported by the repeated image of veiled women ascending the staircase in the apartment building, in various states of distress and anonymity. These incidents, and the lack of significance they are attributed by any of the other characters, underline the way in which the domestic sphere in general is frequently de-politicized. In Rancière's terms the communications and apparitions ('groans or cries') issuing from the domestic space are only deemed capable of 'expressing suffering, hunger or anger' rather than constituting actual speech 'demonstrating a shared aesthesis'[62] that would demand acknowledgement or more broadly indicate a belonging to the realm of the sensible. The ostensible 'de-politicization' of the domestic sphere within *Eight Months*, or rather the refusal by the Saudi State to grant any explicit political significance to what takes place within the 'female' space of the domestic is underlined throughout the novel, both through the actions of State apparatus and the comments of those subject to that apparatus. This can be observed in the early assertion that Saudi police do not enter private homes 'on a whim' (p. 63), an assertion that appears to evidence an official position wherein the space of the home is one in which nothing of legal or political note takes place (an understanding which the 'burglary' of the Shores' home renders specious). Likewise, Andrew's dismissal of Frances's concerns as fabricated and unimportant, emerging as they do from her domestic interactions with her neighbours: 'you sit around the house, confabulating, making plots, and making your dull life brighter' (p. 153), combines with Eric Parsons' patronizing assessment of Frances's relationship with the other housewives in her apartment complex ('I can understand it of course – all you women together in the flats, you've got to know each other, that's nice, and you're sure to talk amongst yourselves' (p. 240)) to reinforce the overt placement of the space of the home as one in which only trivial matters are spoken of and inconsequential events take place.

Yet, the 'veiled ladies' of Ghazzah Street, despite being dismissed as part of the fabric of domestic life in Jeddah and as such not admitted in any meaningful way to the realm of the sensible, possess a powerful significance within the narrative. While, in a strategy which echoes the crime fiction authors Frances reads so avidly, Mantel's 'veiled ladies' turn out to be red herrings, their purpose as misdirection rather than key to a central, highly politicized secret serves not as a formal inscription of the de-politicization of the domestic space but rather allows Mantel to interrogate the culturally freighted difficulties that Frances encounters as she tries to make her interventions in the division of the sensible. As the narrative progresses Frances becomes convinced that the existence of the adulterous couple suggested by the anonymous veiled women she repeatedly encounters in her apartment block is a fiction, that the 'rumour … was tailor-made … for Westerners with their prurient minds' (p. 121). This notion of a narrative 'tailor-made' for 'Westerners' is significant. Rather than a confrontation between a spectre and a subject, the clash between Frances and the veiled figure should be read as signifying an encounter between the Western notion of spectrality, through whose lens Frances views the events that unfold, and a Middle Eastern milieu by which the notion of the ghost and the concept of haunting are not accommodated.

The spectres of Ghazzah Street are profoundly metaphorical, they are the socially dead, the government 'spook'. This knowing deployment of what Peeren would term 'the spectral metaphor' indicates an intersection between the cultural context of the novel and the cultural background of its writer. Many forms of Christianity accommodate the notion of a 'ghost' and ghosts are certainly spoken about with reference to Christian religious practice even if interpretations of scriptural evidence of ghosts forming a part of Christian dogma is conflicted and ambiguous.[63] Islam on the other hand does not have the same familiar relationship with the notion of the ghost and indeed there is no such thing as a ghost mentioned within the Koran, wherein the dead 'can never return, either to right past wrongs or to communicate with the living'.[64] Rather, the Koran describes an impermeable barrier, *barzakh,* raised between the dead and the living until judgement day.[65] The most closely related phenomenon to be found in Islamic culture is that of the *djinn,* a supernatural, shape-shifting creature capable of both disruptive and altruistic magical feats. Crucially, the *djinn* is not understood to be the spirit of a dead person. It stands outside of the binary of life and death as a non-human presence. At one point in the text the lack of superstition within the Wahhabi community is remarked upon by one of Frances's neighbours: 'You must know, Frances, that here they are Sunni Muslims. ... They don't go for shrines and tombs and processions. They call these things superstition' (p. 145). This is echoed in non-fictional accounts of the historical destruction of tomb decorations or visible structures by Wahhabi adherents,[66] supporting the sense of a community in which the dead and their ghosts have no place, as Islam 'hurries to inter the dead' (p. 292) who are immured behind the 'veil' of *barzakh*, incapable of ingress into the world of the living.[67] This being the case, Mantel's creation of a haunted Jeddah populated with manifold spectral inhabitants could be interpreted as an attempt to articulate a culture using terms that do not apply to it, or worse, as an ethnocentric imposition. Yet, to pursue this reading would be to fail to grasp the true extent of Mantel's spectral strategy in this novel, in which no clash or contradiction is orchestrated without purpose.

Lost in translation: turning the screw of ethnocentrism

The notions of translation, of language and of access to knowledge are at the heart of this novel. Frances is a cartographer by training but the impossibility of mapping Jeddah is one of the first things she learns about her new home, her flight attendant assuring her that '[she is] redundant. [The Saudis] don't have maps. ... The streets are never in the same place for more than a few weeks together' (p. 27). This assertion is borne out later when Andrew brings her maps of Jeddah which turn out to be completely inaccurate: 'the shape of the coastline is different', roads run into the sea and the apartment on Ghazzah Street is just a vacant lot (p. 81). This 'CARTOGRAPHY BY KAFKA' (p. 81), as Frances describes it, the inability to translate the geographical reality of Jeddah into a legible document, is just the beginning of a series of difficulties she encounters with 'translations' relating to Saudi culture and society. When her neighbour Yasmin provides her with a translated copy of the Koran she apologizes, saying, 'you must understand that the very language of the Holy Koran is sacred, and so this little Penguin Book is just a little lacking the nuances' (pp. 117–18). Later, upon enquiring how Frances is getting on with the book, Samira reasserts this position, stating 'of course you do not get the full idea in translation' (p. 127). From these interactions a sense emerges of Frances's struggle to translate the Wahhabi beliefs and doctrines that shape Saudi society into an accurate and nuanced form that she, as an outsider, can fully grasp. This struggle repeatedly proves futile as the problems inherent with the process of translation continue to present themselves. By creating Frances in the mode of a gothic heroine, the young female protagonist 'who is simultaneously persecuted victim and courageous heroine',[68] and by casting the apartment building on Ghazzah Street as the classic haunted house, complete with forbidden enclaves, Mantel orchestrates a situation in which the gothic narrative of the search 'for the centre of a mystery ... following clues that pull [the protagonist] onward and inward',[69] can be played out within the context of Saudi society. Unlike the gothic novel, however, *Eight Months* stubbornly maintains its ambiguity until the novel's close, encouraging the epistemological drive towards the resolution of a mystery that typifies gothic narratives but ultimately refusing to show or tell. Nowhere is this more apparent than in the appearance and violent disappearance of Adam Fairfax, one of Andrew's work colleagues. In the context of *Eight Months* Fairfax's name generates a powerful irony, invoking the notion as it does of a 'fair copy', the copy of a document produced after the final corrections and forming the definitive version. *Eight Months* can on one level be understood as a search for such a definitive account which is perpetually thwarted. Frances's expatriate neighbours frequently recount stories which are riddled with omissions and contradictions. For example when the Shores' host a dinner party for Andrew's expatriate colleagues, the attempt to recount the story of the alleged rape of two female tourists at a local souk disintegrates into conjecture, hear-say and contradiction in which the narrative is bolted together with a plethora of 'I heard's, 'what actually happened's and allegations of factual inconsistencies (pp. 162–3). The passage ends with one of Frances's guests concluding: 'I have to say though, I have heard so many versions of that story, I don't know what to believe.' (p. 163) Certainly, this struggle to get a story straight not only forms the basis of the gothic narrative form but also seemingly characterized Mantel's experience of living in Saudi Arabia. She states that 'what really interested me about the Kingdom and interests me even more in retrospect was the way that you never got a story straight, not the simplest thing, and people would tell you versions of public affairs in perfectly good faith and then somebody else would tell you a different version'.[70]

Though productive, Fairfax's significance for the narrative exceeds this ironic provocation to recognize the ubiquity within *Eight Months* of unreliable narrators. His arrival is foreshadowed from the earliest pages of the novel, when Frances overhears two fellow passengers on her flight to Jeddah discussing someone of the same name (p. 27), and his eventual appearance at the Shores' apartment combines the arrival of a romantic hero, bearing flowers, with the entrance of a spectre; he is 'quite insubstantial', possessed of a 'transparent pallor' and a 'transparent smile', even his suit is 'lightweight' and his hair 'as fine as cobwebs' (p. 252). Having celebrated Fairfax's arrival with a meal and several bottles of wine, Andrew and Frances retire to bed leaving Fairfax asleep on the sofa. Frances is awoken to find the front door of the flat open and Fairfax, drunk and distressed, crouching in the stairwell of the apartment building having attempted to get onto the roof for some fresh air. Yet when Frances tries to discover the cause of his shock and fear Fairfax is incapable of articulating what he has seen:

> 'Fairfax, wake up, tell us.' He did open his eyes, for an instant; he looked at her warily, directly. She saw pain and fear. But he said nothing.
>
> 'He's not really all that drunk,' she said. 'Not any more. He's just made a decision I think.' She turned away, distraught. 'He's not going to tell us.' (p. 262)

By the time Frances and Andrew wake in the morning after Fairfax's enigmatic encounter, their guest has disappeared from the flat. This first incident details a somewhat mundane inability to find words to describe a shocking and frightening sight. Yet the scene of 'unspeakability' is more nuanced than this. Fairfax's presence invokes notions of England and Englishness that have been largely absent from the novel previously, though Yasmin's description of the translation of the Koran she gives to Frances as a 'little Penguin book' very much roots their conversation about translation within the context of a translation not only into the English language but via a well-known British publishing house. The group discuss Frances and Andrew purchasing a flat in London and Fairfax describes his home in the village of Cumbernauld. This evocation of Englishness borders on parody as Fairfax is described as looking 'like a schoolboy who had been given the task of imitating ... the governor of the Bank of England' (p. 255). This 'bubble' of Englishness that Fairfax creates, referencing as it does Mantel's own description of expat communities in Saudi Arabia,[71] positions Fairfax's inability to describe what he has seen or explain what has happened to him very specifically as a failure of cultural translation.

Following Fairfax's disappearance Andrew arrives at work to be given a transcription, in Arabic, of a telephone message from Fairfax. Complaining that he can't read the 'Arabic scrawl' (p. 267), he hands the note back to his colleague Hasan who reads it out to him:

> [Fairfax] says, 'I go up to your roof last night and saw two men with box and down the stairs carrying a person who is dead. I am advise you to leave that place.'
>
> Andrew reached out and snatched back the piece of paper. He stared down at it. The loops and squiggles defied comprehension. (p. 267)

Andrew's inability to comprehend, to read from the original source, is both literal and symbolic and the translation provides only enigmatic remains of the original message. Indeed, only two pages later Andrew breaks the news to Frances that Fairfax is dead, apparently killed in a car accident on his way to the airport, at which point Fairfax's corpse comes to profoundly embody these enigmatic 'remains' as Frances and Andrew struggle to obtain an explanation for what has taken place and to locate his corpse. Finding and viewing the corpse can only be achieved through the efforts of a translator and Fairfax's body proves, in itself, 'meaningless' (p. 292), providing no clarity as to the events that led to his death:

> It was a while before the man in charge extricated himself, came out from behind his untidy desk and held some conversation with Hasan.
>
> …
>
> The man made a fussy gesture, to hurry them on; then briefly slid open the mortuary drawer, and showed them Fairfax's dead face. There was no error, no mistake in identity, and for all the inexpert eye could tell, he had died just as the police had given out. The head seemed twisted on the spinal column, the face was clamped, jaundiced, marked by a trickle of black blood; the expression was meaningless. (p. 289–90)

Yet when walking out of the mortuary Frances passes two anonymous, shrouded corpses, their winding sheets knotted around their heads (p. 289). This image, evoking the veils that in themselves prove so ambivalent and problematic in this novel, brings us to what is ultimately at stake in Mantel's use of spectrality to speak about a system in which the spectre is not accommodated. Recall Frances's acknowledgement of the impossibility of tearing off a veil (p. 173) and the failure of her own attempt to do so (p. 235). These scenes provide a powerful metaphor for the inability of any attempt to translate another culture or politico-religious system to be complete, and for such attempts not to result in ambiguous and enigmatic traces that persist and cause discomfort. These traces are inscribed in the image of Fairfax's broken body, refusing to disclose the circumstances of his death. They are found in the empty rooms of the apartment block on Ghazzah Street at the novel's close which retain the residues of lives that were never wholly comprehensible to Frances or the reader, where the 'smell of goatflesh, of onions and herbs, of chemical air-freshener and baby powder' has 'a thick and tangible quality, as if it were a tapestry with which the walls had been draped' (p. 295). The most striking manifestation of these ambiguous remnants is perhaps the final chapter of the novel itself. Describing Frances and Andrew as human leftovers, the last vestiges of a 'golden age' of construction in the Kingdom, living in a 'ghost town' (p. 297) of a compound on the outskirts of Jeddah, the brief chapter provides an enigmatic kernel at the close of the novel which leaves the reader wrong-footed, denied the traditional scene of elucidation which conventionally rewards the reader of the gothic novel. Whichever way they turn the reader, like Frances in the final paragraph of the novel, is left looking down blind alleys and roads that appear to lead nowhere:

> I look out through the glass, on to the landscape, the distant prospect of travelling cars. Window one, the freeway: window two, the freeway. I turn away, cross the room to find a different view. Window three, the freeway, window four: the freeway. (p. 299)

Conclusion

It is not possible for Frances to comprehend what is happening in Jeddah within her own cultural framework; her symbolic universe is insufficient and so despite her attempts to reconcile and interpret what she sees and hears on Ghazzah Street, she is always left with occluded elements whose opacity refuses to yield to interpretation. The significance of this impenetrability and the repeated 'failures of translation' in the text are best elucidated through a consideration of the phenomenon of what is described by Rancière as the 'mute letter'. The text of Fairfax's note, twice translated and unfathomable, provides an excellent example of the 'mute letter', the letter that '[goes] its way without a father to guide it … that [speaks] to anybody without knowing to whom it had to speak and to whom it had not … that [speaks] too much and endows anyone at all with the power of speaking'.[72] Indeed, from the moment when Eric Parsons' driver, Hasan, is asked to read the letter he becomes an articulate subject in the narrative, offering advice and an interpretation of events, stepping from a ghostly background existence into the flow of discourse. It is perhaps one of the most political moments in the novel, a moment in which the accepted order of who can speak and be heard is radically disrupted. By reading *Eight Months* with Rancière it becomes possible to understand the novel not as primarily fictionalized autobiography or conventional thriller, but as political fiction on Mantel's own terms, in which she understands the political as an issue of who and what can be seen and heard. Mantel's propensity for 'privileging the unseen' allows her to 'frame a new fabric of common experience, a new scenery of the invisible and a new dramaturgy of the intelligible'.[73] In other words, *Eight Months* forces the reader to question whose experiences are being excluded from the realm of the socially visible. The text provides a space in which the 'sensory self-evidence of the natural order'[74] is, for a moment, overturned, allowing those subjects, statements and events previously deemed insensible, and thus incomprehensible, by the prevailing social order to be recognized and acknowledged, and permitting them to move from the status of the apparitional to fully appear. Her utilization of the logic of haunting and spectrality achieves a series of acts of dissensus, critiquing the haunted operation of politico-religious authority in Saudi Arabia and bringing to light previously occulted experiences. The narrative skilfully demonstrates that just as 'there is no straight path from the viewing of a spectacle to an understanding of the state of the world',[75] as Frances learns from her multiple encounters with the 'veiled lady' of Ghazzah Street, there is no straight path from an encounter with a spectre to an understanding of the implications of their spectrality. In Chapter 4 I continue to explore, in Mantel's words, 'the defining question of who is human, what is human and what rights therefore adhere'.[76] However, I will be doing so in the context of Mantel's simultaneous engagement with the figure of the traditional ghost, reading her 2005 novel *Beyond Black* as articulating a contemporary rupture with history and the ancestral dead.

4

The princess and the palimpsest: Skin, screen and spectre in *Beyond Black*

In the previous chapter the spectres of *Eight Months on Ghazzah Street* were seen not to be characterized by the post-mortem positioning of the traditional ghost, but rather composed by the 'spooks' of politico-religious authorities and the individuals whose existence is spectralized by those authorities. By contrast, Mantel's *Beyond Black* is a text in which the physically dead continue to circulate within, and forcefully act upon, the realm of the living. The novel, which relates the life of Alison Hart, a spirit medium performing in the orbital towns of southern England in the late 1990s, is populated by a host of ghosts. Perhaps the most striking haunting to occur in the text is the manifestation of the ghost of Princess Diana in the hallway of a detached new-build on a housing estate, as the televised highlights of her own funeral play in an adjacent room.[1] Diana's apparition, clothed in her dishevelled wedding dress and with her press cuttings pinned to her skirts, typifies the novel's preoccupation with the intersections between death and the tele-technological which materialized with greater and greater frequency at the turn of the millennium. *Beyond Black* is a text responding to an uncertainty about the place of the ghost and the moment of haunting in a contemporary period which has in many ways been defined by the ubiquity of tele-technologies, and the hyper-visibility and hyper-connectivity that accompanies that ubiquity. In this novel the Mantelian ghost manifests alongside the figure of the spirit medium in order to pose certain central questions: what happens to the ghost in the millennial moment? What modes of spectrality are made possible and which ones are rendered obsolete in an age of ubiquitous tele-technologies and mass media? How does the contemporary subject relate to the dead?

Possible answers to these questions are provided in the novel through an interplay between the affiliated motifs of the screen and the skin, whose functions are at multiple points in the text demonstrated to be interchangeable.

This interchangeability is articulated in the work of a number of thinkers, both in terms of research around the role of the skin in culture and in terms of the tele-technological screen. Didier Anzieu for example famously described the skin as a screen in his seminal text *The Skin Ego*,[2] while Steven Connor identifies how the skin 'is no longer primarily a membrane of separation but a medium of connection or greatly intensified semiotic permeability'.[3] Conversely, the very notion of the screen is multifarious, invoking both the sense of an obscuring, protective barrier and a medium of display and exposure. *Beyond Black* is a novel structured around a series of 'screening' processes whose nature is by turns deceptive, protective and revelatory. Within the novel both the degree of transparency and the level of robustness possessed by the screen is seen to fluctuate, sometimes becoming permeable, permitting exchange and communication, while at other times hardening into defensive opacity. The objects performing this screening function are also various, exceeding literal computer and television screen to incorporate organic, inorganic and symbolic membranes, formed of flesh, rhetoric and performance. I argue that the heterogeneity of the screening processes and surfaces detailed in *Beyond Black* is tempered by an understanding that they all function, whether by accident or design, to provide a surface upon or against which a variety of spectres and ghosts can become licit and their meanings be discerned. By making available both biological and technological mediums for ghostly inscription Mantel's novel articulates how a plethora of ghosts generated by personal trauma, by historical narratives, by technology, and by society satisfy their requirement for a surface upon which to show themselves in the context of millennial dormitory England.

My analysis of *Beyond Black* begins by exploring how the novel acknowledges and subverts a history of spirit mediumship that has privileged both technology and performativity, reading Alison's spiritualist practice as an ambivalent screening process which recognizes the context of contemporary tele-technological advancement. Building on this understanding of mediumship in the novel, I posit this screening process as forming one element of a critique of how the historical and familial dead are situated in millennial England, demonstrating how Alison's ability to mediate between the living and the dead is increasingly unable to accommodate a contemporary disassociation from history. This disassociation is twinned with a growing prostheticization of memory and affect in the contemporary period facilitated by the proliferation of tele-technologies. In the chapter's third section I return to the question of social ghosting raised in Chapter 3 in order to examine how, in *Beyond Black*, the representation of subjects spectralized by sociopolitical structures is inflected and developed by the presence in the later novel of 'traditional' ghosts (i.e. the manifestations of biologically deceased subjects) and media technologies. Finally, I read *Beyond Black*'s complex intertextual elements as explicitly ventriloquizing the voices of dead authors, situating the novel as addressing the uses to which authors put the dead in contrast to the lack of use *Beyond Black*'s living subjects appear to find for them.

Mediums and media

'The dead won't be coaxed and they won't be coerced. But the public has paid its money and it wants results.' (*Beyond Black*, p. 1)

The protagonist of *Beyond Black*, Alison, is 'a sensitive …, a medium … a clairvoyant' (pp. 7–8). Yet, the spirit medium, most powerfully associated in Britain with darkened Victorian and interwar parlours, is a figure which seems incongruous with the contemporary, secular society depicted in *Beyond Black*, and largely incompatible with 'a culture ruled by hypervisibility'.[4] Indeed, the references to previous modes of spiritualist practice which permeate the novel's second chapter on one level chart what Esther Peeren terms 'the medium's transformation' over the course of the twentieth century 'from being closely associated with mainstream scientific, religious and political discourses to being considered little more than fringe entertainment'.[5] However, despite the spirit medium's anachronistic status, Alison's profession signals the novel's participation in a critical tradition which has identified a close and complex relationship between mediumship and communications technology. An examination of Alison's mediumistic practice reveals a confrontation between media and medium which questions and complicates linkages previously taken for granted between technology and clairvoyance and asks how the evolution of technology shapes our relationship with the dead. Before examining precisely how Mantel nuances Alison's position in relation to the tele-technologies which provided the metaphorical language in which the work of her forebears was couched, it is useful to trace how the novel more generally acknowledges the history of professional mediumship.

Early descriptions of Alison at work make the archaic roots of her profession explicit, depicting her as 'soft as an Edwardian, opulent as a showgirl, … when she moved you could hear (though she did not wear them) the rustle of plumes and silks' (p. 3). A reference to Alison's assistant, Colette, performing the role of 'ladies' maid' in the same passage intensifies the effect of the simile 'soft as an Edwardian' and insists on a historicized understanding of mediumship which spectrally overlays the contemporary narrative, positioning the medium as a relic of another time. During the 'Evening of Psychic Arts', which takes up the second chapter of the novel and gives the reader their first exposure to Alison's mediumistic practice, she assures her audience that '[they're] not going to see anything that will frighten [them]', adding that she 'won't be going into a trance, and [they] won't be seeing spooks, or hearing spirit music' (p. 15). This assurance inserts her into a historic tradition of mediumship in which the hearing of spirit music, the apparition of spirit objects and the apparent materialization of the dead were commonplace,[6] even as she tactfully differentiates herself from that tradition stylistically. Mantel returns to this notion of the evolution of spiritualism in a secular, mediatized and more rampantly capitalist age in the third chapter where Alison observes that, in contrast to her more reticent ghosts, the Victorian dead:

> ... blew trumpets and played portable organs; they moved the furniture; they rapped on the wall, they sang hymns. They offered bouquets to the living, spirit roses bound by scented hands. Sometimes they proffered inconveniently large objects, like a horse. Sometimes they stood at your shoulder, a glowing column made flesh by the eyes of faith. She could see it easily, a picture from the past: herself in a darkened parlour, her superb shoulders rising white out of crimson velvet. (pp. 80–1)

Historical accounts of Victorian spiritualism are consistent with this description, attesting to occurrences of 'musical instruments play[ing] by themselves' and 'flowers fall[ing] in showers from the ceiling',[7] but the compression of these phenomena into a continuous list renders the image carnivalesque and makes the transition to Alison's mode of contemporary spiritualism appear less inconsistent: the public face of spiritualism is presented as always having been the preserve of the performer.

If Mantel deliberately evokes an anachronistic spiritualism defined by theatrical flourishes, to which Alison is indebted, even if she does not emulate it, she also recasts Alison's own theatricality as tailored to the needs and expectations of her audience. In an early draft of the novel Mantel makes explicit how, over time, Alison edits out references to historical spiritual practice, sensing that they mean very little to her contemporary audience: 'So, eventually Alison dropped all her mentions of the reign of Qu. Vic [sic], of the spirit cabinets, the disgorged ectoplasm, the ghostly songs on ghostly banjos.'[8] Through Colette the reader observes Alison's 'public self: a little bit jaunty and a little bit crude, a bit of a schoolmistress and a bit of a flirt' (p. 24). This persona is bolstered by a burlesque aesthetic, with Alison described as 'a genius with make-up' (p. 5) and depicted carefully constructing herself for the stage, donning fake opals and vividly coloured clothing in 'emerald, burnt orange, [and] scarlet' (p. 4). This invocation of bright colours has a specific purpose. Explaining her choice of costume for her performances Alison states that 'the last thing you want, when you go out there, …, is to make them think of funerals' (pp. 4–5). This statement confirms the essentially composite nature of Alison's performance. Her 'Evening of Psychic Arts' is advertised alongside a performance of Faure's *Requiem* and a Christmas pantomime (p. 7), a pairing that implicitly acknowledges Alison's synthesizing of death and entertainment. The vibrant costumes and practiced demeanour which characterize what she calls her 'platform' work are not merely pantomimic devices designed to amuse the 'trade', as Alison refers to her audiences. Rather they are one component of a mediumistic practice constructed to screen off those aspects of death and the dead that are frightening.

This strategy is exemplified in a sustained description of the spirit world as Alison sells it to her customers. This afterlife is one of perfect equilibrium, where everything is in balance and nothing takes place. The temperature is 'moderate', the breeze 'gentle' and the trees 'seasonless' (pp. 43–4). Mantel describes an environment that is free of conflict and contradiction, of painful stimulation of any kind: 'the children never squabble or cut their knees', even the bees are 'stingless' (p. 43). She then nuances this tensionless vision with a calculated representation of a nostalgia for the 'Golden Age' of 1950s Britain: 'There's a certain 1950s air about the dead, or early sixties perhaps, because they're clean and respectable and they don't stink of factories: as if they came after white nylon shirts and indoor sanitation, but before satire, certainly before sexual intercourse' (p. 43).

According to Alison's public account, the afterlife exists in a state of perpetual, post-war propriety in which bodily needs have been eradicated: the dead eat simply for pleasure, never getting hungry, and are immune to sexual desire. Bodily defects possessed in life are corrected in death through a compound process of sanitation; the fiction with which Alison presents her clients is a sanitization of the 'reality' of the existence of the dead and then within this sanitized vision the dead themselves are individually made more appealing than they were in life:

> They all have their own teeth: or an expensive set of implants, if their own were unsightly. Their damaged chromosomes are counted and shuffled into good order; …. Damaged livers have been replaced, so their owners live to drink

another day. Blighted lungs now suck at God's own low-tar blend. Cancerous breasts have been rescued from the surgeons' bin, and blossom like roses on spirit chests. (p. 44)

These rhetorical manoeuvres are placed alongside the vivid colours Alison selects for her theatrical costumes to render her performance a protective screen, utilizing both rhetoric and aesthetics as a barrier designed to shield the general public from the unbearable stimulation of the unpalatable, unsaleable 'reality' of death and the afterlife. This protective screening function is implicitly acknowledged in the following exchange between Colette and Alison. Here Colette is questioning Alison on her apparent deception of her customers:

'You see, I'd have imagined,' [Colette] said, 'that sometimes, once in a while, you'd feel the urge to be honest.'
  Alison gave a comic little shiver, like a character in a pantomime. 'What, with the punters? They'd run a mile, …. It'd kill them.' (p. 32)

While this exchange appears to suggest a robust screening, capable of repelling the fatally stimulating knowledge of the reality of existence 'airside', it is undermined at several points in the text. The final sentence of the rich passage quoted above, describing a publicly palatable afterlife, refers to Philip Larkin's famous poem 'Annus Mirablis' which memorably states that 'sexual intercourse began | in 1963'.[9] In using this allusion here Mantel sets up an intertextual resonance which gives the lie to Alison's construction of an idealized image of airside existence and doubles it with a darker and more troubling alternative since the 'wrangle for a ring | a shame that started at sixteen and spread to everything' which appears later in Larkin's poem sits silently alongside Alison's bucolic rendering of the afterlife in the image of 1950s, early 1960s Britain. Likewise, the synecdoche in Alison's description of the dead subverts her project of idealization. In a passage which overtly aims to communicate a wholeness and coherence, the listing of body parts builds to create an opposing image of fragmentation, amputation and disintegration which operates from a cellular level outwards, from 'chromosomes' through 'teeth' to 'spirit chests'. In so doing the consequences of Alison's acts of redaction are implicitly stated: despite her accomplished performance as spin doctor for the dead, representing them as idealizations of their living selves, the overstimulating and disagreeable elements of the dead and their messages remain as traces, fragments capable of penetrating the protective screen Alison constructs and finding their way into the world of the living.

If Alison's theatrical performance and onstage patter screens off the distasteful reality of the dead rather than providing a surface upon which they can be made manifest, this occlusion takes place in the context of a further screening process that occurs offstage and is rooted in Mantel's troubling of the correlations that have long been drawn between mediums and telecommunications technology. As has been discussed, the spiritualist practice in *Beyond Black* self-consciously references its own Victorian heritage, with the shielding of a rationalist, secular audience against deeply disturbing supernatural truths mirroring the consolatory fictions doled out by mediums in spiritualism's heyday. However, while Victorian society provided the initial milieu for the growth of spiritualism, the references to historic spiritualist practice woven into this depiction of contemporary mediumship carefully track its evolution. It is widely acknowledged that the rise of spiritualism in the nineteenth century ran parallel to a meteoric rise in wireless telegraphy and telephony,[10] and that the concurrence of these developments led to the drawing of an analogous relationship between communications technologies and spiritualism. Jeffrey Sconce astutely observes the equation of the work of the spirit medium with the function of communications technology in the blending of 'supernatural and technological discourses, a model legitimated by the equally incredible yet incontrovertible evidence of the telegraph'.[11] As Jill Galvan notes, 'for many [nineteenth-century] spiritualists, psychical researchers, and the writers who depicted their pursuits, mediumistic contacts were of a piece with the communication technology innovations of the day'.[12]

That the telegraph and the telephone were considered 'functionally analogous' to séance manifestations[13] has been firmly established. However, Galvan goes further, stating that, rather than being merely useful similes, adopted by spiritualist adherents and detractors alike, the relationships between technology and medium, the broadcast situation and the séance situation, were coterminous: 'what happened in the séance was not *like* a technology, but an intricate technological event itself'.[14] Furthermore, she identifies in critical writing on spiritualism a lack of engagement with 'theories of mediums ... as complex, at times faulty communications devices, operated by the spirits'.[15] Galvan's model of the medium as transmitter, which picks up on the communications of the dead and relays them verbatim, is nuanced by her argument that Victorian spiritualists made use of the concept which in communication and information studies is now termed 'noise', to account for anomalies in séance manifestations.[16] The most provocative element of her proposal is the suggestion that it was 'the peculiarities of the medium's own body' which produced the noise that disrupted the transmissions of the dead.[17] For Galvan the Victorian séance was a technological event in which messages were scrambled, garbled or otherwise interfered with due to the idiosyncrasies of the communications device, i.e. the individual physicality of the medium's body and sound of her voice.

Mantel's representation of mediumship resembles Galvan's model to a degree. Yet it also diverges from it in significant ways which allow it to comment upon contemporary, rather than Victorian, technological contexts. Alison herself falls back on tele-technological metaphors in order to offer to her audiences an explanation of what she does, referring to herself as the audience's 'answering machine', and (disingenuously as it will turn out) comparing her access to, and delivery of, the messages of the dead to the mechanism whereby 'you press the button and [the answer machine] plays your messages back' (p. 26). Her recourse to the language of tele-technologies is in keeping with Galvan's description of communications technologies as 'useful similes'.[18] Still, there is a crucial distinction to be made here between the technological metaphor employed by nineteenth-century spiritualists and Alison's spiritualist practice. Rather than the direct real-time transmission of a message, of the kind produced by a telephone line, what Alison is describing is a spiritualist answering service, one that accommodates the idiosyncrasies of contemporary communications technology such as 'wrong numbers' and 'nuisance calls' (p. 27). Alison's conception of her function in *Beyond Black*, as answer machine rather than telephone, is suggestive of an evolution of the public conceptualization of spiritualism which closely corresponds to the evolution of technology itself.

Clearly Alison's performance of being a medium proposes a technological continuum along which the metaphors available to describe the séance situation have developed. However, the reality of her contact with the dead betrays a wholly different technological mechanism, one which chimes with Galvan's discussion of the medium's body as a distorting influence upon the messages of the dead while simultaneously questioning the agency of the medium in controlling or producing that distortion. Prior to relaying the messages she receives during her live stage performances, Alison is depicted sifting through the interference that accompanies it, utilizing 'her peculiar form of listening' (p. 19) to tune out the 'background mutter' (p. 19) and 'confused distant chit-chat that comes from the world of the dead' (p. 17) and tune in to individual voices, 'picking out one and letting the others recede' (p. 20). In contrast to the nineteenth-century séance situation, in which the medium's corporeality in and of itself corrupts the communications of the dead, Mantel represents the contemporary séance as a technological event in which the message itself is always already corrupted and subject to interference before it reaches the medium of communication.

This is not to say that the medium in this text is positioned as having no impact upon the messages of the dead but rather that Alison's interventions in the post-mortem messages she receives are both deliberate, as opposed to a by-product of her physicality, and multifaceted in nature. In this sense Mantel's representation of contemporary mediumship refuses the widely acknowledged conception of the medium as passive transmitter, a technological object lacking agency,[19] and proposes a model which reflects a closer and closer synthesis between subject and tele-technological apparatus. On one level Alison is performing a data cleansing function, removing the 'noise' that comes across the frontier between 'airside' and 'earthside', a cacophony of 'something noisy going on in the background' composed of 'whizzes and bangs' (p. 49), 'hissing ..., startled wails and whistles' (p. 177), to get at the message beneath. On another level, Alison acts as censor with regard to the post-mortem communications she receives, even as she gives the lie to this element of her role, protesting that an answering machine 'doesn't wipe some [messages] out, on the grounds you don't need to know them' (p. 26) and stating that 'if I get a message I don't censor it. I don't ask, do you need it?' (p. 27). As Colette comes to understand, 'there wasn't a necessary tie-up between what [Alison] said on the platform and the true state of affairs. Uncomfortable truths were smoothed over, before Al let them out to the public; when she conveyed soothing messages, Colette saw, they came not from the medium but from the saleswoman, from the part of her that saw the value in pleasing people' (p. 151). Just as the séances in *Beyond Black* provide a sanitized version of the dead and the space they inhabit, the messages that the dead send are similarly sanitized by Alison, who, as mentioned in Chapter 1, reassures a woman who wishes to know if her dead pet would be reunited with her late husband, despite the opposite scenario being true. Nonetheless, the link between noise, interference and the body of the medium proposed by Galvan is not absent in this representation of contemporary mediumship. This link is an extremely potent feature of the mediumship depicted in *Beyond Black*; however, the direction of the agency involved in the process is reversed. Rather than the body of the medium acting upon the messages of the dead as a 'faulty communications device',[20] contaminating the original message with noise, as in the Victorian model, here the words of the dead infiltrate the words of the living medium, scrambling her own communications just as Alison compromises the voices of the dead with her acts of redaction and censorship. Despite describing herself as 'an answering machine', Alison is to a large extent cut off from modern technology. She tells Colette 'I'm not very good with electrical things' (p. 90) and explains that 'whatever message [she] left on her machine was liable to become corrupted. Other messages, quite different ones, would overlay it' (pp. 90–1). Though almost all of her communications are represented as potential vehicles for the voices of the dead, this use of media and communications technology to inscribe the process of contamination and interference to which Alison's communications are subject finds its most powerful expression in the moments where she attempts to record her own voice. Here Alison is recalling her schoolgirl struggle to complete an exam paper:

> All during the maths paper there was a man chattering in her ear. ... The man, the spirit, he was talking just below the threshold, retching and sobbing ... He said, look for my cousin John Joseph, tell our Jo that my hands are bound with wire ... that's what he relied on her to pass on to his cousin, the knowledge of his pain ... so that when Miss Adshead came to flick her paper into the pile there was nothing on it but thin pen scrawls, like the traces and loops of wire with which the hands of this total stranger had been bound. (pp. 181–2)

This hijacking of the medium's spoken and written language is paralleled in the relationship of Alison's own body to the dead subjects who speak to and through her. The body of Galvan's Victorian spirit medium was understood to be acting upon the messages of the dead, with the often uncanny resemblance of manifested spirits to the mediums who were channelling them being attributed to the distorting effect of the medium's own materiality on the spirit's appearance.[21] This relationship between mediumistic corporeality and the messages of the dead (and, indeed, the dead as message) is skewed, though not totally reversed in the novel, as Alison's body becomes a physical medium upon which the dead write their messages. In doing so they perform acts of transformation upon Alison's body which have varying degrees of permanence. For example, in the complete version of the passage quoted above Alison is described as physically experiencing the injuries endured by the murdered paramilitary, 'the crushing of the rifle butts and the men's boots seem[ing] to drive her feet through the floor' (p. 182). Even the recollection of this incident registers itself corporeally as Alison's toes become hot and swollen and her cry of pain is 'bellowed, in somebody else's voice' (p. 185). In this account of contemporary mediumship, then, the medium *is* the message; Mantel's spirit medium becomes the message of the dead, acting as a screen onto which they project themselves.

The situation of communication not only with, but in the presence of, the dead in this novel deliberately cannot be neatly formulated. It is not a straightforward reversal of the traditional understanding of the medium as passive (and possibly, as Galvan argues, faulty) transmitter, though, as we have seen, elements of this formulation find their way into these scenes. The ghost is necessarily a chaotic, disorganizing presence and the possessive effect of the phantom paramilitary on Alison's own voice is striking, capturing the frequent difficulty in identifying who is speaking in this narrative. With reference to her own mediumistic experiences Alison states: 'when famous people pass they attract spirit-impostors, just as on this side you have lookalikes and body doubles' (p. 150). When Alison is speaking it is often ambiguous as to who is using her voice: '"At the mercy of shed merchants," Al said. "Ah dear, ah dear, ah dear." At first she didn't recognise who was speaking and then she realised it was Mrs McGibbet' (p. 283). Ambiguity around who is speaking at any given moment is not restricted to explicit moments in this text but permeates Mantel's writing. The effect of this vocal slippage in *Beyond Black* specifically is to produce a phantasmic multivocality which, as will now be demonstrated, is in part a response to a new, mediatized, relationship with history.

Forgetting the dead: ancestral amnesia and prosthetic memory

'The modern man is he who feels he is free to forget the dead.'[22]

Ferdinand Tönnies's statement here is expressive of a post-Enlightenment divorce from history in which an attempt is made to throw off the sedimented ideas of the past. This rupture is one which has profound implications not only for the status of the ghost but for a whole constellation of attendant notions such as inheritance, legacy and the role of the ancestor. Moreover, this rupture has been contrasted by an emphasis in the contemporary moment on wider and wider spheres of connection facilitated by technological innovation. Marshall McLuhan's statement that 'in the electric age we wear all mankind as our skin'[23] captures strikingly the connectivity brought about by the tele-technological advancements made in the latter part of the twentieth century. McLuhan's description of a quasi-epidermal connection to mankind at large, facilitated by electronic media, proposes that a key feature of existence in the age of ubiquitous communication technologies is being brought into intimate contact with humanity on a global scale, and to be placed within a network of relationships that vastly exceeds the familial and social bonds which were possible in the pre-electric age. This hyper-connectivity, whether facilitated through visual media, telephony or computing, has been argued by a number of scholars to bring about artificial affective consequences.[24]

In the passage above, depicting Alison's reception of the experiences of an Irish paramilitary, the man is described as 'a total stranger'. Yet, through him, she accesses a visceral connection to a past that does not belong to her, obtaining a form of what Alison Landsberg terms 'prosthetic memory': a 'deeply felt memory of a past event through which [she] did not live'.[25] I explored above how Alison's mediumistic practice involves compound acts of screening whose structures share a vexed relationship with various communications technologies. These technologies permeate the novel and their significance exceeds Alison's mediumship. *Beyond Black* presents the proliferation of screens associated with televisual media as, on the one hand, failing to accommodate the manifestation of a certain class of ghost. On the other hand these screens are seen to provide a medium for the appearance of other, mediatized, spectres, radically destabilizing the status of the dead and the nature of memory within the communities Alison serves. It is with the forgetting of the familial dead that I will begin.

The dislocated quality of memory in *Beyond Black* is not limited to prosthetic memories of the kind Alison experiences through her mediumship. It is also registered in her audiences who are shown struggling with the act of listening to the dead, whether historical or personal. This profound decay of ancestral memory is crystallized in the minor character of Leanne, one of Alison's audience members, who fails to receive a message from her own grandmother as she doesn't know her relative's name, stating that she 'didn't think she had a granny' (p. 16). This rupture in family memory is not restricted to the 'kids' who 'don't remember back more than eighteen months' (p. 16). Rather, it is characteristic of the contemporary population of whom Alison observes that:

> It was not uncommon to find family memory so short, in these towns nobody comes from, these south-eastern towns with their floating populations and their car parks where the centre should be. Nobody has roots here; and maybe they don't want to acknowledge roots, or recall their grimy places of origin and their illiterate foremothers up north. (pp. 16–17)

The divorce of the subject from ancestral memory renders the inhabitants of the orbital, dormitory towns Alison frequents incapable of receiving the messages of the dead, since the living do not know if, and by whom, they are being addressed. Leanne's inability to name her own grandmother is indicative of Mantel's confirmation in this novel of Landsberg's statement that 'part of the experience of modernity [is] the disruption of family, kinship and community ties'.[26] An early draft of *Beyond Black* positions this disruption in and of itself spectralizing, stating of subjects such as Leanne, who have no knowledge of their forebears: 'What if you don't know who they are? Who they are and where they dwelled? Then you are beached, stranded, you are washed up on the present moment, you are as significant as a ghost.'[27]

Leanne's disconnection from her family history is absolute. Alison's attempts to spur the girl's recognition of her spectral ancestor through empathic means, emphasizing Kathleen's physically draining existence ('"What about Granny Kathleen walking uphill?"' (p. 16)) and her desperation to speak with her granddaughter, are to no avail. Leanne responds not with recognition but incredulity. It is telling that this attempt to foster an empathic connection between a contemporary subject and their dead forebear is couched in an appreciation of the historical. As Alison describes Kathleen's existence she stresses its otherness, wryly observing that Kathleen's struggle to get home with goods purchased at market 'seems to be before you could order your groceries online', adding rhetorically, 'when you think about how we lived in those days' (p. 16). Thinking about 'how we lived in those days', about the past more broadly, proves to be just as problematic for the characters in this novel as connecting with their own individual histories.

Disengagement from personal heritage is paralleled in *Beyond Black* by a disengagement from history itself, one which Mantel couples with the proliferation of tele-technologies and the ubiquity of mediatization. This rejection of the historical is implicitly demonstrated at the outset of the second chapter, when Colette accidentally treads on Alison's spirit guide, Morris: 'Morris was on the floor, half sitting and half lying, slumped against the wall. ... When Colette stepped back she trampled straight over him' (p. 5). As the narrative progresses it becomes clear that Colette embodies a contemporary attitude towards history that has its roots in an inability to empathize. In the following extract Colette listens to Alison addressing a member of her audience and contemplates her own empathic incapability:

> 'On the mike, darling. Talk to the mike. Speak up, speak out, don't be afraid. There isn't anybody here who isn't sharing your pain.'
> Am I? Colette asked herself. I'm not sure I am. (p. 38)

The significance of these statements becomes clear in a later chapter when Colette recalls being asked in school to 'empathise with the sufferings of cotton mill operatives, plantation slaves and the Scots foot soldiers at Flodden; it left her cold' (p. 52). In this light her trampling of Morris is symbolic of an unwitting flattening of the ghosts that actively embody history in this narrative. Meanwhile Alison struggles to contain the ghosts of deceased members of the royal family as the 'Evening of Psychic Arts' progresses: 'ruthless, she gave the whole tribe the brush-off: Margaret Rose, Princess Di, Prince Albert, and a faint old cove who might be some sort of Plantagenet' (p. 34). This unregulated circulation of history is recognizable from Alison's physically damaging encounter with the ghost of the Irish paramilitary and her clairvoyant colleagues are similarly depicted as being under constant assault from the historical past:

> 'Al? Are you back with us, love? Is she pestering you? The princess?'
> 'No,' Al said. 'It's paramilitaries.'
> ...
> 'I get Cossacks,' Mandy said. 'Apologising for, you know. What they used to do. Cleaving. Slashing. Scourging peasants to death. Terrible.' (p. 182)

In this exchange Alison and her counterparts describe the process of 'tak[ing] on memories of events not naturally their own'.[28] Yet whereas for the community of psychics this memorial appropriation is a result of their profession, Landsberg describes it as being facilitated by what she terms 'the technologies of memory', that is, film, photography and television, and, to a lesser extent, radio. An early draft of the novel captures this mediatized method of affective appropriation neatly, with Al stating: 'They don't live through their own bodies, they live through the TV. That's how they get beyond the limit of their own skin.'[29] This parallel is further drawn out in Alison's depiction as a keen consumer of mediatized images. However, her supernatural insight into historical events is carefully positioned as intersecting with the experience of the casual consumer of media images, introducing a level of instability into the media image by questioning its accuracy: 'It was interesting for Al that you got so many history programmes on TV these days. Many a night she'd sat on the sofa, hugging her plump calves, pointing out people she knew. "Is that really Mrs Pankhurst?" she'd say. "I've never seen her in that hat"' (p. 34). Certainly Alison's ability to pick out discrepancies between mediatized versions of the dead and her own 'lived' contact with them after death is in contrast to the typical viewer's uncritical assimilation of those images. However, her acquisition of somatic and affective memories is still 'prosthetic' in the same way that Landsberg suggests such memories acquired by viewers through 'mass cultural technologies of simulation'[30] are prosthetic. This equivalence confirms *Beyond Black* as representing certain screens as capable of producing their own phantasms, phantom memories which, to paraphrase Michel de Certeau, produce places that do not belong to them.[31]

Following Alison's conversation with her colleagues regarding the intrusive, proximate nature of the historical past for the medium, she and Colette retire to watch the televised highlights of Princess Diana's funeral in a sardonic textual gesture which directs the reader to one of the most remarkable instances of the prostheticization of memory and affect of recent times. Diana's death and the outpouring of public grief that followed it, along with the blanket media coverage of the event, are explicitly alluded to in the novel. This grief possessed for many critics a profoundly prosthetic quality, as individuals who had no actual connection to the dead princess displayed 'a collective sense of loss for something the collective never possessed'.[32] Crucially the scenes of mass mourning formed a 'mediatized epic production'[33] with 'gigantic television screens erected in Hyde Park and various sites around central London to ensure a fully mediatized spectacle'.[34] Reference is made in the novel to the television coverage of the funeral through repeated allusions to the 'highlights' of the coverage but also through a telling statement on the intersection between mourning and the media that Diana's death provokes. On the morning of the funeral Colette and Alison drive to a Psychic Fayre:

> As they turned off the M1 onto the A52, the bells pealed out to mark the end of the National Silence. Curtains were drawn in the Nottingham suburbs. 'That's nice,' Alison said, 'It's respectful, it's old-fashioned.'
> 'Don't be stupid,' Colette said, 'It's to keep the sun out so that they can see the TV.' (p. 167)

Here a traditional gesture of respect for the dead instead functions to facilitate the consumption of mediatized images of the dead, with the indirect reference to those images in this passage causing the 'endlessly recycled photographic effigies of [Diana's] famous face', which 'all enshrined Diana in a ritual economy of post-modern mediatization',[35] to haunt the novel.[36] Diana does not only haunt *Beyond Black* through references to the media spectacle that was made of her death. The two occasions on which her ghost manifests serve to nuance the novel's assertion of the spectralizing potential of tele-technologies. In the novel's representation of Diana, both in life and in death, is found an articulation of the power of the 'technologies of memory' defined by Landsberg not only to depict images of the historical dead, electronically re-animating them for the living, but to render the living themselves spectral.

As discussed at the outset of the chapter, while the highlights of her own funeral are broadcast next door, the newly deceased Diana appears to Alison in the hallway of her home:

> She was wearing her wedding dress, and it hung on her now; she was gaunt, and it looked crumpled and worn, as if dragged through the halls of the hereafter,

where the housekeeping, understandably, is never of the best. She had pinned some of her press cuttings to her skirts; they lifted, in some other-worldly breeze, and flapped. (p. 213)

This description of Diana's post-mortem incarnation emphasizes her thinness, her 'gaunt' appearance invoking images of the skeletal, of bones beneath skin which, alongside the image of Diana's eyes 'roll[ing] beneath her blue lids' (p. 214), generates an image of translucency. Thus far it would appear that Diana's ghost conforms to a recognizably 'ghostly' aesthetic. However, if read alongside Alison's assertion that, airside, the dead are as they were in life,[37] the appearance of Diana's ghost indicates a *pre-mortem* spectralization. Furthermore, Diana's costume suggests that this spectralization results from prolonged exposure to, and representation through, media technologies.

Diana's now tatty and ill-fitting wedding dress, seen by thousands during the televised coverage of her marriage to Prince Charles,[38] is doubled symbolically by the fluttering press clippings in which Diana has partially clothed herself:

She picked up her skirts, and puzzled over a fan of press cuttings, whipping them aside in her search for the name she wanted. 'So many words,' she moaned, then giggled. The hem of her wedding gown slipped from her fingers. 'No use, lost it.' (p. 214)

In this passage Diana lifts up her skirts in an act of exposure that is congruent with the exposing effect of the broadcast media on the princess in life. The fragments of media coverage themselves are attached precariously to the princess's person, only pinned to her wedding dress they flap and lift 'in some other-worldly breeze' (p. 213). On one level this image of the fluttering newspaper clippings conveys the instability of the relationship between the mediatized image and the living referent, an instability which is partly responsible for the spectral quality of media images, as observed in Alison's doubts about the authenticity of the televised Mrs Pankhurst. However, as the passage progresses it becomes clear that the ghost Alison encounters is not merely clothed in media outputs but constructed of them in such a way as to communicate the spectralizing potential of media technologies as a whole.

The statements Mantel places in the princess's mouth knowingly chime with Diana's portrayal in the mainstream media. Her outburst of 'you oiky little greasepot, you're just being hideous. Oh fuckerama' (p. 214) blends caricatured aristocratic idiom with profanity, coupling Diana's upper class background to the derision by the press of 'Diana as a trash icon for our times'.[39] This idea of Diana as contemporary 'icon' is cleverly woven into the passages that describe the aftermath of her death, playing on the idea of the icon as both a religious and technological notion. Here Diana's 'screen goddess'[40]/'media saint' status, which rendered her a quasi-religious icon, is put in dialogue with her flattened, symbolic representation on television and computer screens. Earlier in the novel, as Alison reports Diana's death (in a way which, as will be made clear, further testifies to electronic media as accommodating a certain class of spectre), Colette is seen turning on her computer in order to 'prepare a series of invoices that might take advantage of the event' (p. 146). This manoeuvre parallels the actions of the press towards Diana, both in life and death, selling prosthetic affective connections which found their ultimate expression in the mass-mediatized mass-mourning for the princess. While she is engaged in her attempts to monetize Alison's relationship with the dead, Colette notices that 'the computer was humming and whirring, making from time to time its little sighs, as if deep within its operating system the Princess was gurgling out her story' (p. 147). Diana is positioned as a ghost in the media machine, a compound on-screen icon. This fictional representation clearly communicates the notion that 'each time [Diana] was shot and captured in the imprint of the image there appeared to be a recognition that this was a repetition of events that were yet to come. Every image seemed to configure and confirm Diana as always already dead, catching her imprisoned in the torturous temporality between two deaths – symbolic and real'.[41]

That mediumship in this novel follows a trajectory paralleled by communications technology has been established, as has the novel's exploration of the role of tele-technologies in producing a kind of memorial ghosting in which memory is not tied to first person presence at an event but disseminates prosthetically in an unregulated fashion. Just as technology is understood in *Beyond Black* to be shaping the practice of mediumship, philosopher Bernard Stiegler argues that technology or, more broadly speaking, technics, are constitutive of the human experience generally, radically shaping human behaviour. Stiegler's theory of technics will be put to work at length in Chapter 5 to discuss Mantel's representation of English Reformation print culture. However, presently it suffices to focus on Stiegler's understanding of media technology's effect upon contemporary temporality.

Stiegler conceptualizes media technologies, particularly real-time media technologies, as contributing to the dislocated nature of contemporary memory by making it the object of 'a war of speed: from the computer to the programme industries in general, via the cognitive sciences, the technics of virtual reality and telepresence … the media event to the event of technicized life … new conditions of event-ization have been put in place'.[42] According to Stiegler, this 'war of speed' has the effect of erasing 'the separation between [one's] lived past and [one's] inherited past',[43] facilitating the kinds of prostheticizations of memory that Landsberg defines. The treatment of the moment of Diana's death in the novel serves to interweave both of these notions. It provides a scene in which the merger between medium and media technology is presented as irrevocably linked with the media's acute prostheticization of memorial material while simultaneously dramatizing the 'war of speed' and 'new conditions of "event-ization"' Stiegler describes, in which the here-and-now is suppressed and Diana's death is 'de-rooted from any spatial specificity'.[44]

The event of Diana's death, as distinct from her spectral reappearance, is related through Alison. What is remarkable about this passage are the decisions Mantel makes regarding the timeline of these events. Alison wakes Colette to tell her the news:

> 'It's Diana,' Al said. 'Dead.'
> …
> Al gave a snort of jeering laughter. 'Or as we say, passed.'
> 'Suicide?'
> 'Or accident. She won't tell me. Teasing to the last,' Al said. 'Though probably not quite the last. From our point of view.' (p. 145)

The incident is not only reported as if it has already happened but as if the source for the news is the posthumous Diana herself. It quickly becomes apparent, however, that this is a report of an event that is yet to occur as Alison continues: 'I am sure it will be clearer … when it actually happens' (p. 145).[45] When Colette protests that they should warn somebody, and try to avert the apparently impending accident, Alison does not respond, instead beginning to narrate the events taking place in Paris as if they are happening in real time:

> 'She's getting in the car. She's putting on her seat belt – no, no she isn't. They're larking about. Not a care in the world. Why are they going that way? Dear, dear, they're all over the road!'
> Alison tumbled to the sofa, moaning and holding her chest.
> 'No use waiting around,' she said, breaking off, and speaking in a surprisingly normal voice. 'We won't hear from her again for a while.' (p. 145)

This passage recalls the relentless inescapability ascribed by Stiegler to the television media of which he states, 'one has the feeling that it is impossible to stop',[46] both in the sense that the content delivered by the media possesses a feeling of inevitability, and in the sense that the medium itself has an elusive self-perpetuating quality; switching off the television set does not terminate the broadcast, merely one screening of it. Alison's inability, or refusal, to address Colette's suggestion that they 'warn somebody! Call the police!' (p. 145), reinforces this relentlessness, and conveys her implicit understanding that the night's events are indeed impossible to stop.

What is also implied when Alison states that the princess's death has not 'happened' yet is that the event has not been reported on the broadcast media, the channel through which major world events are brought into being in the contemporary milieu for those people who were not directly involved. Later in the passage Alison's account of the event is situated alongside the broadcast media's account, directly inviting comparison:

> from Al the news arrived piecemeal, but it was more exciting that way. In time the radio, placed beside her, brought the confirming details. The event, in the real world, had actually taken place; [Colette] stopped typing and sat listening. *Lights, a tunnel, impact, lights, a tunnel, black, and then something beyond it: a hiatus, and one final, blinding light.* (p. 146)

This side by side comparison of medium and media reveals a mirroring in which Alison's clairvoyance allows her access to events which have not yet occurred, while the account of the same event provided by the broadcast media, though delayed temporally, brings the event into being in a crucial way. In the age of ubiquitous tele-technological media, it is implied, the 'presence' of a historical event only becomes fully realized in the event of its publication via such media, the real-world occurrence no longer being sufficient.

In addition to the parallels drawn between Alison's reports of the princess's death and those provided by the radio, a disorienting temporal collapse is produced in the 'death-night' passage in which past, present and future events appear to be taking place at once. Alison provides Colette with updates of an event that is occurring and yet to occur simultaneously: 'We're now waiting for the emergency services. We're slightly beyond the paracetamol stage' (p. 146). The princess is apparently both alive, dying and dead, a Mantelian ghost par excellence through her occupation of multiple states which invoke or preclude presence. However, Alison's statement is indicative of another, related, collapse taking place on a subjective level between herself and Diana, a collapse which sees the spiritualist medium ghost the princess in a process comparable to, but distinct from, the broadcast media's spectralization of the princess in life. As the 'death-night' sequence wears on Alison begins to equate herself linguistically with the princess, her use of the pronoun 'we', carrying with it connotations of the royal 'we', setting up a secondary ambiguity regarding whether Alison is speaking as Diana or just experiencing what Diana is experiencing simultaneously. She also begins to exhibit physical symptoms which become progressively worse as the situation unfolds: '[Colette] couldn't stop Al shivering. Over the next hour Alison's face drained of colour. Her eyes seemed to shrink back in her skull' (p. 147). As the princess apparently gets closer to death Alison appears to display the attributes of a corpse – pallor, shrunken eyes and extremely low body temperature – until eventually she begins to smell of decay. Not until the close of the passage is it suggested that she has not taken on the appearance of any corpse but the corpse of the princess herself. Alison is described emerging from the bathroom 'scored all over with faint pink lines ... the cuts on her thighs flared darkest, as if she had been whipped with wire' (p. 149). The description immediately evokes media accounts of Diana's self-harm, though at this stage in the narrative it is ambiguous as to whether Alison has experienced Diana's own memories in the same bodily, sensuous fashion that she experienced the princess's death or whether the scars were pre-existing, physical inscriptions of an event in Alison's own past. The imposition by the dead of their sensuous experiences upon Alison's own body is expressed at length early on in the novel: 'By the end of the evening she'll be sick to her stomach from other people's chemotherapy, feverish and short of breath; or twitching and cold, full of their torsions and strains. She'll have a neck spasm or a foot she can barely put on the floor' (p. 29). However, the physical resemblance Alison comes to bear to Diana in death is not merely a further example of her acquisition of the embodied memories of the dead. Rather, Alison is represented not only as mirroring the mechanism of communications technology but providing an analogue for those subject to that technology, a narrative device which is achieved through a careful twinning of Alison and Princess Diana. The scars on the backs of Alison's legs are first alluded to in the 'death-night' passage analysed above. Later in the same chapter, while Alison is packing to attend the psychic fayre that coincides with the princess's funeral, Colette asks 'Did you do that? ... Like Di, did you cut yourself?' (p. 158). Diana's reported self-harm is thus projected onto Alison's own scars, providing an oblique insight into her screened-off past but also reinforcing the notion that the two women can be equated with one another.

This is not the only moment at which parallels are drawn between Alison and Diana's personal lives as well as their public function. Diana's well-documented eating disorders[47] are paralleled in Alison's own obesity and struggle with her weight. The physical structures of both women's bodies appear to oppose one another diametrically, yet their purpose is concurrent on a symbolic level. Valerie Hey argues that Diana's 'quintessential emptiness enabled her image to host a multiplicity of contradictory demands'.[48] While Diana's hollow quality in the cultural imaginary denotes her ability to receive these projections, Alison's bulk signifies both the host of dead others she is described as physically containing ('I have to house so many people. My flesh is so capacious. I am a settlement, a place of safety, a bombproof shelter' (p. 347)) and the physical structure she attempts to put in place to shield herself from them, her padded flesh 'keep[ing] her from the pinching of the dead, their peevish nipping and needle teeth' (p. 11). This doubling is continued linguistically. Alison observes that in the weeks following her death 'Diana is the queen of hearts; every time the card turns up in a spread, …, she will signify the princess' (p. 191) and in doing so the media's use of the term is mapped onto the symbolism of the tarot, while Alison's full name, 'Alison Hart', invokes not only this public nickname but Diana's own namesake, Diana the Huntress and the deer she pursues. However, the final and most suggestive element of Mantel's doubling of media saint and spirit medium is their interaction with the 'socially dead'.

'Rejects, or anomalies': social death and thingly life

'People assume there are hard and fast distinctions between the living and the dead but within the living there is another very important distinction: are you recognised as human by fellow humans.'

– Hilary Mantel, 'Interview'

Mantel's suggestion above, that to fail to be designated as human by other humans is to be killed off in some crucial way, subjected to a social death that radically compromises your presence, has already been recognized as a key element in the formation of the Mantelian ghost. While in Chapters 2 and 3 my analysis focused on the representation of those socially ghosted individuals in isolation, in the case of *Beyond Black* an opportunity arises to read Alison as a character whose profession charges her with acknowledging not only the biologically dead but those assigned, pre-mortem, to the category of the socially dead. Richard Johnson observes that Diana often 'dealt in "social death" – in recognizing the unrecognizable, touching the untouchable'.[49] This observation is borne out by Diana's work with homelessness charities, the National AIDS trust and the Leprosy Foundation, organizations whose clients, particularly in the 1980s, were frequently, legally or symbolically, excluded from mainstream society. While Alison's primary interactions are with those who are biologically dead, she too characterizes her work as an interaction with the rejected or 'excess' material constituted by the dead, an interaction that the majority of the population are unwilling to undertake:

'I'm like – '
   'A sewage worker?' Colette suggested.
   'Yes! Because the clients won't do their own dirty work. They want it contracted out. They write me a cheque for thirty quid and expect me to clean their drains.' (p. 183)

As Russ Castronovo points out, 'as corporeal fact and political metaphor, death produces bodies' which exist 'at a remove from socio-political life'.[50] Mantel demonstrates a marked awareness of the potentially fatal consequences of marginalization. For Mantel as for Castronovo one does not have to be deceased to be a spectre.[51] Indeed the opening chapter of the novel focuses sharply on a landscape populated by those spectralized by social bankruptcy. It describes a car journey made by Alison and Colette through a post-industrial landscape on the outskirts of London,[52] a wasteland where the only landmarks are defective technology: 'this is marginal land: fields of strung wire, of treadless tyres, fridges dead on their backs' (p. 1). Not only marginal land but the land *of* the marginal, this waste ground is populated with the displaced, the rejected and the dead in all their manifestations, placing refugees and asylum seekers ('Afghans, Turks and Kurds') alongside abandoned animals ('starving ponies, … cats tipped from speeding cars, and the Heathrow sheep, their fleece clotted with the stench of aviation fuel') and criminals ('Perjured ministers and burnt-out paedophiles'). In its focus on the marginal, the passage seeks to reveal those presences who have fallen, or been located, 'beyond the veil' constructed by mainstream social narratives: 'outcasts and escapees … rejects, or anomalies' (p. 1). Strikingly, even the objects that populate this landscape are rendered not broken but 'dead', a description that admits the inanimate into the binary of life and death conventionally reserved for animate beings. In doing so the passage orchestrates a slippage between discrete ontological categories and through its admission of inert objects into the realm of the animate, implies conversely that persons and animals may be capable of joining objects in a state of 'thingliness' facilitated by their combined defects and obsolescence. Building on Heidegger's distinction between an object and a thing, wherein an object becomes a thing when it can no longer perform its designated function, or is put to a use outside of its designated function, Bill Brown comments that 'we begin to confront the thingness of objects when they stop working for us'.[53] Here Mantel is using 'things and thingness … to think about the self',[54] rendering the human and animal subjects in the scene 'things' by virtue of their suggested lack of functionality within society; they have stopped – or been stopped – 'working' in a significant fashion. In this passage the elision of the boundary between persons and things opens up the possibility of such 'thingly' existence being more broadly imposed upon living subjects. As Mantel puts it, 'all sorts of people at different times and places are elected out of the human condition and made things'.[55] By initially describing a landscape so fractured that people, animals and objects occupy the same linguistic and social spaces, the novel articulates a difficulty with 'distinguishing the actually dead from social corpses'[56] as one of its primary concerns.

By depicting this scene, and lingering upon its outcast inhabitants, the screen that obscures the social dead is drawn aside, albeit temporarily. Just as the ghost of Diana Spencer constituted a compound phantom, a result of corporeal death and the spectralizing effects of mediatization, the 'fiends' that plague Alison, ghosts of individuals from her traumatic childhood, and many of the other ghosts that populate the narrative, were marginal figures in life, subject to 'social death': prostitutes, immigrants, drifters and criminals. This focus on the marginalized must be read in the context of the systematic privileging of borderline phenomena in this novel, phenomena exemplified by the multiplicity of screens and the host of ghosts and spectres encountered thus far.

Until now pre-mortem spectralization, whether effected through media technologies or social ghosting, has been read as symbolically mirroring biological death. However, *Beyond Black*'s representation of both forms of death, and the hauntings those subject to them undertake, exceeds mere resemblance and articulates how social death can so easily shade into its biological counterpart. Towards the end of *Beyond Black*, Alison discovers a young homeless man, Mart, living in her shed. Mart is represented as phantasmal from the outset; Colette thinks she dreams his presence in their garden and Alison initially assumes he is a ghost, stating, 'I thought you were a spectral form' (p. 293). It is telling that Alison's ability to acknowledge and listen to the corporeal dead is made analogous with the ability to offer the same act of witnessing to the socially dead. Slowly Mart describes to Alison a life involving child abuse, mental illness, unemployment, homelessness and police brutality. From infancy to adulthood

Mart exists on the outskirts of society, falling through the cracks at every turn: 'I came through the net' he says, 'the list I was on, I think they lost it' (p. 299). Alison's attempts to help Mart, to negate the deathly impact of the existence society has allotted him, are in vain and she eventually finds he has hanged himself in her shed. When interviewed, Mantel stated that Mart is an 'objective of social policy ... nothing just happens to [him], he is always in a policy, he is someone's statistic and he is subject to the ultimate nightmare, he's a marginal and spectral person who is actually murdered by ghosts, they come for him and make him frankly one of their company'.[57] His suicide, which constitutes his transformation from necro-citizen into revenant, strikingly parallels the kind of compound spectrality possessed by Diana Spencer in that it is only through his actual death that his pre-mortem spectrality can be fully comprehended. As Mantel's comments confirm, Mart's suicide is assisted by, or possibly at the behest of, Morris and the rest of the spectral 'fiends' from Alison's childhood who protest that '[they] wanted a laugh, that's all' and opine that 'it's not as if [Mart] was doing much good this side' (p. 411). This moment encapsulates the proliferation of ghosts which has been unfolding throughout the narrative, with physical death exposed as just one spectralizing force among many and where social exclusion can prove literally fatal.

Mart is not the only social spectre to die at the hands of the persecutory fiends from Alison's past, as the persistent and problematic presence in the narrative of a prostitute called Gloria attests. My analysis of Mantel's consideration of mediatization versus mediumship examined the nuanced doubling of Alison with Diana Spencer. However, a crucial element of this doubling remains to be articulated, that is, the trope of the female body as receptacle for the dead and, alternately, death as the only possible container for a certain kind of woman. Certainly these notions were circulating implicitly in the immediate aftermath of Diana's death. In the months leading up to it the press had attacked the princess, dubbing her 'The Queen of England Manqué' and 'a fast woman'.[58] There was a sense in which her death was seen as arresting the 'decay' of the public perception of Diana, enabling the media to transform her from 'a false goddess with loose morals'[59] into a kind of post-modern saint.[60] Mantel voices these moral anxieties through Colette who, upon hearing of the princess's death thinks 'what does she expect? A girl like Diana? There was something so right about it, so *meant*. It had all turned out so beautifully badly' (pp. 146–7). A conversation between Alison and Colette that takes place on the day of Diana's funeral makes explicit the pernicious undercurrents of this media manoeuvre but it also has a sinister resonance within the world of the narrative:

> 'S'funny,' Colette said. 'It's only a fortnight ago – those pictures of her in the boat with Dodi, in her bikini. And we were all saying, what a slapper.'
>
> …
>
> 'I mean, it's not as if it's exactly a surprise. You didn't expect it to last, did you? Not as if she was exactly stable. If she'd been in real life, she'd have been just the sort of slut who'd end up with her arms and legs in left luggage lockers and her head in a bin bag in Walthamstow.' (p. 161)

If Diana's dismemberment is undertaken symbolically by the press, the 'real life' woman Colette describes is also forcefully present in the narrative. The kind of mutilation Colette imagines is the fate of Gloria who, it is implied, is murdered and dismembered by Morris and his friends. Her appearances in the text are marked by a disorienting ambiguity; as Colette complains 'when you're talking about Gloria … I can never tell if she is alive or dead' to which Alison replies 'Nor me' (pp. 128–9). This ambiguity allows Mantel to obscure the precise moment at which Gloria's social death becomes corporeal, reinforcing the assertion that the mode of the ghostly and the mode of the spectral are not simply analogous but contiguous, sharing an unstable border. Like Mart, Gloria's presence is symptomatic of what Sara Knox terms Mantel's 'fleshing of the phantoms, living and dead, that people her fiction',[61] and if Alison's public acts of spirit mediumship establish one screen between the living and the physically dead, her private experiences draw back another, socially constructed, screen designed to obscure the 'unsightly' spectres who form a 'haunting reminder of the complex social relations in which we live'.[62]

Unlike Diana, whose spectral form is unmarred by the precise circumstances of her death, Gloria's anatomization retains a residual presence in her post-mortem existence, as she phases between wholeness and fragmentation:

> [Alison] caught a glimpse of a red-haired lady with false eyelashes, standing at the foot of the stairs. Gloria, she thought, at last; she said, 'Hi, are you all right?' but the woman didn't reply. Another day, as she was coming in at the front door, she had glanced down … and didn't she see the red-haired lady looking up at her, with her eyelashes half pulled off, and no body attached to her neck? (p. 119)

Gloria's head is just one of the phantom appendages that are strewn throughout *Beyond Black* and Alison describes how her spirit encounters with the dead began 'at the age of eight, nine, ten' with seeing 'disassembled people lying around, a leg here, an arm there' (p. 122). In the same passage she anxiously recalls being followed to school by a human eye (p. 123). This reading has thus far focused on the ghosts presented as recognizable incarnations of previously living subjects, how these subjects came to be spectralized in the first place and the mechanisms by which they are variously obscured, disguised and revealed. Thus these amputated remains, re-animated in Alison's recollection of their appearance, bring with them questions about their status and their relationship to the various screening processes operating within *Beyond Black*. If ghostly limbs and organs populate Alison's memories of her childhood, this fragmentation is mirrored in the sinister vacancies present within those memories, rendering Alison's past confusingly occluded. I move now to examine those occlusions, results of another of the screening processes which attempt to contain or accommodate the dead within *Beyond Black*.

Flesh wounds and flash backs: scars as spectral inscription

'The modern man has an epidermis rather than a soul.'

– James Joyce[63]

Despite Alison's clairvoyance and her frequently over-proximate connection to the personal histories of strangers and the historical past more generally, she is herself divorced from significant elements of her own personal history. Though not as stark as Leanne's inability to remember the name of her own grandmother, Alison's memory of her childhood is compromised by haunting lacunae whose impenetrability is as traumatic as the presence of Morris and his ghostly companions. The scars whose origins mystify Alison draw comparisons with the messages of the dead which she is charged with 'cleaning' and interpreting for her customers, with Alison's acts of protective screening undertaken within the séance situation reproduced in the intrapsychic screening which occludes her traumatic past. Moreover, taking Joyce's substitution of internal human essence for external integument as a jumping-off point, it becomes possible to demonstrate how this intrapsychic screening process is structured by and articulated through the dual quality of the skin, not only in terms of its protective yet permeable nature but also in terms of the skin's ability to register both internal and external realities.

> Colette saw the backs of her thighs. 'Christ,' she said. 'Did you do that?'
> 'Me?'
> 'Like Di? Did you cut yourself?'
> Alison turned back to her packing. She was perplexed. It had never occurred to her that she might have inflicted the damage herself. Perhaps I did, she

thought, and I've just forgotten; there is so much I've forgotten, so much that has slipped away from me. It was a long time since she'd given much thought to the scars. They flared, in a hot bath, and the skin around them itched in hot weather. She avoided seeing them, which was not difficult if she avoided mirrors. But now, she thought, Colette will always be noticing them. I had better have a story because she will want answers. (p. 158)

The above exchange between Colette and Alison illustrates neatly Steven Connor's statement that the skin is 'normally invisible except as the bearer of messages written upon or displayed through it'.[64] Made painfully visible through its status as surface for spectral inscription, Alison's skin attests to the way in which the skin as surface is overlooked and taken for granted until it is compromised by the traumatic or scarifying receipt of messages. Colette's blunt 'noticing' of Alison's scarred flesh articulates the insistence of the marks ('now ..., Colette will always be noticing them') and prompts in Alison a need to provide them with a narrative, even as she occupies the same situation as her baffled séance audiences, severed from her past not by a contemporary rupture with the historical but by unknowable trauma.

As has been discussed, Alison's scars first come to light in the text in the aftermath of the death of Princess Diana (p. 149). The 'faint pink lines' that cover Alison's body, alluding to the self-harm practised by Diana, overlay older scars, which 'flare darkest' in a graphic visual representation of what Freud termed *nachträglichkeit*, or as Jean Laplanche has translated, the term *après coupe* or 'afterwardsness'. This term refers to a specific temporal model of trauma in which 'what has been described or deposited as excessive or unassimilable in a first scene is either traumatically repeated, or repressed and symptomatically symbolized, or revived and translated into the terms of a new scene'.[65] The hot bath, in which Alison attempts to scrub away the smell of decay provoked by Diana's death, makes of Alison's body a palimpsest upon which her own trauma is overlaid with the traumas of others which resonate with Alison's own. Rather than resembling a symbolic symptom, however, Alison's scarred flesh forms a 'de-signified signifier',[66] which has been 'stripped of intelligible meaning but [is] nonetheless potent'.[67] As a mode of decayed or residual message, her scars operate to 'signify [that] something real – something exceeding mere signification – has taken place'[68] not merely on a corporeal but also on an intrapsychic level.

Alison's scars symbolize a past trauma, an inscribed testimony that she lacks the tools to translate. She understands that her scars communicate but does not initially have access to the language that would allow her to comprehend their meaning, stating with reference to her attempts to articulate her experiences:

'I can't think how else to talk. I only have the usual words' (p. 200). For both Freud and Laplanche, the concept of *nachträglichkeit* describes a structure of trauma which consists of two moments; the first, in which an overly stimulating message is 'implanted without being understood' and the second, later moment when it is 'reactivated from within'.[69] This kind of 'reactivation' is embedded textually in the novel through the repetition of oblique or enigmatic images and phrases at a remove from their original context until the point at which they become intelligible. The most obvious manifestation of this motif can be found in the references to Alison's scars in which Morris's enigmatic assertions are echoed:

> She fingered her damaged flesh; the skin felt dead and distant. She remembered Morris saying, we showed you what a blade could do! For the first time she thought, oh, I see now, that was what they taught me; that was the lesson I had. (p. 159)

This moment of realization, in which Alison is able to translate the semiotic messages of her scars into a coherent narrative of a childhood trauma, possesses a doubleness that characterizes the approach to symbolism in this text. If, in her platform work, Alison's skin displays the messages of her ghostly contacts, it also serves to record haunting messages issuing from her own past. In Alison's case, it is her own past which is incomprehensibly set down upon her skin and it is only through a concurrent understanding of the message-carrying quality of her skin and the quality of the messages born by the literal spectres of her past that she can begin to penetrate the intrapsychic scar tissue that has formed an obscuring screen across her childhood.

To fully understand the significance of the image of the skin within *Beyond Black* it is necessary to acknowledge the intrapsychic significance that image has been granted, particularly within psychoanalytic thought. Didier Anzieu defines the titular concept of his book, *The Skin Ego*, as being a psychical envelope, the origin for which is the biological skin of the infant which comes to be represented phantasmally in the psyche as a projection of, or metaphor for, the body's surface.[70] Indeed, Anzieu argues that 'the skin ego is the original palimpsest, the erased, scratched and written-over outlines of an "original", pre-verbal writing made up of traces upon the skin'.[71] The skin ego surrounds the psychical apparatus and functions in an analogous fashion to the physical skin, providing protection, registering excitation and more broadly facilitating a differentiation between inside and outside. However, in *Beyond Black* the boundaries between inside and outside, whether of a mind, a body, an identity, even of life itself, are continually transgressed and confused. As such the relationship between Alison's physical skin and her psyche is compressed, and both its internal and external surfaces are subject to 'scarifying acts of signification'.[72] These twinned surfaces both come to possess the originary palimpsestic function Anzieu describes, and thus map the 'early encroachments, cumulative traumatisms and prosthetic idealisations that gave rise to them'.[73] If we consider Anzieu's assertion that 'the extent of the damage done to the skin is proportionate to the depth of psychical harm done'[74] the scar tissue on Alison's thighs comes to correspond directly with the inaccessible sites within her psyche. It is the interpretation of both sets of cryptic traces which drives *Beyond Black*. The trajectory of the novel is revealed in the words of its title which contain, like the tarot cards that are drawn and drawn again throughout the narrative, a multiplicity of meanings simultaneously. Taken literally the title refers to the post-mortem space that Alison refers to as 'airside', announcing the novel's focus on the dead and the space they take up while also wryly alluding to the quality of the novel's humour. Yet the phrase 'beyond black' also implicates symbolically both a series of concealments and repressions, of 'blacking' and 'blanking' out, and the necessity of seeing these occlusions as open to challenge and capable of reversal. The space 'beyond black' towards which the narrative of the novel is inexorably drawn is formed at least in part by the compound blackness that Alison experiences as her own past: '[Alison] couldn't see the past clearly; only an outline, a black bulk against black air' (p. 317).

Initially only alluded to, Alison's childhood is recalled in a halting and fragmentary fashion as a confused montage of sexual, physical and emotional abuse of which she is both victim and witness. She describes 'walk[ing] in on her mum, rolling on the sofa with a squaddie' (p. 115) and after witnessing this adult sexual behaviour Alison goes on to describe how 'a few nights later she woke suddenly. It was very dark outside, as if they had been able to shut off the street lamp. A number of ill-formed, greasy faces were looking down on her. … She closed her eyes. She felt herself lifted up. Then there was nothing, nothing that she remembers' (p. 116). This nothingness, both an absence of memory and a memory of absence, is key. Alison recalls, in detail, multiple instances of abuse but crucially is denied access to specific scenes. As the novel progresses it becomes apparent that her attempts to access her personal history are hampered by a series of embargoes, persistent intrapsychic screening processes that take a number of forms. Formally, these are inscribed through Mantel's use of the tape transcripts that Colette produces with the intention of using them as the basis of a book about Alison's work. Often when Alison approaches a particular childhood memory the recordings stop, indicated by a 'click' in the text. The gaps in the transcripts often remain blank, concealing what Alison wishes to omit from the recording or alternatively cannot record because she has no conscious access to it. This process of screening or censorship is not only indicated formally. Alison is also warned off speaking about certain material by a series of literal and metaphorical guard dogs. As she tries to articulate her experiences of being a 'sensitive' she is drowned out:

> ALISON: … Oh Colette, what's that? Can you hear it?
>
> COLETTE: Just carry on.
>
> ALISON: It's snarling. Somebody's let the dogs out? … I can't carry on over this racket. (p. 98)

When Alison tries to talk directly about her childhood this censorship becomes explicit and she asks Colette, 'can we switch the tape off, please? Morris is threatening me. He doesn't like me talking about the early days. He doesn't want it recorded' (p. 124). Morris's statements are deeply enigmatic and repeatedly make inscrutable references to events in Alison's own past. For example, when Alison inquires about the identity of her father, Morris replies:

> 'Speak the name of MacArthur!' He mimicked her voice: '*I think he's my dad.* Suppose he is? Is that how you treat a dad? Is it? Got to hand it to her, she has some cheek, that girl.'
>
> 'How?' She said. 'How did I treat him?'
>
> …
>
> 'I'll tell you something about that bugger' he said. (pp. 127–8)

Initially, it appears that Mantel is establishing Alison as ultimately being haunted by a void in her knowledge, with the spectral 'fiends' functioning to demarcate the limits of this void. Indeed, Morris refuses to reveal who Alison's father is, or her 'treatment' of him. However, he does affirm that Alison suffered some kind of retribution for this 'treatment': 'Still girl, you got paid out. You got a lesson eh? They taught you what a blade could do' (p. 128). Through this statement Mantel creates an incision in the text, an opening which begins to allow both reader and protagonist access to what lies beyond the spectrally supervised intrapsychic screen. The blade's cutting action, implied by Morris, is revealed to be the source of the most intimate inscriptions of the enigmatic events of Alison's childhood: the scars she bears on her thighs. These scars are not simply signifiers of physical injury. Rather they emerge as the unintegrated, unbound remainders of an original trauma which are reproduced intrapsychically, the skin itself standing as a surface upon which the haunting traces of Alison's past are made available for interpretation. This process of interpretation in turn allows Alison to compromise the spectrally supervised intrapsychic screen which obscures the reality of her experiences.[75]

In the final chapter of *Beyond Black* Alison undertakes to remember her past, an undertaking which is framed as an act of self-protection: 'at some point on your road you have to turn and start walking back towards yourself. Or the past will pursue you and bite the nape of your neck, leave you bleeding in the ditch' (p. 418). Alison's regression to her childhood is specifically framed as an interaction between the psychical and the physical, and elegantly encapsulates the ability of the skin as metaphor to speak to internal and external realities: 'With each step backwards she is pushing at something, light, tensile, clinging. It is a curtain of skin. With each step the body speaks its mind' (p. 419). The metaphor which conveys Alison's breaching of the screen erected between her conscious mind and certain scenes from her childhood relies on the corporeal reality of the skin, giving credence to Anzieu's theorization of the skin as the basis for an intrapsychic equivalent. Alison's regression takes her back to the moment at which she received the injuries that originated her scars:

> … back to the hut where she lies and howls. She peeps in, she sees herself, lying bleeding on to newspaper they've put down: it will be hygienic, Aitkenside says, because we can burn them once she's clotted. … She hears the men saying, we said she'd get a lesson, she's had one now. (pp. 427–8)

Anzieu argues that the skin functions 'as the interface which marks the boundary with the outside and keeps the outside out; it is the barrier which protects against penetration … from others, whether people or objects'.[76] This function as protective screen against excessive external excitation is acknowledged early on in *Beyond Black* through a discussion of the fabric Alison ritually drapes around her professional portrait during her clairvoyant demonstrations: 'with the silk around her studio portrait, she loses the sensation she is shrinking inside her own skin. It blunts her sensitivity, in a way that is welcome to her; it is an extra synthetic skin she has grown to compensate for the skins the work strips away' (p. 175). Yet, paradoxically, the skin also acts as 'an inscribing surface for the marks left by those others'.[77] The piercing of Alison's skin by her abusers constitutes such an act of inscription, but one in which the skin's ability to receive the messages of others is perversely exploited to such a degree that its quality as mediating interface breaks down. The scars record a sadistic attack not only upon Alison's body but upon her subjective integrity. As Alison puts it 'there on the ground they operated on me, took out my will and put in their own' (p. 209). This attack sets a precedent for Alison's adult relationship with the dead which she experiences as invasive, unregulated and over proximate: 'Al talked then about the perfidy of the dead, their partial, penetrative nature, their way of dematerialising and leaving bits of themselves behind or entangling themselves with your inner organs' (p. 153). The notion of the dead as fragment or remainder, whose quality may well be misleading or duplicitous, is given form through the treatment of Alison's own skin. Yet this concept is at work on another level in the novel where the dead are insinuated into the text not thematically but formally.

This spectred isle: spectrality as intertextuality

Wagstaffe: This sceptred isle ...

Morris: My sceptred–

...

Wagstaffe: This other Eden –

Morris: My sceptred arse. (*Beyond Black*, pp. 214–15)

The kind of intermingling described by Alison as she defines 'the perfidy of the dead' is symptomatic of the failure, or permeability, of boundaries, membranes and surfaces which, appropriately, pervades *Beyond Black*. However, there is a way of positioning this intermingling as a gesture that is broader still, a gesture which has significant implications for understanding Mantel's conception of subjectivity and authorship. As the borders between bodies, selves, even life and death are questioned through Alison's mediumistic practice and *Beyond Black*'s representation of social death, also in operation in the novel is a questioning of the boundaries of a text. In my opening chapter I explored the intertextual play that Mantel undertakes in *Giving up the Ghost*, noting how she mines her own texts as sources of intertextual material in order to articulate the synthetic, patchwork nature of life narratives. While the recurrence in *Beyond Black* of the same sentences in a variety of different contexts creates intra-textual resonances, careful attention must be paid to the self-conscious and complex use of intertextuality in the novel. The text's use of a quotation from Philip Larkin's 'Annus Mirabilis' has already pointed to a conventional mode of literary intertextuality. However, this explicit textual reference forms only one facet of *Beyond Black*'s intertextual strategy, one of the most striking elements of which are the recurrent, implicit references to the myth of Oedipus which are woven through the text, creating a sophisticated textual interface.

As John Fletcher astutely observes, the eponymous protagonist of Sophocles' *Oedipus the King* 'carries around with him an unknown but still active past, in both his name and wounded body'.[78] Fletcher is referring here to the scars that Oedipus bears on his heels, the 'old pain'[79] caused by the yoking and piercing of the tendons in the infant Oedipus's feet by his parents. Both Alison and Oedipus bear the scars of parental/quasi-parental abuse, deliberate physical damage caused by a piercing or penetration of the skin constituting an enactment of trauma in both its original and contemporary medical sense. Like Alison's injuries, Oedipus's scars signify obliquely for the majority of the text and can only be translated with the input of a third party; in Oedipus's case the messenger who arrives from Corinth with news of his father's death and in Alison's case Colette with her probing questions and desire for a narrative, 'a story' (p. 159). For both of these characters it is their scars that alert them to occulted portions of their past. Multiple elements of the Oedipus narrative are playfully mobilized throughout *Beyond Black*, conflating characters, and reversing directions of agency. Alison is constructed as a hybrid Oedipus, with whom she shares a troubling ambiguity about her parentage and a name that stubbornly links back to her origins and cannot be shaken off. Just as Oedipus's own name refers to both his gift of reason but also to the childhood injury to his feet,[80] linking him irrevocably to his abandonment by his parents, Alison succeeds in changing her surname (the problematically revealing 'Cheetham' with its implication of the phrase 'cheat them' which speaks to the reality of Alison's platform work) but cannot shake off her first name, crucially the name given to her by her mother: 'She managed to lose "Cheetham" but her baptismal name kept sliding back into her life' (p. 138).

The comparisons continue as the plague on Thebes which drives Sophocles' Oedipus to begin the search for King Laius's murderer is mirrored in the rumours of radioactivity, the 'white worms' and 'seepages' from the drains on Alison and Colette's housing estate which escalate as the narrative moves towards its close (p. 252). Jocasta's suicide by hanging is paralleled in Mart's suicide in Alison's garden shed, while the observation of one of Alison's fellow psychics that 'in antiquity they didn't have tiepins. Brooches, I grant you' (p. 257) recalls Oedipus's use of his mother's brooches to put out his eyes. The motifs of blinding and castration are also brought to bear as the implication that Alison castrated one of her abusers and stabbed out the eye of another is made increasingly explicit. Yet this intertextual invocation is not simple or predictable, the analogues are not direct. Rather, the individual tropes are appropriated, dislocated from their original context to reappear in bizarre situations. Even when considered in the light of the Oedipus myth's Freudian afterlives, *Beyond Black* is not a standard primal scene narrative in that the threat of blinding/castration is actualized and the agent of these punitive acts, which are carried out upon the quasi-parental adults in the scene, is a child. This reversal of the direction of agency and the fact that Mantel draws a symbolic equivalence between the act of blinding and the act of castration necessitates another observation, namely that Mantel conflates the mythical Oedipus, the Sophoclean Oedipus and the Freudian Oedipus. The equating of blinding with castration in this context was a Freudian observation about the original myth that has since become irrevocably associated with the figure of Oedipus in the cultural imaginary. This plastic use of Oedipal imagery serves to reinforce the novel's assertions about the inescapability of the haunting residues of the past. No matter how hard the characters in the Oedipal narrative strive they cannot evade the consequences of their past actions and, importantly, the past actions of their families.

Oedipus is not the only literary figure to haunt this text. On the contrary, the multiple references to his eponymous tragedy are characteristic of a broader intertextual strategy. In addition to Sophocles and Larkin, sustained reference is made to Shakespeare, who appears to speak lines from *Richard II* and *Hamlet* on the recordings of Alison and Colette's conversations and who is repeatedly referenced by Morris who refers to Shakespeare as 'Wagstaffe': 'bloody Bill Wagstaffe, he owes me, I'll give him Swan of bloody Avon' (p. 164). As the novel draws to a close allusions are made to Shelley's poem 'To Edward Williams' and, significantly, to Tennyson's 'The Charge of the Light Brigade'. These phantasmic literary echoes function in the same fashion as Alison's mediumistic performances which give voice to familial predecessors. Just as the tapes Colette makes of Alison 'all [speak] on top of one another … like a compost heap' (p. 320), the profusion of intertextual material allows Mantel to comment on the act of writing as inherently haunted by one's literary forebears and to make explicit how a literary lineage must necessarily speak through an author, sometimes without their control and perhaps even without their knowledge.[81] In *The Skin Ego*, Anzieu describes the two modes in which the skin can be marked, with lateral inscriptions upon its surface or vertical penetrations through the dermis.[82] The direct literary references and indirect allusions operate upon the skin of this novel in an analogous fashion, constituting intertextual scars upon 'the space of [the] writing' whose texture encourages the reader to 'range over' rather than attempt to 'pierce' the text with interpretation.[83]

The complex textual veiling and unveiling undertaken in this novel is more than the parlour trick of a sham medium and, ultimately, the literary intertexts under discussion here form one mode of intertextuality among many. Alison's interventions in the messages of the dead, blending her voice with their own, result in a message that is intertextual in nature. Likewise, the numerous surfaces present within the novel, Alison's own skin, the skin-screen that obscures her past, tele-technological screens and the membranous surface of the novel itself, form palimpsestic planes upon which a multiplicity of ghosts and spectres, be they familial, historical, textual or mediatized, can manifest. This sophisticated textual interface develops the kinds of work already analysed in *Giving up the Ghost* and *Learning to Talk* and sets the scene for the complex exploration of authorship and authority undertaken in *Wolf Hall*.

5

'If the dead need translators': Heresy, haunting and intertextuality in *Wolf Hall*

It's the living that turn and chase the dead. The long bones and skulls are tumbled from their shrouds, and words like stones thrust into their rattling mouths: we edit their writings, we rewrite their lives.[1]

So concludes Thomas Cromwell at the close of *Wolf Hall* in a gesture which acknowledges accusations frequently levelled at writers of historical fiction. Mantel herself 'hold[s] up [her] hands' and states 'you might think that what I am doing in this book is dubious – it might even be thought to be reprehensible'.[2] Nevertheless, the Booker prizes awarded to her Tudor novels clearly evidence a positive critical reaction. Certainly, *Wolf Hall* has been received by the popular press as first and foremost a paradigm-shifting example of historical fiction.[3] Writing in the *Guardian* Christopher Taylor describes *Wolf Hall* as 'a non-frothy historical novel',[4] situating the text in opposition to a prevalent critical discourse in which the genre is 'frowned on' and 'disapproved of', dismissed as 'escapism' concerned with 'cloaks, daggers, crinolined ladies, ripped bodices [and] sailing ships in bloody battles'.[5] The academic attention the novel has garnered has focused on the text as a seminal example of its genre, seeking to use *Wolf Hall* as a vehicle for analysing the tropes of historical fiction.[6] Contrastingly, those studies which depart from this generic approach decry the text for an apparent lack of historical veracity while neglecting its status as literary production. This is exemplified in P. I. Kaufman's 2010 article 'Dis-Manteling More'.[7] Kaufman's piece is symptomatic of what A. S. Byatt terms 'the refusal of narrative by contemporary historians'[8] who are 'suspicious of history which concentrates on the fates and motives of individuals'.[9]

The critical landscape outlined above is formed of two problematically reductive reading strategies. The critical voices engaging in debate around the novel have either attempted to aggressively situate the text as an account of the Tudor period without meaningfully recognizing its status as a work of literature, or else used the book as an exemplar through which historical fiction as a genre can be validated. In opposition to these strategies, I offer a reading that privileges *Wolf Hall*'s status as primarily a literary text whose project is both more subtle and more expansive than these previous critical viewpoints have allowed. Taking into account two key contextual details arising from the novel's setting within the upheavals of the Protestant Reformation, namely the invention of the printing press and the move within Protestant theology to abolish Purgatory, I argue that *Wolf Hall* is ultimately a book that, rather than displaying the 'complex self-consciousness about the writing of history itself',[10] which Byatt argues has accompanied the renaissance in historical fiction, displays instead a complex self-consciousness about *writing* itself. *Wolf Hall* dramatizes the linkages between textuality and spectrality, foregrounding the spectres that emerge from the evolution of technologies of inscription. Simultaneously, I explore the ways in which the written word is capable of producing myriad spectres and facilitating a variety of hauntings that refract the more traditional phantoms with which the narrative is also populated.

The matrix of connections and resonances between writing and haunting which this chapter draws out of *Wolf Hall* is complex, often resisting a schematic organization. Nevertheless, for the sake of clarity this chapter is formed of three distinct sections. The first discusses the presentation in the novel of the book as object, both in the form of manuscript and incunabula, decoupling the physical object from the text it contains and positing a relationship in the novel between corporeal bodies and material books, between corpses and corpuses. In the second section of the chapter I build on this decoupling in order to analyse how *Wolf Hall* presents a vision of text as spectral and in turn argue that this spectrality is specifically freighted by the developments in writing technologies which saw the advent and rapid growth of print culture in the period immediately prior to, and during, the English Reformation. Finally, I move to demonstrate the significance of this presentation of corpse-like books and ghostly texts for our understanding of intertextuality in *Wolf Hall*, not only as authorial strategy but as object of critique and enquiry.

I posit that to define *Wolf Hall* as 'simply' (or, as Byatt's puts it, 'innocently'[11]) an example of the realist historical novel, whose haunted quality is a given thanks to its resurrections of the historical dead, is to overlook a multiplicity of less traditional spectres which saturate *Wolf Hall*. To do so is to fail to appreciate the subtle and nuanced discussions orchestrated within the text, discussions whose impacts are felt far beyond questions of genre and historical veracity. However, to fully understand the scope of the debates in which *Wolf Hall* is engaged, and to articulate the novel's contribution to those debates, it is necessary to place the text in conversation with one of Mantel's earlier works – not its apparent predecessor, Mantel's first experiment with the historical novel, *A Place of Greater Safety* (1992), but the critically neglected and elusive *Fludd* (1989). *Wolf Hall* is not the first of Mantel's texts to dissect the process of religious reformation, or even the first to represent the conflicts inherent in the Henrician Reformation. Published in 1989, *Fludd* satirizes the religious schisms of the 1530s through the microcosm of Catholic practice in a fictional Lancashire village, Fetherhoughton, in the 1950s. That a relationship exists between the two texts has, until now, failed to be recognized and explored, yet the extensive and specific intellectual project undertaken in *Wolf Hall* clearly has its origins in *Fludd's* idiosyncratic exploration of the English Reformation, textuality and spectrality. Both *Wolf Hall* and *Fludd* contain an atmosphere of pervasive haunting. From the rectory in Fetherhoughton, where ghostly presences pace empty rooms and slam doors (p. 23), to the 'aggregated mass' of the dead that Thomas Cromwell senses on All Hallows Eve (p. 154), these are narratives where the hinterland between the dead and the living is permeable. *Fludd* forms one of *Wolf Hall's* most potent intertexts but for the present moment it suffices to say that *Fludd* returns throughout this chapter to inform and complicate the discussion, acting as a phantom forerunner which, through *Wolf Hall*, repeatedly 'arrives', drawing our attention again and again to the textual spectrality and spectral textuality which, I will argue, define the later novel.

The critical neglect of *Fludd* as a textual counterpoint capable of opening up *Wolf Hall* to more expansive and accommodating reading strategies is just one example of how the critical approaches discussed in the opening of this chapter have occluded the statements Mantel is making in the later text about the links between writing and heredity, history and the imagination, and the position both writer and reader might occupy with regard to the past: that of legatee. Jacques Derrida understands the act of inheritance as 'not essentially to receive something, a *given* that one may then *have*' but 'an active affirmation [which] answers an injunction, but also pre-supposes an initiative, … presupposes the signature or counter signature of a critical selection. When one inherits, one sorts, one sifts, one reclaims, one reactivates'.[12] With regard to Mantel's historical fiction, it is necessary to add to this inventory of responsibilities: 'one translates'.[13] *Wolf Hall* is produced through Mantel's occupation of the position of legatee, one who inherits the past and then sorts, sifts, reclaims and reactivates, translating the dead into fictive life, translating the material of historical 'fact', and its many lacunae where 'fact' breaks down into multiple ghostly potentialities that make up the 'shifting shadow-mesh' (*Wolf Hall*, p. 27) of fiction. As Jerome de Groot has succinctly put it: 'the translation and revoicing of history in uncanny and ultimately queer ways: these are what the historical novelist participates in'.[14] By expanding the terms of my reading strategy beyond the genre of 'historical fiction' and by reading *Wolf Hall* as nuanced literary product preoccupied with literary production, indeed, as a text in which 'popular historical fiction dramatizes textual reception itself',[15] it is possible to understand this novel as coupling imagination and testimony productively without admitting any incompatibility between the two concepts. Mantel insists 'we can't help but imagine the past; we have no choice. It is part of us and we must acknowledge that it is *we* who reimagine it'.[16] If the dead need translators then, Mantel suggests, it is the writer who must translate. Before embarking upon a sustained analysis of the more obvious literary and textual works referenced in the novel, and the attendant phantoms through which we see this discharging of responsibility and act of creative heredity, I begin with a moment in *Wolf Hall* that encapsulates the concerns of this chapter through its preoccupation with inheritance.

'To Rafe Sadler his books': inheritance, technology and textuality

> 'Rafe,' he says, 'do you know I haven't made my will? I said I would but I never did. I think I should go home and draft it.'
> 'Why?' Rafe looks amazed. 'Why now? The cardinal will want you.'
> 'Come home.' He takes Rafe's arm. On his left side, a hand touches his: fingers without flesh. A ghost walks: Arthur, studious and pale. King Henry, he thinks, you raised him; now you put him down. (p. 147)

Early on in *Wolf Hall*, Thomas Cromwell's apparent encounter with the 'dead hand' of King Arthur prompts him to return home and compose a will, a document activated by death and enabling the dead to exert a little post-mortem power over their inheritors. The account given in *Wolf Hall* of the fictionalized Cromwell's will is fascinating for a variety of reasons.[17] However, the most interesting elements in terms of the present discussion are the final two sentences: 'To God his Soul. To Rafe Sadler his books' (p. 148). The first sentence accords with the religious and legal conventions of the time and is present early on in the original historical document. However, the last sentence is buried in the body of the original text, among 'markes of lawful yngllish money' and Cromwell's 'Seconde gowne Jaquet and Doblet'.[18] Its positioning adjacent to Cromwell's 'bequest' of his soul to God in Mantel's version gives the two acts of passing on a powerful equivalence. Cromwell's legacy to Rafe is particularly notable since the books he bequeaths number among them a copy of William Tyndale's translation of the New Testament, printed 'in octavo, [on] nasty cheap paper: on the title page, where the printer's colophon and address should be, the words "PRINTED IN UTOPIA"' (p. 40). Two important observations can be made, based on this fictional account of Cromwell's will.

The first is that writing of all kinds in *Wolf Hall* should be understood as being subject to the logic of inheritance. By structuring the close of Cromwell's fictional will in this way, Mantel demands an understanding of inheritance which incorporates the notion of the written word as something that can be passed down and – bearing in mind the fact that Rafe Sadler is not a biological heir to Cromwell – that can bypass systems of genetic or familial inheritance. This more expansive understanding of heredity is underscored early on in the book, in a passage where Cromwell conjectures about the reformist leanings of his mother-in-law:

> Mercy, he suspects, comes from a family where John Wycliffe's writings are preserved and quoted, where the scriptures in English have always been known; scraps of writing hoarded, forbidden verses locked in the head. These things come down the generations, as eyes and noses come down, as meekness or the capacity for passion, as muscle power or the need to take a risk. (pp. 41–2)

In this passage, written texts, in both physical and memorial form, are equated with bodily features and characteristics of personality in terms of their ability to be in some way 'inherited'. Through being understood as heritable these writings sit alongside Cromwell's fictionalized will to constitute what Bernard Stiegler terms 'tertiary memory'. As part of his theorization of technicity, Stiegler insists that, alongside genetic and epigenetic memory, there exists a kind of memory or inheritance which is epiphylogenetic,[19] comprised of the inorganic traces left behind in the form of objects, tools or writings and not dictated by genetic inscription. It is through these traces, Stiegler argues, that each successive generation is able to inherit the historical past of their forebears despite not having lived that past themselves.[20] Cromwell's suspicions about Mercy articulate the idea of epiphylogenesis as the process which 'bestows its identity upon the human individual: the accents of his speech, the style of his approach, the force of his gesture, the unity of his world'.²¹ While I would not go so far as to assert that the model of inheritance present in *Wolf Hall* follows Stiegler's exactly or deliberately, the expansive understanding of heredity we see demonstrated, both in the extract above, and in Cromwell's will, can be usefully mobilized alongside Stiegler's thinking to highlight the crucial but overlooked relationship between writing technologies and inheritance at work in the novel. However, the literary legacy included in Cromwell's fictional Last Will and Testament is only one element of a wider questioning of the relationship between writing and dying, between literature and inheritance.

Indeed, the second implication of *Wolf Hall*'s account of Cromwell's will is the association between death and technologies of writing. The mention of the printed book within the handwritten, autographed document, specifically designed to communicate in the event of the author's death, deftly reminds us that the technologies of inscription during the Reformation were by no means solely defined by the dominance of print. Yet the will also serves as an exemplar of the intrinsically posthumous quality of written words, traces, or 'survivals' as Derrida terms them,²² which always inscribe the eventual death of their author: 'all the figures of death with which we people the "present", which we inscribe (among ourselves, the living) in every trace ...: figures we inscribe because they can outlast us, beyond the present of their inscription: signs, words, names, letters'.²³ Indeed, in *Wolf Hall* and *Fludd*, often all that is left of the dead are their inscribed traces; annotations, dedications, tracts and notes, seemingly confirming Derrida's assertion that 'there is no inheritance without technics'.²⁴ Yet, as was made clear in Chapter 4, to inscribe demands a surface to receive the inscription and it is to the physicality of the books left to Rafe Sadler, and of the multiple other volumes that accompany them, that I turn now in order to examine how their presence and possession in this novel is specifically freighted.

In the body of the text: corpses, corpora and the Bible in the age of mechanical reproduction

'We are always dying – I while I write, you while you read' (Petrarch in *Wolf Hall*, p. 648)

In response to the use of printed material within Christian religious practice, the seventeenth-century oration priest Bernard Lamy complained that 'the words on the page are like a dead body stretched out on the ground',²⁵ arguing that the use of typography 'devocalized' and 'desocialized' Christian teaching.[26] His striking statement provides a powerful formulation of the ways in which the posthumous is implicated in all acts of writing as the fact of the inscription being reproducible, quotable in our absence, renders us 'haunted by [a] future which brings our own death'.[27] As Derrida succinctly puts it, 'our disappearance is already there'.[28] This interaction between physical inscription and death is powerfully present in *Wolf Hall* where the act of writing is, I argue, positioned as involving in a crucial way the passage from subject (the author) to object (the document they produce), and thus implicating dying and the dead in the process of writing. Specifically, I examine here the complex relationship between corporeal bodies and physical books within the novel in order to establish its significance for *Wolf Hall* as a novel about writing, haunting and inheritance.

The historical moment of the Protestant Reformation, rather than limiting the impact of the essential linkages between writing and dying, provides an ideal crucible within which these associations can be complicated and explored in the novel. Before a detailed analysis of the concomitance between books and the dead in *Wolf Hall* can be undertaken it is useful to establish one of the two contextual points which drive the text's intellectual project: the changing status of the dead in Reformation England. As Cromwell confirms early on in the novel, *Wolf Hall* depicts a period in which 'with every month that passes, the corners are knocked off the certainties of this world: and the next world too' (p. 39) as debates around previous theological orthodoxies gather pace. As Anthony Low observes, while 'many things were repudiated at the English Reformation, including Transubstantiation, Confession as a sacrament, the monasteries and the primacy of Peter ... few things were ended as absolutely as Purgatory'.[29] The abolition of Purgatory wrought a drastic change in the relationship between the individuals who made up Reformation society and their dead, as they no longer had recourse to an intermediate space which 'enabled the dead to be not completely dead – not as utterly gone, finished, complete, as those whose souls resided forever in Heaven or Hell'.[30] *Wolf Hall* is concerned with the period immediately antecedent to the official abolition of Purgatory effected by Chantries Act and Royal Injunctions of 1547, a time when the writings of reformist thinkers like Martin Luther were beginning to put pressure on Purgatory as a concept and to bring into question a previously 'legitimately sanctioned belief in ghosts'.[31] The cause of this relocation of the dead can on one level be attributed to disputes over interpretations and translations of religious texts. When Cromwell demands, 'show me where it says, in the Bible, "Purgatory"' (p. 39), he articulates how previously approved religious tenets were stripped away during the Reformation on the basis of their lack of scriptural underpinnings. Thus the fate of the Reformation dead is decided, or rather destabilized, through acts of reading. Yet, rather than rendering the division between the living and the dead impenetrable, as they were intended to, these reforms apparently had the effect of increasing rather than decreasing the permeability of the barrier between the living and the dead. In the face of the impending abolition of Purgatory the regulatory structure whereby the dead could appear to the living to specific ends was beginning to give way, not to a ghost-less landscape in which the dead were unable to manifest, but rather to an unregulated ingress of the dead into the world of the living.[32] In *Wolf Hall* this questioning of the location of the dead through religious literature is deftly acknowledged with physical books repeatedly providing the conduits through which the dead are able to infiltrate the world of the living, both symbolically and intellectually. Yet, as we shall see, the object and status of the book was undergoing a similar transformation during this period. It is necessary then for this analysis to remain responsive to the specific effects that the print and manuscript technologies within the novel have upon the dead and the living alike. I begin my exploration of the relationship between the physical book and the dead with an analysis of a haunted moment of reading.

> Halloween: the world's edge seeps and bleeds. This is the time when the tally-keepers of Purgatory, its clerks and gaolers, listen in to the living, who are praying for the dead.
> At this time of year, with their parish, he and Liz would keep vigil. They would pray for Henry Wykys, her father; for Liz's dead husband, Thomas Williams; for Walter Cromwell, and for distant cousins, for half-forgotten names, long-dead half-sisters and lost step-children. (p. 154)

In this way Mantel introduces the religious practices that surrounded the Catholic feast of All Hallows day, capturing succinctly how Purgatory accommodated the admission of the dead into the world of the living[33] while also facilitating the partial entry of the living, their prayers and pleas, into the world of the dead. Initially it is not the individual dead that trouble Cromwell but rather 'a solid aggregated mass, their flesh slapping and jostling together, their texture dense like sea creatures, their faces sick with an undersea sheen' (pp. 154–5). Then comes a moment of transition as Cromwell 'stands in a window embrasure, Liz's prayer book in his hand' (p. 155);[34] the Book of Hours which 'his daughter Grace liked to look at' (p. 155). The homogenous dead fall away to leave the individuated phantoms of Elizabeth and Grace Cromwell. In this moment, when the dead stand alongside the living, it is a manuscript book that is placed at the centre of the scene, seemingly as the provocation for the return of Cromwell's familial dead. As he progresses through the religious offices and their illustrations he 'feel[s] the imprint of [Grace's] small fingers under his own. ... He turns a page. Grace, silent and small, turns the page with him' (p. 155). The materiality of the book produces a post-mortem materiality for Grace, whose fingers seem to combine with the page under Cromwell's hands. This image of merger between flesh and page echoes the prayer book's illustration of the Annunciation, in which a scroll 'unfurls from [the angel's] clasped hands, as if his palms were speaking' (p. 155), scroll and flesh appearing as irrevocably conjoined, complicating where one ends and the other begins and reinforcing the link between books and bodies. Through their invocation alongside the vividly illustrated Book of Hours, whose images were intended to communicate in situations where the vernacular was not permitted, the phantoms of Liz and Grace become symbols of a religious status quo about to be changed forever. The Protestant Reformation's emphasis upon print transformed religion for the laity, performing a 'shift from image towards word'.[35] As Cromwell puts it '[the laity] have seen their religion painted on the walls of churches, or carved in stone, but now God's pen is poised, and he is ready to write his words in the book of their hearts' (p. 516).

Yet if the moment of haunted reading above captures the ambiguous status of Purgatory, and of the relationship of the living to the dead via the object of the book, whose status as surface for inscription and container of scriptural truth unites both issues, there is also something of the manuscript book's uniqueness, its singularity, which Mantel is harnessing here.[36] The book's origins as 'a wedding present ... from [Liz's] first husband' who 'wrote her new married name in it' (p. 39) obliquely inscribes the ability not only of texts but of material books to conjure up the dead. Both Elizabeth Cromwell and, through the frontispiece inscription, her dead husband, are invoked through the act of reading the book, which records denotations not of authorship but of ownership through its handwritten annotations.[37] In this moment, as the process of religious reform and its impact upon the relationship between the dead and the living is being refracted through the object of the manuscript prayer book, Mantel is also recognizing the manuscript Book of Hours as a literary object that routinely underwent adaptations and personalizations in a way, and on a scale at which, printed volumes did not. This is recognized in Cromwell's acting upon this impulse to adapt and annotate: 'he has taken out Liz's book of hours, and on the page where she kept the family listed he has made alterations, additions' (p. 583).

This is not the only moment in *Wolf Hall* when the presence of a material book belonging to a deceased subject provokes or accompanies a spectral apparition of that subject. However, the second extract examined here marks a movement from manuscript to print productions and concerns another Book of Hours, this time belonging to Thomas More.[38] Displaying the temporal slippages which are characteristic of Mantel's writing, *Wolf Hall*'s account of More's execution moves quickly back and forth between the present moment in which Cromwell waits to learn of More's death, and the process of accusation, arrest and trial for treason that led to it. As Cromwell waits 'Thomas More stands before him, more solid in death than he was in life' (p. 644). Yet this apparition has significantly less impact within the text than the approach and appearance of More's book:

> The window rattles; it startles him, and he thinks, I shall bolt the shutter. He is rising to do it when Rafe comes in with a book in his hand. 'It is his prayer book, that More had with him at the last.'
> He examines it. Mercifully, no blood specks. He holds it up by the spine and lets the leaves fan out ....
> More has written his name in it. There are underlinings in the text: *Remember not the sins of my youth.* ...
> The whole house is rocking about him; wind in the eaves, wind in the chimneys, a piercing draft under every door. (p. 646)

This instance of pathetic fallacy, stressed almost to the point of cliché, makes manifest the haunting power of books. More's book comes to stand in for him posthumously, the analogue all the more powerful because of the presence of his annotations. These are crucial when we consider that, unlike Liz Cromwell's prayer book, the book to which the above passage refers is a printed text and thus More's book constitutes an amalgamation of writing technologies. More's process of reading and interpretation is preserved through his manuscript inscriptions which surround and infiltrate the printed text. If we compare the two scenes of haunting, one serene, poignant, taking place within the contained space of the window embrasure, the other unsettling, disruptive, causing Cromwell to seek to secure his home against the ingress of the disruptive but unseen wind, a contrast can be seen between the kinds of haunting that print and manuscript technologies are able to provoke, even as the presence of annotations in both passages underscore the posthumous quality implicated in all modes of inscription. That these annotated books are accompanied by the apparitions of their dead owners potently underlines the fact of the inscriptions surviving their author. However, it is the printed book whose presence (and by extension Thomas More's) is depicted as capable of causing disruption. The space of Cromwell's house is seemingly destabilized by its presence while the invasive power of the wind, which penetrates ubiquitously, captures the disruptive and uncontainable quality of print. The unruliness of print will be examined in more detail below but for the moment I would like to address the corporeality implied by the 'merciful' absence of the blood specks tentatively sought by Cromwell.

Alongside the linkages already analysed between books and haunting, present in *Wolf Hall* is a persistent analogue between the physical body and the object of the book that usefully articulates the play the novel is engaging with through the various meanings of the word 'corpus' and its innate relationship to the 'corpse'. We saw above how Thomas More's book arrives on Cromwell's desk as evidence of his death, a substitute for More's corpse. An even more striking manifestation of the corpse-like book is found in the account given of the confiscation of Cardinal Wolsey's books in the wake of his fall: 'they are packing [the cardinal's] gospels and taking them for the king's libraries. The texts are heavy to hold in the arms, and awkward as if they breathed; their pages are made of slunk vellum from stillborn calves, reveined by the illuminator in tints of lapis and leaf-green' (pp. 48–9). In this description there is a sense of the books hovering phantasmally between life and death which is made particularly striking by Mantel's description of the vellum in which they are bound being produced from the flesh of 'stillborn' calves, creatures whose entry into the world of the living takes place only in death. The books appear to breathe and struggle against their removal, the veins of the original material suggested through the artifice of the illuminator's brush. These books are depicted as being possessed of a quasi-animate life specific to them which underlines their power to haunt. While in the previous two examples the book's owner is deceased, in this passage, the undead quality of the cardinal's library acts as a harbinger of the cardinal's own death, apparently brought about by his ill-treatment at the hands of the king; the confiscation of the books only a precursor to the forfeit of the cardinal's body. In the emphasis on the origins of the vellum can be detected a tongue-in-cheek inversion of the notion of 'the word made flesh' as the 'flesh' constituted by the skin used in binding is obscured by the words inked upon it. This inversion, which implies that flesh can also be reduced to words, that it can offer (or be rendered) a surface of inscription, has profound implications which are realised in *Wolf Hall*'s representation of the relationship between an author and their work as distinct from the relationship between a book and its owner or series of owners.

The relationship between the doomed Cardinal Wolsey and his strangely undead gospels exemplifies how *Wolf Hall* depicts books and bodies as having a consonant relationship. Considering Rembrandt's painting 'The Anatomy

Lesson of Dr Nicholas Tulp', Derrida observes how the focus of the figures within the painting is not upon the body being dissected but upon the open book lying at the cadaver's feet. He comments: 'this book stands up to, and stands in for, the body: a corpse is replaced by a corpus, a corpse yielding its place to the bookish thing'.[39] This form of substitution, of 'standing in', is active within *Wolf Hall's* presentation of the relationship between authors and their texts. An equivalence is repeatedly drawn between an author and their works through the use of the former's name to refer also to their written output, and this effacement builds throughout *Wolf Hall* to form a notion of the object of a book as analogous with the human body. This analogue is confirmed in an extract from the novel's closing chapters: 'I hear they are burning the books from the city libraries. Erasmus has gone into the flames. What kind of devils would burn the gentle Erasmus?' (p. 591). Likewise, giving an account of how Cardinal Wolsey will respond to the influx of heretical texts arriving in England from Germany it is stated that 'Wolsey will burn books, but not men. He did so, only last October, at St Paul's Cross: a holocaust of the English language, and so much rag-rich paper consumed, and so much black printers' ink' (p. 40). This refusal carries within it an acknowledgement that the destruction of the book could stand in for the destruction of its author, an equivalence which has significant consequences as the novel progresses and men are burned in the place of their books.

What are the implications, then, of the embodied life of books, their unique connection to the dead and their shifting status within the economy of inheritance and authority brought about by the advent of print? As I have illustrated above, the effects produced by printed and manuscript books are variously and subtly different but the unifying factor in all of these cases is the presence of annotations and edits by the owners of the books in question. Alongside making licit and active the posthumous quality of the written word through the representation of the 'corpse-like' book, the references to handwritten material found throughout the novel prompt a consideration of the afterlife of reading, graphically charting as they do the processes of interpretation and adaptation undertaken by readers. In so doing, the physical object of the written document in *Wolf Hall* lays the groundwork for an interrogation of the nature and status of the text, both in the historical moment of the Reformation and in Mantel's work more broadly. It prompts, above all, a consideration of the afterlife of ideas.

As we have seen, *Wolf Hall* does not attempt to impose an irrevocable split between printed texts and their manuscript predecessors, presenting hybrid objects, like that of Thomas More's heavily annotated printed prayer book. A less direct but nonetheless striking example of the novel's blurring of the boundaries between manuscript and print can be found in a detail of the description of

Protestant reformer James Bainham's arrest, interrogation and execution for heresy. The passage describes how Bainham is burned alongside the leather seller, John Tewkesbury, who 'had possession of Luther's *Liberty of a Christian Man*, the text copied out in his own hand' (p. 335). This hand-copied version of a printed text echoes those 'scraps of writing' encountered earlier with reference to Cromwell's mother-in-law, a material representation of the 'hidden verses locked in the head' that acknowledges the unstoppable circulation of texts. The 'pall of human ash' (p. 335) that Bainham and Tewkesbury are reduced to foreshadows a similar passage 20 pages later in which Cromwell recalls his childhood experience of watching as a Lollard is burned for heresy. The macabre and visceral description of the event is striking but the most pertinent moment of the passage comes in the aftermath of the execution as the Lollard's remains are disposed of:

> [Cromwell] watched the officers strike with their iron bars at the human debris that was left. The chains retained the remnants of flesh, sucking and clinging. …
>
> The Loller's skull was left on the ground, the long bones of her arms and legs. Her broken ribcage was not much bigger than a dog's. A man took an iron bar and thrust it through the hole where the woman's left eye had been. He scooped up the skull and positioned it on the stones, so it was looking at him. Then he hefted his bar and brought it down on the crown. Even before the blow landed he knew it was false, skewed. Shattered bone, like a star, flew away into the dirt, but the most part of the skull was intact. …
>
> They threw down their iron bars amid what was left of the Loller. It was just splinters of bone now, and thick sludgy ash. …
>
> The stink of the woman was still in the air. He wondered if she was in Hell now, or still about the streets, but he was not afraid of ghosts. (pp. 355–6)

I quote this passage at length because it demonstrates a doubleness which is provocative. Even as the passage describes an attempt to utterly obliterate a subject whose body, as the container of her religious beliefs, functions as a threat to religious orthodoxy, it begins to acknowledge that the destruction of ideas is not so simple. The smell of the burned flesh combines with the splinters of bone and 'sludgy ash' to resist the officers' acts of destruction. Far from destroying the Loller, the passage renders her beyond destruction, atomized, dispersed, along with the religious ideas that her body is made to represent. Mantel goes further though, turning the moment of execution into a moment of inscription as the executed woman's friends and family gather up what is left of her:

> He saw now that the men and women were not praying. They were on their hands and knees. They were friends of the Loller, and they were scraping her up. One of the women knelt, her skirts spread, and held out an earthenware pot. …

> When they had got a bowlful, the woman who was holding it said, 'Give me your hand.'
> Trusting, he held it out to her. She dipped her fingers into the bowl. She placed on the back of his hand a smear of mud and grit, fat and ash. 'Joan Boughton,' she said. (p. 357)

The smear on the back of Cromwell's hand acts as a form of inscription that moves beyond the posthumous permanence of the written word to attest to the afterlife of an idea. The marking of Cromwell's skin with Joan Boughton's remains produces an internalization of the moment, and by association the tenets of Lollardy.[40] Though the mark is not physically indelible it produces a permanent memorial and affective trace for Cromwell; the narrative states that he 'ha[d] never forgotten the woman' (p. 357) and the memory of this instance of religious intolerance 'floods into his body' (p. 352), contributing to a sense that this instance of inscription has been internalized, defying physical or corporeal containment or inscription. Above I discussed the material object of the book and its analogous relationship to the body in *Wolf Hall*. Having established this analogue, the harbouring of ideas and beliefs within the body of the subject comes to parallel the inscription of those ideas and beliefs within the pages of the book. The depiction, in the Lollard passage, of an inscription whose ideational content remains though its material form no longer persists points towards the unpredictable circulation of ideas, and more specifically, the texts that express those ideas, whose existence is not predicated upon 'cheap parchment' or 'slunk vellum'. It is to the unbound or, perhaps, disembodied text that this analysis now moves.

Pressing matters: technology, textuality and ghosts from the machine

Thus far I have discussed the undead lives of books and the hauntings those books facilitate. I have also examined how the image of book as corpse articulates the act of writing as negotiating the boundaries between pre- and post- mortem, with the writer producing work that will outlive them, creating a bibliographic cadaver that anticipates and mirrors the physical body in death. Yet, as the analysis of the Lollard passage in conversation with this concept of the corpse-like book indicates, a material book is merely the physical container for a text whose existence is not prescribed by bindings and pages but has a disembodied quality which renders it unregulatable and unruly. What then is the status of the text in *Wolf Hall* and how does it develop the linkage that has already been established between writing and death? In order to answer these questions it is necessary to outline the second contextual element upon which the novel grounds its intellectual and creative project: the advent of print.

The Protestant Reformation is a period inextricably linked with the proliferation of print culture, though the nature and strength of that link are subjects of complex and ongoing debate.[41] In Germany in the 1500s the rapid expansion of print enabled unprecedented access to education among urban populations, which led to significantly increased levels of functional literacy.[42] This in turn allowed an 'astonishing wave of religious heterodoxy to sweep across [the country],'[43] a wave that subsequently broke onto the shores of England. As is observed in *Wolf Hall*:

> when the last treason act was made, no one could circulate their words in a printed book or bill, because printed books were not thought of. [Cromwell] feels a moment of jealousy towards the dead, to those who served kings in slower times than these; nowadays the products of some bought or poisoned brain can be disseminated through Europe in a month. (p. 492)[44]

Cromwell's frustration and envy of those living in the 'slower times' of the pre-print era articulate a broader association between print, heresy and sedition; as Jesse Lander points out 'a printed book cannot be dismissed as the solitary ravings of a singular heretic, disgruntled reader or political dissident'.[45] As Lowenstein notes, the 'Henrician Reformation of the 1530s' perceived heresy 'not simply in terms of evangelical individuals but in terms of proliferating texts … capable of quickly disseminating dangerous and unorthodox doctrine and seditious opinion to the people'.[46] During Thomas Cromwell's lifetime, to possess certain publications, such as William Tyndale's English translation of the New Testament, which was later to go on to form the basis of much of Cromwell's own officially sanctioned and commissioned Bible, was grounds for arrest and prosecution for heresy. Indeed, the flood of reformist literature into England so concerned Henry VIII that in 1538 'he issued a proclamation banning the importation of any book printed in English'.[47] The strategy failed and, as Richard Rex points out, Protestant texts continued to be printed, imported and circulated 'by those who were already on the wrong side of the law'.[48]

Circulation, proliferation, dissemination; these words emerge repeatedly in the literature that has grown up around early print culture. Cromwell's jealousy of his pre-print predecessors articulates all three concepts either implicitly or explicitly but it also captures another common quality attributed to print technology at this time – that of carrying disease, being contagious or else poisonous. Harold Weber observes how 'the printed word becomes … a power unhealthy, infectious, subtly and mysteriously contagious .... A plague has invaded the body of the kingdom fragmenting a unity ..., a dark and secret realm of books which mysteriously propagate themselves'.[49] Despite pertaining to the reign of Charles II, Harold Weber's analysis of various proclamations responding to print culture offers a picture of print that is instantly recognizable within *Wolf Hall* with the novel acknowledging how the press emphasized the disembodied nature of textuality and in so doing 'gave new vitality to ghosts'.[50] The present reading does not propose that *Wolf Hall* is merely offering a literary rendering of these debates around print. Rather, I argue that the novel presents the printing press and print culture as changing the nature of spectrality and by doing so, generating new forms of haunting.

> The Castile soap came. And your book from Germany. It was packaged as something else. I almost sent the boy away. (p. 37)

Here Liz Cromwell informs her husband of the delivery to the house of a copy of William Tyndale's testament, printed in English. This seemingly offhand comment captures Mantel's nuancing of the compromised presence of the material books in *Wolf Hall* through an acknowledgement of how, during the Reformation, banned religious texts were frequently smuggled into the country by Dutch and German textile merchants under false titles, cheaply reprinted and covertly circulated. By examining how these objects are established as only partially present, wavering between visibility and invisibility, it becomes clear how, through compromising the physical forms of the books which contain them, Mantel sets the scene in the novel for an understanding of text as spectral. I have already observed how Cromwell's copy of Tyndale's testament is described through a privileging of its physicality, its size, the poor quality of the paper, the capitalized typesetting of the colophon registered through its uppercase rendering in the novel (p. 40). Yet following this description, it is not these kinds of scholarly descriptions of the printed products of the Reformation which are foregrounded; indeed we never again see a Protestant book being read. Rather, the occult life of Reformation publications is emphasized as Cromwell is described 'keep[ing] up with what's written and with what's smuggled through the Channel ports, and the little East Anglian inlets, the tidal creeks where a small boat with dubious cargo can be beached and pushed out again, by moonlight, to sea' (pp. 39–40). The vernacular religious books that formed the primary drivers for the Protestant Reformation flicker in and out of the novel, spoken of, alluded to, yet hidden and compromised, frequently destroyed by the time they appear within the narrative. This representation is exemplified by the fate of the books belonging to Humphrey Monmouth, the master draper thought to have sheltered William Tyndale before his flight from England:

> When Monmouth's house is raided, it is clear of all suspect writings. It's almost as if he was forewarned. There are neither books nor letters that link him to Tyndale and his friends. All the same, he is taken to the Tower. His family is terrified ... They have to let him go, for lack of evidence, because you can't make anything of a heap of ashes in the hearth. (p. 125)

The physical presence that confronts the reader is that of 'a heap of ashes' (foreshadowing the fate of Joan Boughton, and others like her, reduced to 'a pall of human ash' (p. 335)) rather than a complete book, and is paralleled in a later passage in which the wife of John Peyt, another Protestant Reformer arrested for heresy, recounts the raid on their house by Thomas More. Lucy Peyt describes her husband 'cast[ing] his Testament under his desk' where it remains for the hour-long search for incriminating publications, 'Tyndale lying there, like a poison stain on the tiles' (p. 300). Ashes, stains; this preoccupation with remains sits alongside the compromised physical presence of Protestant books more generally to depict a process of disembodiment with regard to texts and ideas. By occulting the material object of the book, showing it burned, hidden and smuggled, and in doing so creating a parallel with the fates of their readers and writers, Mantel provokes her own reader to ask what is left over when book and body are destroyed? The answer can be found in Protestant reformer Hugh Latimer's explanation of how he evaded his heresy charge: 'bare walls my library. Fortunately, my brain is furnished with texts' (p. 360).[51] Latimer's description of his mind as 'furnished with texts' underscores the futility of the attacks on Joan Boughton's skull discussed above, reaffirming as it does the immunity of texts and ideas to material destruction. Such a formulation powerfully articulates an understanding of the text as exceeding the physical bounds of the book and possessing a discarnate persistence.[52] The Reformation texts discussed in *Wolf Hall* are possessed of a spectrality which is given potency by their production in print. Unbound, they form the persistent haunting presences that characterize not only the emergent print culture of the Reformation but Mantel's work more generally.

> 'He cannot lock us all up.'
> 'He has prisons enough.'
> 'For bodies, yes. But what are bodies? He can take our goods, but God will prosper us. He can close the booksellers, but still there will be books. They have their old bones, their glass saints in windows, their candles and shrines, but God has given us the printing press.' (p. 301)

The exchange above, which takes place between Thomas Cromwell and Lucy Peyt, captures the shifting relationship between books and bodies, how the former have recourse to evasion and survival in ways that the latter do not. Lucy Peyt is, I suggest, using the term 'book' as a synonym for text. Such synonymous usage is supported by the differentiation implied in her question 'what are bodies?', suggesting a belief in something beyond the body which cannot be contained, something that is given an equivalence in the books that will survive even if the booksellers are closed. The 'books' referred to here are in fact texts of the kind Hugh Latimer's brain is furnished with, texts which are passed down and 'locked in the head'. The idea that a printed text, once read, might be internalized and memorized, capable of being quoted and misquoted regardless of the presence of a physical inscription is repeatedly emphasized throughout the novel. Cromwell himself 'knows the whole of the New Testament by heart' (p. 104). This distinction is crucial; he is not said to know the Bible by heart only the portion available to him in print, implying that print is somehow more memorable, more persistent, than its manuscript counterparts. Likewise, William Tyndale, whose association with print publication is definitive, is repeatedly quoted in the narrative. That Tyndale is ventriloquized is indicative in itself of *Wolf Hall*'s understanding of text as discarnate and it should be noted that this incorporeality is given a doubly phantasmal gloss thanks to the slippery narrative voice whose identity cannot satisfactorily be located. As a result the reader must constantly ask who is speaking when another is quoted, with the secondary question, of where to locate the author in relation to their text, in close attendance. This reading of *Wolf Hall* is predicated upon an understanding of the author as both testator and legatee, one who inherits and translates the past and in turn leaves a legacy of their own. This troubled position, in which the questions of responsibility and authority are vexed, is played out in the novel's treatment of Tyndale's translation of the New Testament. Indeed, it is Tyndale's testament that facilitates the second facet of Mantel's spectralization of text.

> Show me where it says, in the Bible, 'Purgatory'. Show me where it says relics, monks, nuns. Show me where it says 'Pope'. (p. 39)

Unsurprisingly, Cromwell forms the mouthpiece for increasingly vocal demands made during the Protestant Reformation for proof of the scriptural validity of certain tenets of Catholicism. If the incorporeal afterlives of a printed text are stressed throughout *Wolf Hall*, the spectral quality of the texts produced by the printing press is compounded by a repeated return to the discrepancies which arise between various translations and editions of the same publication which are made so readily available through the process of printing. Through exposing the lack of scriptural underpinnings for practices such as indulgences, purgatory, the worship of saints and the necessity of monks and nuns, Mantel establishes texts as being composed of additions and omissions, depicting them as shifting and unreliable. The unstable quality of a text is remarked upon at various moments in the novel, both in terms of instability caused by the process of interpretation ('leases, writs, statutes, all are written to be read, and each person reads them by the light of self-interest' (p. 228)), and in terms of the process of textual production.[53] Stephen Gardiner's response upon hearing that Cromwell 'antiquated a statue' is to quip, 'statue, statute, not much difference' to which Cromwell answers 'one letter is everything in legislating' (p. 329). This brief exchange captures not only the idea that a text may be 'antiquated', edited in such a way as to imply a historical precedence which is actually non-existent, but also how texts are spectralized through the process of editing which creates a wealth of possibilities composed of omissions, deletions and discrepancies. As has been established, for Mantel this process, with its emphasis on potentiality, is a fertile breeding ground for ghosts.[54]

A more expansive examination of textuality's inherent play with potentiality, and its resulting spectral quality, can be found in the novel's treatment of the translations which generated the texts at the heart of Reformation controversies. This is most specifically undertaken with reference to William Tyndale's New Testament.[55] As Cromwell's demands indicate ('Show me where it says ...'), Tyndale's testament is presented as a document in which certain extracts are redacted and certain concepts rejected on the basis of their not possessing any sufficient authority, absent as they are from the Bible as written in Hebrew, Aramaic, Greek and latterly the Latin vulgate.

> Tyndale says, now abideth faith, hope, and love, even these three; but the greatest of these is love.
> Thomas More thinks it is a wicked mistranslation. He insists on 'charity'. He would chain you up, for a mistranslation. He would, for a difference in your Greek, kill you.
> He wonders again if the dead need translators; perhaps in a moment, in a simple twist of unbecoming, they know everything they need to know.
> Tyndale says, 'Love never falleth away.' (p. 152)

A number of things are taking place in this depiction of the oppositional relationship between Thomas More and Tyndale which evidence the ghostings inherent in textuality, ghostings which render texts spectral. Firstly, through the controversy over Tyndale's use of the word 'love', the play of potentiality which takes place during the process of translation is exposed. Mantel's dramatization of the disagreement between More and Tyndale over the translation of the word *agape* in the Greek translation of 1 Corinthians 13 similarly enacts the way that, in translation, the choice of one word leaves a host of other possible words in a state of suspension. In this case More is correct to assert that *agape* means charity, just as Tyndale is correct in his translation of it as 'love'. However, it also has the sense of compassion, and affection. *Wolf Hall* adeptly expresses the ghostly existence of these other potential translations, ghosts of meaning which form a 'shifting, shadow-mesh of ... possibilities' (p. 27).

By now it is clear that *Wolf Hall* understands print as having facilitated a dramatic spectralization of textuality. It has also been established that the discarnate quality of print is underscored in the novel's treatment of translation as a play of ghostly potentialities. Subsequently, it has been possible to analyse translation as a process taking place between the living and the dead, not merely with regard to the characters within the novel but with regard to Mantel's writing practice as a process of inheritance that brings with it an attendant responsibility to translate and interpret. Having examined how print allowed for a medium-specific spectralization of text that amplified questions of authority and authenticity, it is necessary to examine what impact this bibliographic development had upon textual practice, both during the Reformation and within Mantel's contemporary work, and how this spectral quality manifests itself in specific textual hauntings.

Paratextual activity: textiles, (inter)textuality and haunting

> Suppose within every book there is another book, and within every letter on every page another volume constantly unfolding; but these volumes take no space on the desk. (*Wolf Hall*, p. 482)

These 'volumes [that] take no space on the desk' attest to the phantasmal quality given to textuality in *Wolf Hall*, their 'volume' seeming to refer more to a billowing and voluminous textual mass rather than to any physical binding. Furthermore, these lines adeptly capture the supposition which drives not only *Wolf Hall* but many of Mantel's other writings, the supposition that all works of literature harbour within them myriad moments where the influence of, or references and allusions to, other texts make or attempt to make themselves known.⁵⁶ In short, this scene of discarnate textual multiplication refers to the notion of intertextuality. In what follows I lay out the relationship between print technology and intertextual practice, interrogating how this relationship affords Mantel the opportunity to critique intertextuality while establishing the multiplicity of intertextual drivers which exceed marked quotation to encompass allusion, translation, paraphrase, unmarked and misquotation.⁵⁷ Having situated intertextuality in a Reformation context I demonstrate how, when read alongside that which appears in *Fludd*, the intertextual material present in *Wolf Hall* establishes intertextuality as an inherent quality of textuality itself, an understanding which resonates with Julia Kristeva's definition of the text as 'a productivity … a permutation of texts' in the space of which 'several utterances, taken from other texts, intersect'.⁵⁸ Furthermore, I explore how Mantel's intertextual play constitutes a potent and deliberate mode of haunting, her intertexts acting 'as ghosts passing through the text'.⁵⁹ An examination of early drafts of *Wolf Hall* reveals this haunting to be multivalent, with a reference to T. S. Eliot's 'The Love Song of J. Alfred Prufrock' making an anachronistic appearance in the text only to be effaced in the published novel.⁶⁰

Before embarking on an analysis of the various manifestations of intertextual play within *Wolf Hall* it is necessary to understand how the medium of print influenced the message of the texts it produced. One of the most striking elements of this transformation is the variety of ways in which print accommodated and amplified intertextuality. Firstly, it is vital to note that, with the advent of print, the practice of textual quotation was significantly altered. In the pre-print age quoted material was indicated by a change in font,⁶¹ a clear and unavoidable visual indicator of the presence of a voice discrete from that of the putative author of a text. The invention of print brought with it the invention of the quotation mark,⁶² and while the symbol's usage differs from contemporary convention, this formal change should be seen as significant, denoting a partial occlusion of quoted material which made it less immediately identifiable. Secondly, the printed material of the Protestant Reformation should be understood as predominantly paratextual: vernacular Bibles were produced but alongside them were printed a wealth of glosses, marginalia and exegesis. As Scribner notes, 'expanding lay-interest in printed works of piety' was satiated by the publication in print of texts 'recycled from the predominantly scribal pre-print era'.⁶³ These recyclings sat alongside vernacular translations of the Bible which were not unmediated but rather 'increasingly filtered through marginal glosses, sermons, catechisms and devotional literature'.⁶⁴ Thus it is important to recognize the printed texts of the Protestant Reformation as being multivocal, amalgamating and reworking texts in a way which was neither as pronounced nor as commonplace before the advent of the press.[65] This is not to deny the intertextual play already present in the texts of the pre-print era but rather to acknowledge that the 'borrowings, re-workings and enhancements that manuscript took for granted as its very substance became the problem of intertextuality' following the advent of print.[66]

It is necessary, then, to consider the ways in which intertextuality, as concept and as technique, is at work within *Wolf Hall*. The novel's treatment of translation as productive of intertextuality has already been established. However, as Cromwell captures in his assertion that 'I am always translating, …: if not language to language, then person to person' (p. 421), translation is a slippery concept. As was demonstrated in the opening of this chapter, the *Oxford English Dictionary* definition of the term attests to this, revealing that it refers not only to the rendering of one language as another, but also has the sense of the 'removal or conveyance from one person, place, or condition to another' and 'the expression or rendering of something in another medium or form, e.g. of a painting by an engraving or etching'. However, the most pertinent definition for the current discussion is translation as meaning 'transformation, alteration, change; changing or adapting to another use; renovation'.[67] An examination of the way in which Mantel uses textile imagery within the novel illuminates how this understanding of translation is at play in *Wolf Hall*, working to elegantly articulate the unavoidably 'textile' nature of text, its availability for alteration, repurposing and transformation.

> October comes, and his sisters and Mercy and Johane take his dead wife's clothes and cut them up carefully into new patterns. Nothing is wasted. Every good bit of cloth is made into something else. (p. 120)[68]

The quotation above, while referring to a poignant act of recycling in the wake of Elizabeth Cromwell's death, also serves as an example of the way in which textiles are predominantly foregrounded in the novel in order to discuss acts of repurposing and remaking. Earlier I noted *Wolf Hall*'s acknowledgement of the role played by German and Dutch textile traders in importing banned Reformation texts. This link to the textile industry is expanded throughout the novel from a contextual detail to a significant metaphorical vehicle which allows the reader to think about text as textile, about 'the generative idea that the text is made, is worked out in a perpetual interweaving'[69] producing a fabric composed of many strands, capable of possessing flaws, patches, of being re-cut and re-fashioned to fit the taste of the times. The language of the textile industry, the processes of weaving, dying, tailoring and adapting fabrics, saturates the novel as a way of talking about textuality, intertextuality and the signifying power of words. Cromwell returns repeatedly to tapestries which depict Biblical and mythological texts, and identifies flaws in the weave of fabrics which interrupt their ability to signify or signal inauthenticity as in the case of his identification of the flaw in a rug belonging to Thomas More: 'he walks forward, puts a tender hand on the flaw, the interruption in the weave, the lozenge slightly distorted, warped out of true. At worst, the carpet is two carpets, pieced together. At best it has been woven by the village's Pattinson, or patched together last year by Venetian slaves in a backstreet workshop' (p. 228). Even written dispatches are sewn into their envelopes (p. 239). Yet, the most notable manifestations of this use of the textile metaphor are the discussions of the deceased Cardinal Wolsey's clothes. After the Cardinal's death it is observed:

> The cardinal's scarlet clothes now lie folded and empty. They cannot be wasted. They will be cut up and become other garments. Who knows where they will get to over the years? Your eye will be taken by a crimson cushion or a patch of red on a banner or ensign. You will see a glimpse of them in a man's inner sleeve or in the flash of a whore's petticoat.' (p. 265–6)

This brief passage provides an elegant metaphor for the kinds of intertextuality that became recognizable during the explosion of printed texts during the Protestant Reformation. Some borrowing is obvious and attributed (symbolized by the banner or ensign), some decorative, like the marked quotation[70] (symbolized by the 'crimson cushion') while still others are allusive, easy to miss or fail to recognize (as in the examples of 'a man's inner sleeve', 'the flash of a whore's petticoat'). This recruitment of the language of textiles is not limited to providing an (albeit nuanced) analogy for intertextual play. It is also found in the way that texts and ideas themselves are spoken about. The following extract describes the strategies used by Cromwell in order to facilitate conversations with Cardinal Wolsey about the so-called bad books imported from Germany:

> Heresy – [Cromwell's] brush with it – is a little indulgence that the cardinal allows him. [The cardinal] is always glad to have the latest bad books filleted, and any gossip from the Steelyard, where the German merchants live. He is happy to turn over a text or two, and enjoy an after-supper debate. But for the cardinal, any contentious point must be wrapped around and around again with a fine filament of words, fine as split hairs. Any dangerous opinions must be so plumped out with laughing apologies that it is as fat and harmless as the cushions you lean on. (p. 134)

The presence of the word 'filament' brings with it the sense of threads amassing to obscure or 'embroider' the more 'dangerous' content of the Protestant texts. These threads combine with the simile of the plumped cushion to confirm the interwoven relationship between the text and the textile in *Wolf Hall*. The circulation of the dead Cardinal's clothing in a variety of new forms, then, articulates not merely a description of Tudor household practice but an articulation of how recycled 'material', be it textile or textual, possesses a spectral presence for Mantel. In the case of literary productions, the intertextual material has the effect of haunting the primary text, unavoidably drawing past utterances into the present, the intertext acting as 'the locus of simultaneously magnetic (centripetal) and counter magnetic (centrifugal) force'[71] which refers outward to other texts while concurrently being drawn into the body of the main text, permitting the creation of new meanings and new contexts.

This exploration of text as textile, or rather textile as text, in *Wolf Hall* is valuable in that it makes licit an awareness within the novel not only of the changing nature of Reformation textual practice but also of the structures created through textuality's intrinsically intertextual quality and the spectral effects of that quality. Yet Mantel's consideration of intertextuality exceeds an articulation of the phenomenon as a structural property of writing. To more fully appreciate the complexities and idiosyncrasies of her own intertextual strategy, and in turn locate that strategy as symptomatic of her positioning as simultaneous literary legatee and textual testator, it is necessary to examine one of *Wolf Hall*'s most striking intertexts and the site of some of Mantel's most audacious and overt intertextual play.

Après moi, le deluge: *Wolf Hall* as the great *Fludd*

One of the crucial elements that lends the use of intertextuality in Mantel's work its unique quality is the way in which she utilizes self-quotation. In accordance with Mercy and Johanes's reworking of Elizabeth Cromwell's clothes, previous works are 'cut up carefully into new patterns'. *Fludd* was positioned at the outset of this chapter as a precursor to *Wolf Hall*. In turning to look at *Wolf Hall*'s intertexts it is necessary to bring *Fludd* to the fore, not only to demonstrate its powerful influence upon the later novel and its significance for our current reading, but also to map the evolution of Mantel's intertextual play from the earlier book into the present day. I begin by looking at two moments of intertextual resonance in which it is apparent that, if *Fludd* anticipates *Wolf Hall*'s broad intellectual concerns, this anticipation is also registered at the level of textual exposition. Before doing so it is necessary to provide an introduction to what is a critically neglected and idiosyncratic text.

In her review of *Fludd* in the *New York Times* Patricia O'Connor describes the novel as Mantel's 'contribution to a long and worthy line – the English clerical novel'[72] and certainly, the book coalesces around the representation of the life of rural parish priest, Father Angwin, in all of its quotidian detail. More broadly *Fludd* depicts the spiritual upheavals which take place in the lives of various members of the religious communities associated with the Roman Catholic Church of St Thomas Aquinas, in which all is not well. The faith of the novel's protagonists is complex and compromised; Father Angwin, the local priest, has lost his faith in God but still believes in the devil (p. 53). Miss Agnes Dempsey, housekeeper to Father Angwin, holds a plethora of superstitious beliefs. To make matters worse, the vicarage in which they both live is seemingly haunted: '[Miss Dempsey] heard footsteps above, in the passage, in the bedroom. It is ghosts, she thought, walking on my mopping. Angelic doctors, virgin martyrs. Doors slammed overhead' (p. 23). Meanwhile Catholic nun, Sister Philomena, has been exiled to the convent of St Thomas Aquinas for being unfortunate enough to have had dermatitis misdiagnosed by an Irish clergyman as stigmata (pp. 96–7). Against this background of lapsed and heretical faith, Mantel orchestrates a parodic playing out of the debates which structured the Protestant Reformation, through pitting the staunchly traditionalist Father Angwin against the modernizing Bishop Aiden Croucher. Introduced into this complex and heterodox scene is the eponymous Fludd. Based on seventeenth-century alchemist and Rosicrucian Robert Fludd,[73] the novel's protagonist provides the catalyst for the disruptions and reformations that take place within the text, complicating the narrative through the fact of his literary resurrection, straddling the scientific and the supernatural, the historical and the fictional.

Following the visit of Bishop Croucher to the vicarage, and the focusing of his reformist zeal upon the sacred statuary of St Thomas Aquinas, Father Angwin is faced with the dilemma of how to dispose off the plaster saints. Unwilling to destroy them completely he opts to 'keep them together', deciding to 'bury them in the church grounds' and stating, 'I shan't have a service,' …. 'Just an interment' (p. 27). Sister Philomena assists with the burial and as she does so discusses with Father Angwin the life and death of her aunt, Dymphna (pp. 37–8). Following their conversation the nun and the priest make for the convent and vicarage respectively:

> As they left the church, he thought that a hand brushed his arm. Dymphna's bar-parlour laugh came faintly from the terraces; her tipsy, Guinness-sodden breath, stopped by the earth these eleven years, filled the summer night. (p. 39)

This ghostly encounter, partial and indistinct but nonetheless a moment of haunting, is seemingly called forth by Philomena's poignant recollection of her aunt's life and death. We have already encountered the structure of this moment, resurrected in *Wolf Hall*, as Cromwell returns with his ward from a meeting with Cardinal Wolsey and is prompted to write his will.

> 'Rafe,' he says, 'do you know I haven't made my will? I said I would but I never did. I think I should go home and draft it.'
> 'Why?' Rafe looks amazed. 'Why now? The cardinal will want you.'
> 'Come home.' He takes Rafe's arm. On his left side, a hand touches his: fingers without flesh. A ghost walks: Arthur, studious and pale. King Henry, he thinks, you raised him; now you put him down. (p. 147)

At first glance the resonance between the two passages might appear circumstantial, yet these *mains mortes* are performing an analogous purpose. In both cases the ghost in question appears not to the individual most closely related to them but to a stranger, their descriptions synecdochical as the ghostly hand comes to stand in for the whole, and their manifestations apparently prompted by discussion of their lives (in particular their sexual relationships) and the manner of their deaths. Even so, this provocative instance of self-quotation could be dismissed as incidental if it were not for a further passage in which the spectre of *Fludd* seems to be attempting to manifest itself within the space of *Wolf Hall*. In the following passage Thomas Cromwell is standing in the house in Chancery Lane, traditionally given to the Master of the Rolls and left all but vacant for years:

> He rests his hand on the banister of the great staircase, looks up into the dust-mote glitter from a high window. When did I do this? At Hatfield, early in the year: looking up, listening for the sounds of Morton's household, long ago. If he himself went to Hatfield, must not Thomas More have gone up too? Perhaps it was his light footstep he expected, overhead?
>
> …
>
> He hesitates, looking up into the light: now gold, now blue as a cloud passes. Whoever will come downstairs and claim him, must do it now. His daughter

Anne with her thundering feet ... Grace skimming down like dust, drawn into a spiral, a lively swirl ... going nowhere, dispersing, gone.

Liz, come down.

But Liz keeps her silence; she neither stays nor goes. (pp. 583–4)

This scene recalls the ghostly footsteps which pace the upper floor of the vicarage, unsettling Agnes Dempsey and interfering with her mopping. When Agnes confesses her experiences of these phantom disturbances to Father Angwin, the priest's response is striking:

'Father – I must alert you. I can hear a person walking about upstairs, when nobody is there.'

...

'Yes, it happens,' Father Angwin said. He sat on a hard chair at the dining table, huddled into himself, his rust-coloured head bowed. 'I often think it is myself.'

'But you are here.'

'At this moment, yes. Perhaps it is a forerunner. Someone who is to come.' (p. 26)

Father Angwin attributes these phantom perambulations and doors slamming to 'a forerunner. Someone who is to come'. This temporally ambivalent moment, in which an anonymous ghost's presence is signalled by footsteps from upper stories and their identity is guessed at, finds itself reanimated in the *Wolf Hall* passage, as Cromwell fantasizes about the various ghosts who might emerge upon the staircase to 'claim him': his daughters, Anne and Grace, his wife, Liz. Mantel's use of self-quotation here, in which a scene of haunting from one novel spectrally erupts through the text of another, generates an uncanny resonance, as *Wolf Hall* takes the place of the 'someone who is to come' in relation to *Fludd*'s 'forerunner'.

Derrida famously posited that 'a phantom's return is, each time, a different return, on a different stage, in new conditions, to which we must always pay the closest attention, if we don't want to say or do just anything'.[74] Derrida's phantoms are not the 'aggregated dead' of *Wolf Hall*, or the 'discarnate entities' of *Fludd*. Rather they are those from whom we must inherit, actively and responsibly. Working with Derrida's formulation it is necessary to understand the revenant fragments of *Fludd* which haunt *Wolf Hall* as similar spectres, indicative of an active process of inheritance undertaken by Mantel, even with regard to her own work. These moments of self-quotation are composed of miniature ghost stories and, when lifted from their original context and reanimated in *Wolf Hall*, the hauntings they depict become compounded by their status as haunting intertextual fragments. This compound nature prompts us in turn to remain alert to the linkage in Mantel's work, between intertextual material and the concept of haunting. Allowing *Fludd* to manifest fully, I now move to examine the earlier novel's intertexts in order to contrast the strategies at work in both novels, strategies which are predicated upon the formulations of the book as corpse and the text as spectre posited previously. I do so in order to illustrate how *Fludd*'s intertexts, and Mantel's treatment of them, demonstrate a schematic playing out of the writer as occupying a position of responsibility and creativity with regard to literary heredity.

'I have come to transform you': *Fludd* and its intertexts

There are those, it is said, who have entertained angels unawares; but Miss Dempsey would have liked notice. (*Fludd*, p. 44)

Miss Dempsey's recollection, in response to Fludd's unexpected arrival at the vicarage, invokes the biblical story of Tobias and the angel,[75] one of a host of intertextual references that orbit Fludd as character and permeate *Fludd* as text. From the novel's first moments the reader is aware of multiple intertextual presences hovering at the text's peripheries, not only through the complex, quasi-fictional status of *Fludd*'s protagonist but also via Mantel's description, placed before the opening of the novel's first chapter, of Sebastiano del Piombo's painting 'The Raising of Lazarus'.[76] Before the narrative has gotten underway intertexts are already multiplying with this reference to a painting that itself depicts a Biblical narrative. Perhaps one of the most striking manifestations of the density of *Fludd*'s intertextual strategy comes early on in its first chapter when Fetherhoughton, its environs and inhabitants, are initially described:

> The people of Fetherhoughton kept their eyes averted from the moors with a singular effort of will. They did not talk about them. Someone – it was the mark of an outsider – might find a wild dignity and grandeur in the landscape. The Fetherhoughtonians did not look at the landscape at all. They were not Emily Brontë, nor were they paid to be ... (p. 12)

The central sentence of this passage alone ('they were not Emily Brontë ...') is a misquotation of the line 'I am not Prince Hamlet, nor was meant to be', taken from T. S. Eliot's 'The Love Song of J. Alfred Prufrock'.[77] Mantel's revision refers to three separate literary texts, taking in Emily Brontë's *Wuthering Heights* and, through 'Prufrock', Shakespeare's *Hamlet*. While each of these intertexts has a complex and resonant relationship with Mantel's *Fludd*, it is the intertextual ground of the 'Prufrock' poem which provides the most striking illustration of the relationship that Mantel establishes between haunting, intertextuality and the debates of the English Reformation.

Eliot's poem alludes repeatedly to Andrew Marvell's 'To His Coy Mistress' and this scene of unconventional wooing, with one eye on the grave, makes its own coy appearance in *Fludd*. We have already encountered Father Angwin's solution for the removal of the statues whose presence in the Church of St Thomas Aquinas Bishop Croucher decries as idolatrous: the interment of them in the church grounds. Yet, the execution of his plan is not as emotionally or intellectually uncomplicated as Father Angwin's statement appears to suggest. Faced with holes prepared in the churchyard to receive the statues, the priest is gripped with 'a nameless, floating anxiety' as the excavations become 'a graveyard prepared for some coming massacre or atrocity' (p. 34). This comment serves viscerally to connect the removal of the statues and the parodic religious schism in Fetherhoughton to historical accounts of the Reformation and religious reform more generally, the atrocities and associated corpses that these events brought with them, corpses like those of Joan Boughton and John Tewkesbury. Unlike those incinerated bodies, however, these objects are available for resurrection and do not remain interred for long, as Fludd proceeds to the churchyard to reverse this act of iconoclasm by inhumation. As the statues are gradually disinterred and light is shed on the face of the statue of St Agnes, Sister Philomena makes a startling observation:

> this interval, this suspension, this burial had brought about a change. She did not mention this change to the others; she realised that it might be something only she could see. But the virgin's expression had altered. Blankly sweet, she had become sly; unyielding virtue had yielded; she gazed up, with a conspiratorial smile, into Heaven's icy vault. (p. 137)

The statue Philomena scrutinizes depicts the patron saint of virgins, and when this status is combined with the discussion of worms earlier in the passage and the dark observation from Agnes Dempsey that 'as for worms, we all know where they are coming from and going to', the narrator's deduction that 'unyielding virtue had yielded' completes an oblique textual reference to Marvell's lyric in which the amorous poetic speaker contemplates the possibility of his love dying a virgin, ghoulishly conjecturing that 'then worms shall try|That long preserved virginity' (ll.27-8). The origins of this reference are present in Mantel's misquotation of 'Prufrock' whose line 'there will be time' refers to the opening lines of Marvell's own verse ('Had we but world enough and time' l.1). That the reference persists throughout the novel is indicative of the haunting quality of the intertextual fragment as it insistently revisits the narrative, even while subject to partial occlusion.

The readings above demonstrate the multilayered treatment of intertextual material within *Fludd*, a novel which alludes to biblical, alchemical, literary and visual texts, and places historical narratives alongside folk devils (the 'real bodies' buried on the Fetherhoughton Moors making implicit reference to the Moors Murders of the 1970s) within an intertextual crucible. The resulting textual effects are manifold. On the one hand the unmarked quotations which make up the bulk of *Fludd*'s intertextual material repeatedly direct the reader's attention beyond the text to a phantasmal network of paratextual sources. In these instances the novel activates what Giovani Nencioni dubs 'recognition', a term describing 'the moment I perceive in a text the unsuspected presence of another text ... intertextuality at the moment of revelation – the moment of recognition ... as if a space suddenly opened up behind the text, and a new face emerged'.[78] These moments serve to disorientate, acting as they do as sudden apparitions, whose appearance disturbs the narrative through their implication of a textual space beyond the primary text. They serve to destabilize the reader's assumptions about who is speaking as the narrative voice becomes possessed by the voices of other authors and other texts. The following passage from *Wolf Hall* obliquely speaks to this kind of paratextual activity, introducing characters from other stories, temporarily re-routing the path of the narrative.

> In the forest you may find yourself lost, without companions. You may come to a river which is not on a map. You may lose sight of your quarry, and forget why you are there. You may meet a dwarf, or the living Christ, or an old enemy of yours; or a new enemy, one you do not *know until you see his face appear between the rustling leaves*, and see the glint of his dagger. You may find a woman asleep in a bower of leaves. For a moment, before you don't recognise her, you will think she is someone you know. (p. 224, my italics)

In context the passage forms, if not a non-sequitur, then a sharp change of direction, following as it does a discussion of the king's hunting activities, which takes place in the third person, in contrast to this extract's direct address. In doing so it formally produces the effects it self-consciously discusses, disorientating the reader even as the passage speaks to experiences of confusion, misrecognition, of being lost and of unexpected or inexplicable encounters.

On the other hand, Mantel's frequent use of unmarked quotations has the effect of rendering her work as always populated by these hidden texts, even when they cannot be immediately identified by the reader. The idea of the quotation that is missed, the extract that is not recognized as quotation, is played upon several times within *Fludd*. In this first exchange, Fludd, intertextual referent and revenant, despairs of Sister Philomena's inability to recognize the presence of quoted material within their conversation:

> '*My days have passed more swiftly than the web is cut by the weaver, and are consumed without any hope.*'
> The girl did not recognise a quotation. 'Have you no hope?' (*Fludd*, p. 95)

This failure to recognize is played out explicitly twice in the novel, and in the second incident it is Fludd who is oblivious:

> 'I am ill,' [Father Angwin] said. 'My soul chooseth hanging, and my bones death.'
> 'My dear fellow,' said Fludd, removing his gaze from the fire, and fastening it anxiously on the priest's face.
> 'Oh, a quotation,' Angwin said. 'A biblical quotation. The Old Testament, you know. Book of somebody-or-other.' (p. 127)

In these two brief extracts we see the kinds of confusions and anxieties provoked in the reader by the unmarked quotation as intertextual technique within *Fludd*. When encountering certain passages the reader senses an intertextual presence whose identity cannot be easily made out and whose borders cannot easily be defined, an absent presence manifesting in an apparently empty room in a moment comparable to that experienced by Father Angwin as he sits and ponders his tea leaves:

> Nothing in particular could be seen in the leaves, but for a moment Father Angwin thought that someone had come into the room behind him. He lifted his face, as he did in conversation, but there was no one there. 'Come in, whoever you are,' he said. 'Have some stewed tea.' … Somewhere else in the house, a door slammed. (p. 8)

Conclusion

That the intertextual fragments found not only in *Fludd* but in Mantel's work as a whole should be understood as spectres, possessed of a haunting power, is not merely a useful metaphor to enable discussion of her intertextual play, but rather a conscious and central element of her writing practice. This deliberate positioning of intertexts as spectres is indicated through the sources chosen, which frequently allude to narratives of haunting, to spectres, to the dead and the undead, as has been demonstrated. However, this spectrality is also registered in the structure of the intertextual eruptions, which are generally partial, composed of the kinds of unmarked quotations, anonymous quotations or misquotations explored with reference to *Fludd* and observed in *Wolf Hall*'s treatment of Reformation print culture. That these intertexts speak of and to the dead, to the persistence of the dead, and do so most frequently without fully manifesting themselves and declaring their origins, demands an understanding of them as spectres, more specifically the spectres of influence, from which Mantel inherits and, as inheritor, sifts, interprets, translates. From an examination of the extended textile metaphor employed in *Wolf Hall* to talk about textuality itself and to indicate how textuality always already implies intertextuality, through an analysis of self-quotation as a key element of Mantel's intertextual strategy, to understanding the intertexts within her work as functioning as spectres, a conceptualization emerges of Mantel as a writer whose intertextual play dramatizes the dual forces of creativity and responsibility that she understands to be implicated in the process of literary and historical inheritance.

I began this chapter by exploring the affinity between the material book and the corporeal body in *Wolf Hall*, examining how that affinity produced moments of haunting in which not only the key players in the mainstream narrative of Tudor England, but those figures that formed the footnotes and deletions of history – for example Liz, Anne and Grace Cromwell and Joan Boughton – are resurrected, are given life, friends, interests and preferences. Mantel renders them, as far as is possible, human, and central, if only for a moment. At the same time her depiction of the object of the book as conceptually mirroring the dead body nuances her role as inheritor (interpreter and translator) of the past, recognizing that to write is always to inscribe one's own death, to render one's words a phantom that will take possession of the living and speak to and through them in your absence.

Indeed, such absences, their recognition and partial amelioration, are what drive *Wolf Hall*'s intellectual project. Just as Tyndale's translation of the New Testament is held up as revealing the power of textual practice to occult certain ideas or alternatively occlude certain absences, Mantel should be understood, through her establishment of the spectralized text, to be producing through *Wolf Hall* the 'occult history of Britain' (p. 65) that is found in knowing précis in the novel's fifth chapter. The novel provides an account of British history 'occulted' by traditional processes of historiography that insist upon one 'approved' translation of the past. The 'buried empire' (p. 575) of hobs and boggarts, ghosts and outlaws, which Cromwell's commissioners cannot reach, captures the material lost to conventional recordings of history, unaccounted for through a drive for veracity. In closing it is useful to turn to this 'buried empire' for in mapping its territory it is possible to reassert the significance of *Wolf Hall*'s literary project and its multiplicity of hauntings.

> Beneath the sodden marches of Wales and the rough territory of the Scots border, there is another landscape; there is a buried empire where [Cromwell] fears his commissioners cannot reach. Who will swear the hobs and boggarts who live in the hedges and in hollow trees, and the wild men who hide in the woods? Who will swear the saints in their niches, and the spirits that cluster at holy wells rustling like fallen leaves, and the miscarried infants dug into unconsecrated ground: all those unseen dead who hover in the winter around forges and village hearths, trying to warm their bare bones? For they too are his countrymen: the generations of the uncounted dead, breathing through the living, stealing their light from them, the bloodless ghosts of lord and knave, nun and whore, the ghosts of priest and friar who feed on living England and suck the substance from the future. (*Wolf Hall*, p. 575)

In this passage Cromwell is seen acknowledging the importance of the dead and supernatural to the lives of the living as he considers how this haunting mass are unaccommodated by the process of swearing allegiance to King Henry, and as such form a problematically unaffiliated, unregulatable quantity. The space inaccessible to Cromwell and his commissioners is populated by the hidden, the miscarried, the unseen and the uncounted whose partial and precarious existence is provided only by acts of appropriation from the living. Such appropriation, Cromwell appears to suggest, may be depleting, as these unacknowledged dead 'feed on living England and suck the substance from the future'. Yet simultaneously the passage suggests an alternative mode in which the living might relate to the dead, one that is not parasitic but based upon a recognition which would flesh the 'bare bones' of the historical dead. Early on in this chapter I demonstrated the importance of notions of heredity and legacy to *Wolf Hall*'s understanding of writing as associated with and generative of ghosts. The various interactions between writing and haunting and between writers and ghosts that I have examined here are produced out of the necessity of literary inheritance, and the responsibilities and possibilities associated with it; to reanimate the dead, to give voice to literary and historical predecessors alike and allow them to speak while avoiding the muffling of one's own voice. They are results of what de Groot has termed 'an ethical mediation' and 'a moral practice'.⁷⁹ In producing a new text, in the act of inheriting, Mantel demonstrates a simultaneous awareness that she is producing her own legacy, ghosting her authorial self and acting as legatee and testator in one. This interrogative passage, with its repeated 'who will?' prompts an ultimate understanding that the one who will swear the dead, the spectral and the hidden, who has the capacity to do so, is the writer. In *Wolf Hall* Mantel is answering her own question of 'who will swear?'

Afterword

'There are no endings. If you think so you are deceived as to their nature. They are all beginnings. Here is one.'
— Hilary Mantel, *Bring up the Bodies*

In early drafts of *Beyond Black* we find the protagonist Alison's approach to apparently empty houses documented:

> She checks the quality of the silence and how populous it is. Don't hold back, she will say to the floorboards, to the uncurtained windows … Then the little scratchings begin, that another woman might mistake for mice: and the clearing of throats, in cavity walls, behind chimney breasts, the shy … modest dead, making themselves known Perhaps they're out of practice because no-one has asked after them in years, perhaps someone's told them not to talk to strangers.[1]

Alison implores these ghosts: 'don't be shy, come out and let's see if we could live together'. It is a plea present throughout Mantel's corpus to date, a plea which brings together these writings as spaces in which those vocalizations mistaken for, or written off as, noise find their status as meaningful communications, spaces in which the forgotten, the neglected and the invisible are returned to presence, spaces in which prohibitions on speech and visibility are exposed and lifted. As my epigraph suggests, this book acts as an intervention into an 'invisibility' of Mantel's work within the academy which is only now beginning to be robustly challenged, securing a mode of visibility for these writings which foregrounds the significance and heterogeneity of the Mantelian ghost as a key trope within Mantel's canon. The preceding chapters have demonstrated that the situation of haunting and the motif of the ghost do not merely form one theme among many within Mantel's writing. Rather, both formally and thematically, haunting and spectrality form a principle which has shaped her work, from her experiments with the gothic form through her autobiographical writing to her best known works of historical fiction.

My opening chapter reads Mantel's life-writing alongside her first volume of short stories. In doing so I establish how *Giving up the Ghost* self-consciously positions the documents produced through life-writing as unstable and hybrid – engaged in a project of writing the self into being which is perpetual – through a series of formal and thematic hauntings. Alongside demonstrating the presence in the memoir of a spectral 'I' speaker who refuses ultimately to fully manifest, the chapter identified a key element of Mantel's intertextual strategy, that is, her use of self-quotation. These explicit interactions between her own texts act to articulate the patchwork and haunted nature of life-narratives. Through invoking Jacques Derrida's conceptualization of the secret, and the role it might play in mediating between fiction and testimony, I established the need to accommodate and privilege the enigmatic gaps and untellable secrets within those texts, phenomena which emerge as key elements of Mantel's narratives of haunting. Finally, I proposed a mode of reading Mantel's work which was predicated on the maintenance of the texts' haunting secrecy rather than an exorcism of their ambiguity.

With this in mind, my second chapter explored how Mantel's debut duology uses the situation of haunting within the gothic mode to articulate the complex and potentially deadly shortcomings of Thatcherite social care policy and, more broadly, of the familial domestic milieu. I demonstrated how Mantel's duology understands care-giving relationships and environments to incubate both the potential for horrific abuses and collapses, and contains an ethical imperative whose demand is for acts of empathic witnessing. Maintaining a focus on the interaction between the political and the spectral, my third chapter analysed Mantel's *Eight Months on Ghazzah Street* in the context of Jacques Rancière's theory of the 'partition of the sensible'. Here Mantel's re-engagement with the gothic mode was established, alongside a depiction of groups of subjects (women, domestic servants) who are so marginal as to be rendered spectral, resulting in a novel which is profoundly political in Mantel's terms. The deliberate clash between the Western mode of the gothic and the Saudi Arabian setting of the novel is shown to be orchestrated in order to reveal the profoundly artificial quality of the politico-religious systems in which only certain voices can be heard and certain subjects can be seen and acknowledged as subjects, systems which produce ghostly excesses in the forms of individuals denied the status of being meaningfully visible and audible.

My fourth chapter established the status of the Mantelian ghost within a contemporary moment in which hyper-connective tele-technologies are ubiquitous, and so too is a mode of hyper-visibility seemingly antithetical to the existence of the ghost. My reading of Mantel's 2005 novel *Beyond Black* proposed that the screens boasted by numerous tele-technologies are doubled and re-doubled throughout the novel as surfaces through which, and upon which a multiplicity of familial, memorial, historical and intertextual ghosts could manifest themselves. This work puts at stake the contemporary subject's relationship with any number of lived and unlived pasts. Appropriately, in my final chapter I turned to the historical past, moving away from haunting as a prerequisite for the genre of historical fiction and instead demonstrating Mantel's use of the Tudor milieu to play out the intricate interactions between the textual and the spectral. Through an examination of the duology's treatment of the advent of print culture in Europe and Tudor England I proposed that *Wolf Hall* is at its heart a book about writing and what it means to be an author, books which recognize the moments of haunting and acts of inheritance which accompany authorship and the responsibilities such acts and moments might bring with them.

This study makes licit how Mantel's literary ghost stories make meaningful ethical interventions into social, historical and political debates, demonstrating that her work acts at numerous points as social theory which, as Janice Radway puts it, 'use[s] imaginative fiction both to diagnose the political *dis-*ease of our historical moments and to envision just what it will take to put things right'.[2] Numerous hauntings have formed the basis for this book which tracks myriad ghosts and spectres formed not only of the dead, but the unborn, the marginal, the silenced and the invisible, potentialities, intertexts and secrets. While, in closing, it is important to avoid imposing upon this diverse host an artificial homogeneity, falling into the trap of rendering the Mantelian ghost uselessly ubiquitous, 'the ungrounded ground of representation and key to all forms of storytelling … both unthinkable and the only thing worth thinking about',[3] it is also necessary to articulate what unites the meanings of ghosts within Mantel's corpus. In *Ghostly Matters*, Avery F. Gordon argues that 'following … ghosts is about making a contact that changes you and refashions the social relations in which you are located. It is about putting life back in where only a vague memory or a bare trace was visible to those who bothered to look'.[4] It is this transformational change that the Mantelian ghost is charged with effecting. When speaking about her research for *Wolf Hall*, Mantel stated that 'once you know that the spaniel keeper was called Humphrey he is going to appear in half a line. I conceive of that as an act of reverence'.[5] Whether the spectralized citizens of a conservative politico-religious regime, as in *Eight Months*, the forgotten historical dead of the Cromwell duology, the words of long-dead writers, or traumatizing personal enigmas, an encounter with the Mantelian ghost is first and foremost an ethical encounter where an act of mourning, reverence or simple recognition has the potential to take place. The hauntings to be found in Mantel's writing are united through their status as situations in which not only are previously occluded people, voices, events and other phenomena revealed, but the fact and mechanism of their occlusion is also rendered licit and available for dispute and debate. As Mantel puts it, 'even if you are documented you can vanish from the imagination. But you can be reinstated in the imagination … the need to mourn and do reverence is not a sentimental impulse, it's a political impulse. It's about doing justice, no matter how many years that might take'.[6]

In Mantel's short story 'Terminus'[7] a rush hour traveller spots her dead father on a passing train. Disembarking at Waterloo, she seeks him throughout the station, growing increasingly distressed and suspicious about what proportion of the commuter crowds around her are 'connected at all points, … are completely and utterly what they purport to be: which is alive?' (p. 198). She questions the status of a 'lost, objectless, … man, a foreigner with a bag on his back' and of a woman 'whose starved face recalls a plague-pit victim', of commuters, high-rise inhabitants and suburbanites, asking 'how many … are solid, and how many of these assumptions are tricks of the light?' (p. 198), a questioning which echoes a conception of the dead posited in early drafts of *Fludd*:

> Mostly, when people see ghosts, they don't know anything's amiss. But <u>later</u> you learn that the person in question, on the day in question, was dead: Calcinated perhaps, inhumed, at any rate no longer of this world. What you took to be a solid man, was a dead man. You thought you saw your neighbor, perhaps, but where is your neighbor now? Not, for sure, in the house next door. If you can't tell the dead from the living, what can you tell? What do you know?[8]

Alongside the ghost whose appearance provides the story's catalyst, all those figures upon whom the speaker's suspicion lands recall the host of ghosts and spectres whose presence and meanings have been traced throughout this book, the familial and historical dead, the alien, the lost, the deracinated mass. The protagonist's demand obliquely acknowledges how to be living is no guarantee of being deemed 'alive' while her frantic and ultimately unproductive search for her father among the mundane structures of a modern train station – 'W. H. Smith' and 'Costa Coffee' (p. 196), photo booths and bureau de changes (p. 199) – recalls the dormitory inhabitants of *Beyond Black* and their ambivalent quest for contact with the dead. In the image of 'a court of shadow ambassadors, with shadow portfolios tucked within their silks' (p. 197) the world of *Wolf Hall* and *Bring up the Bodies* begins, intertextually, to resonate.

I invoke this crowded ghost story not simply because it holds within its limited space a striking display of the multiplicity accommodated by the Mantelian ghost. After casting doubt upon her fellow citizens' animate existence the story's speaker asks:

> For distinguish me, will you? Distinguish me 'the distinguished thing'. Render me the texture of flesh. Pick me what it is, in the timbre of the voice that marks out the living from the dead. Show me a bone that you know to be a living bone. Flourish it, will you? Find one, and show me. (p. 198)

This rhetorical demand inscribes both the richness and the difficulty of Mantel's literary project, its double aspect in which the reader, though presented with traditional ghosts – those formed of the speaker's father, *Wolf Hall*'s Anne and Grace Cromwell, Morris and his fellow 'fiends from Aldershot' who populate *Beyond Black*, Jack Mantel's 'baffled spirit' (*Giving up the Ghost*, p. 429) and countless others – is required to acknowledge that these narratives are not intended to 'give up' their ghosts so easily, to simply mark a dividing line between the living and the dead. Rather the Mantelian ghost acts to disavow the possibility of such a line, such a distinction, to insist, in myriad ways, that the meaning of ghosts cannot be 'rendered' and 'shown' and 'flourish[ed]'. Rather, such meaning as can be gleaned must be allowed to manifest in the ethical encounters the Mantelian ghost prompts: acts of literary, personal and moral reverence to that which isn't quite, which never was, or is no more, to that which 'shivers between the lines, where the ghosts of meaning are' (*Giving up the Ghost*, p. 222).

Notes

Introduction

1. Hilary Mantel, MN1528, Hilary Mantel Papers, The Huntington Library, San Marino, California.
2. Hilary Mantel, *Wolf Hall* (London: Fourth Estate, 2010), p. 649.
3. Hilary Mantel, *Interview*, in 'Where the Ghosts of Meaning Are: Haunting and Spectrality in the Work of Hilary Mantel' (PhD Thesis, University of Leeds, 2016), p. 291.
4. Avery F. Gordon, *Ghostly Matters: Haunting and the Sociological Imagination* (London; Minnesota: University of Minnesota Press, 1997), p. 8.
5. Hilary Mantel, MN1805, Hilary Mantel Papers, The Huntington Library, San Marino, California.
6. Hilary Mantel, MN1092b, Hilary Mantel Papers, The Huntington Library, San Marino, California.
7. Hilary Mantel, *Giving up the Ghost: A Memoir* (London: Fourth Estate, 2010).
8. Roger Luckhurst critiques the term in his essay 'The Contemporary London Gothic and the Limits of the "Spectral Turn"' (Roger Luckhurst, 'The Contemporary London Gothic and the Limits of the "Spectral Turn"', *Textual Practice*, 16 (2002), 527–46 (p. 527)). Yet already embedded within Luckhurst's critique is a problematic elision of the borders between the gothic, the spectral and the ghostly.
9. Esther Peeren and Maria del Pilar Blanco, 'Introduction: Conceptualizing Spectralities', in *The Spectralities Reader: Ghosts and Haunting in Contemporary Cultural Theory*, ed. by Esther Peeren and Maria del Pilar Blanco (London: Bloomsbury, 2013), pp. 1–28 (p. 1).
10. Ibid., p. 15.
11. Ibid., p. 1.
12. Mantel, *Giving up the Ghost*, p. 20. All further references to this edition are given in parentheses within the text.
13. Mantel, *Interview*, p. 294.
14. This is most marked in Eileen Pollard's repudiation of the gothic as a useful critical tool in reading Mantel's work, particularly in her response to Avril Horner and Sue Zlosnik's reading of Mantel's novel *Fludd* as comic gothic in their article '"Releasing spirit from matter": comic alchemy in Spark's *The Ballad of Peckham Rye*, Updike's *The Witches of Eastwick* and Mantel's Fludd' (*Gothic Studies*, 2 (2000), 136–47). Eileen Pollard, '"What is Done and What is Declared: Origin and Ellipsis in the

Work of Hilary Mantel' (PhD Thesis, Manchester Metropolitan University, 2013), pp. 28–38.

15 Sarolta Marinovich, 'The Discourse of the Other: The Female Gothic in Contemporary Women's Writing', *Neohelicon*, 21 (1994), 189–205 (p. 193).

16 Colin Davis, *Haunted Subjects: Deconstruction, Psychoanalysis and the Return of the Dead* (Basingstoke: Palgrave, 2007), p. 8.

17 Luckhurst, 'The Contemporary London Gothic and the Limits of the "Spectral Turn"', p. 527.

18 Martin McQuillan. This is particularly apparent in Peggy Kamuf's admission in response to McQuillan's question 'are you a scholar who deals with ghosts?' that she was, 'though [she was] not sure [she] would have said so with as much conviction before *Spectres of Marx*'. Peggy Kamuf, 'Translating Spectres: An Interview with Peggy Kamuf', *Parallax*, 7 (2001), 43–50 (p. 45).

19 As highlighted in Luckhurst's article, examples of this body of work include Jean Michel-Rabat's *Ghosts of Modernity* (Gainsville: University Press of Florida, 1996), Julian Wolfrey's *Victorian Hauntings: Spectrality, the Gothic, the Uncanny and Literature* (London: Palgrave Macmillan, 2001), Carla Jodey Castricano's *Cryptomimesis: The Gothic and Jacques Derrida's Ghost Writing* (Montreal; London: McGill-Queens University Press, 2003) and Davis' *Haunted Subjects*.

20 Luckhurst, 'The Contemporary London Gothic and the Limits of the "Spectral Turn"', p. 534.

21 Jacques Derrida, *Spectres of Marx: The State of Debt, the Work of Mourning and the New International*, trans. by Peggy Kamuf (New York: Routledge, 1994), p. 161.

22 Martin Jay, *Cultural Semantics: Key Words of Our Time* (London: Athlone Press, 1998), p. 162.

23 Gordon, *Ghostly Matters*, p. 25.

24 Ibid., p. 7.

25 Ibid., p. 8.

26 Ibid., p. 17.

27 Ibid. Italics author's own.

28 Esther Peeren, *The Spectral Metaphor: Living Ghosts and the Agency of Invisibility* (London: Palgrave, 2014), p. 6.

29 Clive Bloom, *Gothic Horror* (London: Macmillan, 1988), p. 7.

30 Hilary Mantel, *Email Interview – Answers*, 'Where the Ghosts of Meaning Are: Haunting and Spectrality in the Work of Hilary Mantel' (PhD Thesis, University of Leeds, 2016), p. 255.

31 Hilary Mantel, 'P.S. Ideas, Interviews, Features', interview by Fanny Blake, in Hilary Mantel, *Giving up the Ghost: A Memoir* (London: Harper Perennial, 2004), p. 8.

32 A. S. Byatt, 'Fathers', in *On Histories and Stories: Selected Essays* (London: Chatto and Windus, 2000), pp. 9–35 (p. 9).

33 Hilary Mantel, *Bring up the Bodies* (London: Fourth Estate, 2012), p. 414.

Chapter 1

1. Hilary Mantel, *Giving up the Ghost: A Memoir* (London: Fourth Estate, 2003). All further references to this edition are given in parenthesis in the body of the text.
2. *Giving up the Ghost* is the only example of Mantel's life-writing to be published in print. *Ink in the Blood: A Hospital Diary* (London: Fourth Estate, 2010) is also autobiographical but was published only as an e-book and comprises a single essay.
3. This inexorable growth is illustrated convincingly in Yagoda's observation that 'according to Nielsen BookScan, which tracks about 70 percent of US book sales, total sales in the categories of Personal Memoirs, Childhood Memoirs, and Parental Memoirs increased more than 400 percent between 2004 and 2008'. Ben Yagoda, *Memoir: A History* (New York: Riverhead, 2009), p. 7.
4. Yagoda, *Memoir*, p. 1.
5. Ibid., p. 2.
6. Ibid., p. 3.
7. Max Saunders, *Self-Impression: Life-Writing, Autobiografiction and the Forms of Modern Literature* (Oxford: Oxford University Press, 2013), pp. 6–7.
8. Yagoda, *Memoir*, p. 103.
9. Hilary Mantel, MN1802, Hilary Mantel Papers, The Huntington Library, San Marino, California.
10. Kathryn Hughes, 'Ghost Stories', *The Guardian*, Saturday 10 May 2003, <http://www.theguardian.com/books/2003/may/10/featuresreviews.guardianreview18> (accessed 03 September 2015).
11. Inga Clendinnen, 'Unsuited to Everything', *The New York Times*, 05 October 2003, <http://www.nytimes.com/2003/10/05/books/unsuited-to-everything.html?pagewanted=all> (accessed 16 November 2012).
12. Marianne Brace, 'Hilary Mantel: The Exorcist', *The Telegraph*, Saturday 10 May 2003, <http://www.independent.co.uk/arts-entertainment/books/features/hilary-mantel-the-exorcist-590258.html> (accessed 03 September 2015).
13. 'The Devil's Work: Hilary Mantel's Ghosts', *The New Yorker*, Monday 25 July 2005, <http://www.newyorker.com/magazine/2005/07/25/devils-work> (accessed 03September 2015).
14. 'Giving up the Ghost: A Memoir', *Publisher's Weekly*, 14 July 2003, <http://www.publishersweekly.com/978-0-8050-7472-7> (accessed 03 September 2015).
15. Amy Prodromou, 'Writing the Self into Being: Illness and Identity in Inga Clendinnen's *Tiger's Eye* and Hilary Mantel's *Giving up the Ghost*', in *Identity and Form in Contemporary Literature*, ed. Ana Maria Sánchez-Arce (London: Routledge, 2014), pp. 195–209.
16. Ibid., p. 195. Here Prodromou is adapting a term first coined by Anne Hunsaker Hawkins in her book *Reconstructing Illness: Studies in Pathography*, 2nd edn (West Lafayette: Purdue University Press, 1999).

17 The onset of a chronic period of the illness is described in *Giving up the Ghost* as follows: 'a pain sliced through me, diagonal, from my right ribs to my left loin. It was a new pain: but not new for long. It stole my life: it stole it for ten years and for a double term, and then for ten years more' (p. 173).
18 Sara Knox, 'Giving Flesh to the "Wraiths of Violence": Super Realism in the Fiction of Hilary Mantel', *Australian Feminist Studies*, 25 (2010), 313–23.
19 Hilary Mantel, *Beyond Black* (London: Fourth Estate, 2005). All further references to this edition given in parenthesis in the body of the text.
20 Knox, 'Giving Flesh to the "Wraiths of Violence"', p. 320.
21 Ibid., p. 319.
22 In the moments before the memoir's speaker begins to relate a traumatic childhood encounter she notes: 'you are aware that readers – any kind readers who've stayed with you – are bracing themselves for some revelation of sexual abuse. That's the usual horror' (p. 106). This statement alludes to the preponderance of autobiographical narratives of child abuse which came to prominence with David Pelzer's *A Child Called It* (2000) and which continue to dominate the non-fiction paperback charts. For a detailed discussion of the evolution of the misery memoir see Esther Addley, 'So Bad It's Good', *The Guardian*, 15 June 2007, <http://www.theguardian.com/society/2007/jun/15/childrensservices.biography> (accessed 15 January 2016).
23 Writing in his essay 'Demeure: Fiction and Testimony', Derrida usefully identifies how 'a distinction between fiction and autobiography ... not only remains undecidable but, far more serious, in whose indecidability, ..., it is impossible to *stand*, to maintain oneself in a stable or stationary way' Jacques Derrida, *Demeure: Fiction and Testimony*, trans. by Elizabeth Rottenberg, (Stanford: Stanford University Press, 2000), p. 16.
24 Yagoda, *Memoir*, p. 109.
25 Saunders, *Self-Impression*, p. 511.
26 Linda Anderson in Saunders, *Self-Impression*, p. 504.
27 Hilary Mantel, MN1517, Hilary Mantel Papers, The Huntington Library, San Marino, California.
28 Eileen Pollard, '"But at second sight the words seemed not so simple" (Virginia Woolf, 1929): Thickening and Rotting Hysteria in the Writing of Hilary Mantel and Virginia Woolf', *The Virginia Woolf Miscellany*, 80 (2011), 24–6 (p. 24).
29 Virginia Woolf, *A Room of One's Own and Three Guineas* (London: Chatto and Windus, 1984), p. 4. The above understanding of the autobiographical 'I' does, however, have implications for the terminology used to speak about the author of *Giving up the Ghost* in contrast to its speaker. To that end, in this chapter the name 'Hilary' refers to the memoir's narrator while 'Mantel' will be used to refer to the book's author.
30 Shari Benstock, *The Private Self: Theory and Practice of Women's Autobiographical Writings* (Chapel Hill: University of North Carolina Press, 1988), p. 11.

31 Hilary Mantel, 'Destroyed', in *Learning to Talk* (London: Harper Perennial, 2006), pp. 21–44 (pp. 21–2). All further references are given in parentheses in the text.
32 Nancy Miller speaks provocatively about the unstable frontiers of fiction with regard to its place within memoir: 'I could write down what I remembered; or I could craft a memoir. One *might* be the truth; the other a good story … When I sit down to reconstruct my past, I call on memory, but when memory fails, I let language lead … As a writer, the answer to the question of what "really" happened is literary – or at least textual. I will know it when I write it. When I write it, the truth will lie in the writing. But the writing may not be the truth; it may only look like it. To me.' Nancy Miller in Yagoda, *Memoir*, p. 3.
33 Mantel, *Interview*, p. 267.
34 Derrida, 'Demeure', p. 29.
35 Ibid., p. 26.
36 Liam's childhood resonates with the account of Irishness given in the memoir in which Hilary frequently asserts the Protestantism of objects, animals and people in contrast to her own Irish Catholicism and recalls 'a Protestant boy across the road point[ing] and jeer[ing]' at her as she stands in her communion dress, preparing 'for one of the Feasts of the Church' (*Giving up the Ghost*, p. 102). The details of the troubles in Northern Ireland, and how they impacted her, are skated over in a brief reference to her great aunt's sectarian views: 'she could not fail to hate … a black and tan. And for people of the Orange persuasion she can't care' (p. 48).
37 Rupert Brooke, 'The Old Vicarage at Grantchester', in *The Complete Poems of Rupert Brooke* (London: Sidwick and Jackson, 1934), p. 93.
38 William Butler Yeats, 'The Lake Isle of Innisfree', in *The Collected Poems of W. B Yeats*, ed. by Richard J. Finneran and George Mills Harper, 1st edn (London: Macmillan, 1981), p. 44.
39 Alisa Miller, 'Rupert Brooke and the Growth of Commercial Patriotism in Great Britain 1914-18', *Twentieth Century British History*, 21 (2010), 141–62 (p. 152).
40 Ibid., p. 162.
41 Marjorie Howes, 'Introduction', in *The Cambridge Companion to W.B. Yeats*, ed. by Marjorie Howes and John Kelly (Cambridge: Cambridge University Press, 2007), pp. 1–18 (p. 3).
42 Ibid., p. 4.
43 Miller, 'Rupert Brooke and the Growth of Commercial Patriotism in Great Britain 1914-18', p. 10.
44 Contrary to Saunders's insistence that the novelist's memoir traditionally constitutes a coda of sorts to the author's writing life and forms a commentary upon that author's oeuvre (Saunders, *Self-Impression*, pp. 516-7), *Giving up the Ghost* sits stubbornly at the centre of Mantel's writing career, refusing this traditional position and thus significantly complicating the work of the memoir.
45 Saunders, *Self-Impression*, p. 6.

46 In fact, during one of the more expansive passages detailing the Brosscroft hauntings, the term 'dead centre' is used twice in quick succession, once to describe the lightless and troubling space of the stairwell in the middle of the house and then again to describe the positioning of a front door key, mysteriously lost and just as mysteriously returned to the top of the china cabinet (pp. 87–8). Such a repetition is one of many indications that not merely the dead, but the enigmas they leave behind, are the key to understanding this text.

47 In *Giving up the Ghost*'s account of the emergence of the apparent household ghosts, it is interesting to note that they are reported to manifest from, among other locations, 'the glass-fronted cupboards to the right of the fireplace' (p. 96), rather than the left hand side described in the short story. This mirror image offers a succinct example of the transformative effect of relocation on textual material.

48 Derrida, 'Demeure', pp. 42–3.

49 Ibid., p. 47.

50 Jacques Derrida, *Resistances of Psychoanalysis*, trans. by Peggy Kamuf, Pascale-Anne Brault and Michael Naas (Stanford: Stanford University Press, 1998), p. 44.

51 Ginette Michaud, 'Literature in Secret: Crossing Derrida and Blanchot', *Angelaki: Journal of Theoretical Humanities*, 7 (2002), 69–89 (p. 78).

52 Derrida, 'Demeure', pp. 72–3.

53 Ibid., p. 29.

54 Jacques Derrida, 'Passions: "An Oblique Offering"', in *Derrida: A Critical Reader*, ed. David Wood (Oxford: Blackwell, 1992), pp. 5–35 (p. 21).

55 Simon Baron-Cohen and John E. Harrison (eds), *Synaesthesia: Classic and Contemporary Readings* (Oxford: Blackwell, 1997), p. 3.

56 Danko Nikolić, 'Is Synaesthesia Actually "Ideasthesia": An Investigation into the Phenomenon', in *Proceedings of the Third International Congress on Synaesthesia, Science and Art* (Granada, Spain, 2009), <http://www.danko-nikolic.com/wp-content/uploads/2011/09/Synesthesia2009-Nikolic-Ideaesthesia.pdf> (accessed 14 September 2015).

57 Richard E. Cytowic, *The Man Who Tasted Shapes* (Cambridge: MIT Press, 2003), p. x.

58 Siri Carpenter, 'Everyday Fantasia: The World of Synaesthesia', *Monitor on Psychology*, 32 (2001), <http://www.apa.org/monitor/mar01/synesthesia.aspx> (accessed 14 September 2015).

59 'Synaesthesia, n.' OED Online. Oxford University Press, June 2015. Web. 27 July 2015.

60 Reuven Tsur, 'Issues in Literary Synaesthesia', *Style*, 47 (2007), 30–52 (p. 30).

61 Richard E. Cytowic and David M. Eagleman, *Wednesday Is Indigo Blue: Discovering the Brain of Synaesthesia* (Cambridge: MIT Press, 2011), p. 166.

62 Tsur, 'Issues in Literary Synaesthesia', p. 30.

63 Ibid.
64 This sublimating of words and concepts into gaseous presences is repeated later in the novel in a similarly inextricable blending of clinical and literary synaesthesia wherein it is not clear whether the synaesthesic image is a metaphor created by Mantel or an account of 'Hilary's' perceptual reality: 'We are talked about in the street. Some rules have been broken. A darkness closes about our house. The air becomes jaundiced and clotted, and hangs in gaseous clouds over the rooms. I see them so thickly that I think I am going to bump my head on them' (p. 86).
65 In a reflection on R. D. Laing's *Sanity, Madness and the Family*, Mantel states of her family: 'we ran on lies like a cooker runs on gas', a fragment which transforms Hilary's synaesthesic compression into a quotidian simile capable of controlling the confusion between the aural, emotional and conceptual material she experiences. Hilary Mantel, MN1745, Hilary Mantel Papers, The Huntington Library, San Marino, California.
66 It is useful to note that many of the manifestations of synaesthesia within *Giving up the Ghost* are concerned with eating. The marzipan incident is accompanied by a rich paragraph in which Hilary describes a dream of eating bees and notes 'their milk-chocolate sweetness' and texture 'like lightly cooked calves' liver' (p. 3). While this description constitutes a disordering within one sensory modality, that of taste, it prompts, in a fashion analogous to the marzipan incident, consideration of the anxiety produced by the notion that in the process of ingesting or otherwise internalizing, something unexpected and extraneous may also be taken in. This notion is acknowledged by Mantel as also occurring at the point of transmission: when discussing how the process of writing frequently exceeds the author's intentionality she observes: 'look at what I said, without meaning to'. Mantel, 'In Conversation', in Eileen Pollard, '"What Is Done and What Is Declared": Origin and Ellipsis in the Writing of Hilary Mantel' (Phd Thesis, Manchester Metropolitan University, 2013), pp. 201–30 (p. 197).
67 Prodromou, 'Writing the Self into Being', p. 195.
68 Yagoda, *Memoir*, p. 180.
69 Linda Anderson, 'At the Threshold of the Self: Women and Autobiography', in *Women's Writing: A Challenge to Theory*, ed. Moira Monteith (Brighton: Harvester, 1986), pp. 54–71 (p. 56).
70 The title of this story resonates with the description given in the memoir of one of Hilary's childhood toys, the 'magic slate', 'a rectangle of carbon paper covered by a sheet of plastic' (p. 69). Despite seeming to offer the possibility of a 'clean slate', the surface's inscriptions apparently wiped away after use, Hilary reports that 'when [she] held the slate away from [her] and turned it, [she] saw that the pen left marks in the plastic sheet, like the tracks of writing on water. It would have been possible, with some labour and diligence, to discover the words even after they had been

erased' (pp. 69–70). The discovery of this palimpsest casts the search for a definitive account of a family history within 'The Clean Slate' as doomed to failure, positing instead a multiplicity of possible accounts laid one on top of the other. As the narrator confirms, her mother 'has her own versions of the past, and her own ways of protecting them' (p. 131).
71 Hilary Mantel speaking at 'An Evening with Hilary Mantel', Manchester Metropolitan University, Manchester, 30 September 2015.
72 Blake, 'P.S. Ideas, Interviews, Features', p. 8.
73 Benstock, *The Private Self*, p. 11.

Chapter 2

1 Hilary Mantel, *Every Day is Mother's Day* (London: Harper Perennial, 2006) and Hilary Mantel, *Vacant Possession* (London: Harper Perennial, 2006). All subsequent references to this edition are given after quotations in the text.
2 The relationship between the literary gothic and the ghost is one that is frequently taken for granted. However, while maintaining an awareness of the close connection between the mode and the trope, it is important to recognize that not all literary ghosts are gothic and not all gothic narratives contain ghosts. As Julia Briggs puts it, 'ghost stories constitute a special category of the Gothic and are partly characterised by the fact that their supernatural events remain unexplained'. Julia Briggs, 'The Ghost Story', in *A Companion to the Gothic*, ed. by David Punter (Oxford: Blackwell, 2000), pp. 122–31 (p. 123). Briggs's assessment of the place of the ghost within the gothic, and the gothic ghost's inexplicability, encourages a reading of the ghosts present in the duology as specifically inflected. In other words, the ghosts present in a gothic text can be argued to function in a way which is distinct from the ghosts found in other fantastic or supernatural modes.
3 This attitude is exemplified in Hephzibah Anderson's 'Hilary Mantel: On the Path from Pain to Prizes' in which she asserts that 'attempts to define [Mantel] and her work fall invariably short' before going on to dismiss the gothic as a potentially useful category to apply to Mantel's fiction, speculatively coining her own description of 'Northern gothic?' before rejecting it, concluding 'No, not really'. Hephzibah Anderson, 'Hilary Mantel: On the Path from Pain to Prizes', *The Observer*, Sunday 19 April 2009, <http://www.theguardian.com/books/2009/apr/19/hilary-mantel-man-booker≥ (accessed 15 December 2015).
4 Pollard, 'What Is Done and What is Declared', p. 10. Pollard refers specifically to Victoria Nelson's study of Mantel's work in her book *Gothicka* (Cambridge: Harvard University Press, 2012).
5 Knox, 'Giving Flesh to the "Wraiths of Violence"', p. 313.

6 Fred Botting, 'In Gothic Darkly: Heterotopia, History, Culture', in *A Companion to the Gothic*, ed. by David Punter (London: Blackwell, 2000), pp. 3–14 (p. 4).
7 Ibid.
8 Kate Ferguson Ellis, *The Contested Castle: Gothic Novels and the Subversion of Domestic Ideology* (Urbana: University of Illinois Press, 1989), p. ix.
9 Ibid., p. 13.
10 Marinovich, 'The Discourse of the Other' p. 191. Though Marinovich is here considering contemporary female gothic, such confrontations with motherhood are to be found in some of the earliest gothic texts. For example both Sheridan Le Fanu's 'Carmilla' (1871) and Coleridge's 'Christabel' (1816) feature motherless protagonists persecuted by replacement mother/lover figures.
11 Rodney Lowe, *The Welfare State in Britain since 1945* (London: Palgrave Macmillan, 2005), p. 320.
12 Margaret Thatcher, 'Speech to the Canadian and Empire Clubs in Toronto', 27 September 1983, <http://www.margaretthatcher.org/document/105443> (accessed 27 May 2016).
13 Indeed the roles of 'housewife and mother' were held up by Thatcher as almost unmatched in terms of 'long term satisfaction and importance'. Margaret Thatcher, 'Speech to the Conservative Women's Conference', 25 May 1988, <http://www.margaretthatcher.org/document/107248> (accessed 27 May 2016).
14 Thatcher, 'Speech to the National Society for the Prevention of Cruelty to Children', 16 May 1984, <http://www.margaretthatcher.org/document/105682> (accessed 27 May 2016).
15 Margaret Thatcher, 'Speech to the Conservative Women's Conference'.
16 Ibid.
17 Margaret Thatcher, 'Speech at Conservative Party Conference (plus address to overflow meeting)', <http://www.margaretthatcher.org/document/104717> (accessed 27 May 2016).
18 Thatcher, 'Speech to the Conservative Women's Conference'.
19 Lowe, *The Welfare State in Britain since 1945*, p. 349.
20 Marinovich, 'The Discourse of the Other', p. 193.
21 Gordon, *Ghostly Matters*, p. 8.
22 Margaret Thatcher, 'Speech to the Conservative Political Centre Summer School', 6 July 1979, <http://www.margaretthatcher.org/document/104107> (accessed 16 January 2016).
23 The physical space of the family house occupied a crucial place within Thatcherite rhetoric. Multiple policies were introduced to promote the purchase of council housing, including the 1986 Housing and Planning Act. Thatcher herself deemed council estates to be 'breeding grounds of socialism, dependency, vandalism and crime' while 'home ownership, in contrast, encouraged all the virtues of good

citizenship'. Lowe, *The Welfare State in Britain since 1945*, 3rd edn. By 1983, 'what was called a "property owning democracy" in 1979 was called a "home owning democracy"' in that year's manifesto. Geoffrey K. Fry, *The Politics of the Thatcher Revolution: An Interpretation of British Politics, 1979-1990* (London: Palgrave Macmillan, 2008), p. 23. This emphasis on private home ownership is recognized in the duology by patriarch Colin Sidney who, reminiscing about his childhood home, muses 'Ah, property … that is what they are, not merely houses but a statement of values. But surely, he thought in mild surprise, those are not the values I hold?' (*Every Day*, p. 67).

24 Fry, *The Politics of the Thatcher Revolution*, p. 108.

25 As Ros Coward has pointed out, while during the 1960s and 1970s a 'demystification of the joys of self-sacrificing motherhood was crucial in the formulation of feminist politics' which 'led feminists to call for men to be more involved in parenting, for the state to provide better child-care facilities, and for the provision of proper benefits for mothers who lost the support of men … throughout the 1980s this discourse was eroded. … A reaction set in. During the 1980s motherhood was romanticised again, so much that the "*Kinder und Küche*" images of the 1950s now look like social realism'. 'The Heaven and Hell of Mothering: Mothering and Ambivalence in the Mass Media', in *Mothering and Ambivalence*, ed. by Wendy Holloway and Brid Featherstone (London: Routledge, 1997), pp. 111–18 (p. 116).

26 Peter Jenkins, 'How the Policies of Decay may Stir Britain towards a New Beginning', *The Guardian*, 28 December 1984.

27 Peter Riddell, *The Thatcher Decade: How Britain Has Changed in the 1980s* (Oxford: Basil Blackwell, 1989), p. 148.

28 Hilary Mantel, 'Author, Author', *The Guardian*, 24 May 2008, <http://www.theguardian.com/books/2008/may/24/1> (accessed 11 April 2016).

29 Marinovich, 'The Discourse of the Other', p. 191.

30 Florence Sidney's ill-judged Christmas visit to 2 Buckingham Avenue offers an insight into the squalor of the house: 'the upholstery of the suite was greasy and worn, the wallpaper yellow with age. What a way to live, Florence thought; creating a slum, here in this neighbourhood. What was the need for it? She tried to place the smell. Cats?' (*Every Day*, p. 111).

31 Roszika Parker, *Torn in Two: The Experience of Maternal Ambivalence* (London: Virago, 1995), p. 40.

32 Knox, 'Giving Flesh to the "Wraiths of Violence"', p. 314.

33 Ibid., p. 316.

34 Mantel, *Beyond Black*.

35 Hilary Mantel, MN173, Hilary Mantel Papers, The Huntington Library, San Marino, California.

36 Parker, *Torn in Two*, p. 1.

37 D. W. Winnicott, 'Hate in Countertransference', *International Journal of Psychotherapy*, 30 (1949), 69–74 (p. 73).
38 Parker, *Torn in Two*, p. 6.
39 Ibid., pp. 86–7.
40 James Hill, 'The Bad Mother, An Archetypal Approach', in *Fathers and Mothers*, ed. by P. Berry (Dallas: Spring Publications, 1990), p. 107.
41 Parker, *Torn in Two*, p. 92.
42 Welldon in Parker, *Torn in Two*, p. 220.
43 Mary Jacobus, *First Things: The Maternal Imaginary in Literature, Art and Psychoanalysis* (London: Routledge, 1995), p. 28.
44 Parker, *Torn in Two*, p. 78.
45 Leonard Shengold, *Soul Murder: The Effects of Childhood Abuse and Deprivation* (London: Yale University Press, 1989), p. 21.
46 D. W. Winnicott in Parker, *Torn in Two*, p. 59.
47 Colin Sidney, recalling his own childhood, fantasizes an idyllic domestic scene in which his mother greets him after school, provides a snack and a cosy environment in which to do his homework before admitting that 'the past had not been like that. It was negligence, not sentiment, that kept things in their place year after year' (*Every Day*, p. 92). This contrasts starkly with a description given by Margaret Thatcher of her own childhood, in an interview with *The Sun* newspaper in which she recalls walking home from school 'to a living room with a nice warm fire' and states: 'my mother was there. She'd want to know what happened at school. We'd toast bread for tea. … Then there would be homework to do.' Margaret Thatcher, 'TV Interview for HTV *George Thomas in Conversation*', 13 September 1983, <http://www.margaretthatcher.org/document/105188> (accessed 27 May 2016).
48 Parker, *Torn in Two*, p. 73.
49 Margaret Thatcher, 'Interview for *Woman's Own*', 23 September 1987, <http://www.margaretthatcher.org/document/106689> (accessed 27 May 2016).
50 Parker, *Torn in Two*, p. 39.
51 For a detailed exploration of the treatment of sexual abuse and social work in particular in the duology see Eleanor Byrne's 'Mantel's Social Work Gothic: Trauma and State Care in *Every Day is Mother's Day* and *Vacant Possession*', *Hilary Mantel: Contemporary Critical Perspectives* (London: Bloomsbury, 2018), pp. 213–27.
52 This essay, which is included in the 2006 edition of *Every Day is Mother's Day* details this period of Mantel's life and the two specific house calls that provoked the novel. Mantel's recollection of attempting to dismiss how 'profoundly' troubled she is by her encounter with an elderly lady and her mentally ill adult daughter ('But I said to myself, the household is fine, the trouble is all in your head', p. 11) is particularly striking when compared to Isabel's experience of trying to care for Evelyn and Muriel.

53 This tradition is mapped skilfully in Charley Baker's *Madness in Post-1945 British and American Fiction* (London: Palgrave, 2010).
54 Erving Goffman, *Asylums: Essays on the Social Situation of Mental Patients and Other Inmates* (New Brunswick: Aldine Transactions, 2007), p. 17.
55 Ellis, *The Contested Castle*, p. 45.
56 Ibid.
57 Notable examples of the 'lunatic asylum' as setting in gothic fiction can be found in Wilkie Colins' *The Woman in White* (1859), whose heroine is wrongfully incarcerated in a psychiatric hospital, and in Bram Stoker's *Dracula* (1897), in which the character of Renfield is detained in an asylum. It is interesting to note that this particular intersection between gothic and psychiatry gave rise to a parodic clinical term, namely 'Renfield Syndrome', coined by Richard Noll in his book *Vampires, Werewolves and Demons: Twentieth Century Reports in the Psychiatric Literature* (New York: Bruner/Mazel, 1992).
58 Peter Bartlett and David Wright, 'Community Care and Its Antecedents', in *Outside the Walls of the Asylum: The History of Care in the Community 1750-2000*, ed. by Peter Bartlett and David Wright (London: Athlone Press, 1999), pp. 1–18 (p. 1).
59 Sarah Payne, 'Outside the Walls of the Asylum? Psychiatric Treatment in the 1980s and 1990s', in *Outside the Walls of the Asylum: The History of Care in the Community 1750-2000*, ed. by Peter Bartlett and David Wright (London: Athalone Press, 1999), pp. 244–65 (p. 247).
60 Though widely associated with Thatcher's economic policy, the phrase 'there is no alternative', or TINA as it came to be called, was first used by Margaret Thatcher in the Press Conference for American Correspondents in London on 25 June 1980. <http://www.margaretthatcher.org/Speeches/displaydocument.asp?docid=104389&doctype=1≥ (accessed 12 April 2016).
61 Thatcher's association with the term 'Victorian values' originated during a televised interview with Brian Walden for London Weekend Television's *The Weekend World* on 16 January 1983. During the interview Walden put it to the prime minister that she subscribed to and approved of 'Victorian Values' to which she replied 'Oh exactly. Very much so.' <http://www.margaretthatcher.org/document/105087> (accessed 12 April 2016). The prime minister went on to repeat Walden's term, and her endorsement of it, in a number of other speeches and interviews that year.
62 Margaret Thatcher, 'Remarks on Becoming Prime Minister (St Francis's Prayer)', <http://www.margaretthatcher.org/document/104078> (accessed 21 April 2016).
63 John Welshman, 'Rhetoric and Reality: Community Care in England and Wales, 1948-1974', in *Outside the Walls of the Asylum: The History of Care in the Community 1750-2000*, ed. by Peter Bartlett and David Wright (London: Athlone Press, 1999), pp. 204–26 (p. 223).
64 Ben Nelson, '"Inadequate" Community Care Attacked: House of Lords, Parliament', *The Times*, 8 December 1988.

65 Jane Brotchie, 'Do We Care Who Cares? - The Neglect of Those Who Look After the Ill at Home', *The Guardian*, 7 September 1988.
66 Polly Toynbee, 'Just One Cry for Help / Focus on the Association of Carers', *The Guardian*, 10 December 1984.
67 Mrs Sidney's status as an animated corpse is confirmed while she is still resident at her hospital, as the staff nurse addresses her but concludes: 'expect a mummy to answer you …. Expect Tutankhamun to boogie into the sluice' (*Vacant Possession*, p. 92).
68 Word of Phillip's death is reported anonymously, the last in a series of snippets of news regarding patients who had recently been discharged: 'Phillip got a council flat,' someone said. 'How did he like it?' 'He hanged himself' (*Vacant Possession*, p. 57). His suicide is not merely an authorial conceit but reflects the real outcome for a significant minority of patients who were discharged from long-term care into the community. In 1985 Brian Brown, a twenty-three-year-old man who had recently been discharged into the community from a psychiatric ward in West Lothian, threw himself from a bridge to his death. David Henke, 'Suicide Claim leads to Social Security Debate', *The Guardian*, 21 June 1985. Likewise, in 1986 an enquiry was called for following the suicides of fifteen patients of St John's psychiatric hospital Lincoln, of whom ten had been recently discharged into the community. Jill Sherman, 'Fears for former patients / Mental health association calls for greater supervision of people discharged from psychiatric hospitals', *The Times (London)*, 11 August 1986.
69 It is telling that the rest of the original line, in which the winter is rendered 'glorious summer', is absent from the description, leaving Sholto's proposed winter of discontent unthawing.
70 Margaret Thatcher, 'Remarks on becoming Prime Minister (St Francis's Prayer)', 4 May 1979, <http://www.margaretthatcher.org/document/104078≥ (accessed 20 May 2016).
71 The return of the dead, whether literal or metaphorical, to homes which have been destroyed or negated is a trope which recurs insistently in Mantel's writing. *Beyond Black*'s protagonist, Alison, asserts the impossibility of returning to her childhood home on the grounds that 'its been knocked down. It's the car supermarket now' (Hilary Mantel, MN1162, Hilary Mantel Papers, The Huntington Library, San Marino, California) while in a speech for the Dublin Trinity Burke Historical Society Mantel recalls how her grandparent's house had been bulldozed with the exception of the front wall whose doors and windows were bricked up to form the perimeter of a new mill: 'When I was a child this row of houses, one layer thick, struck me as sinister. They were ghost houses, with a ghost on the doorstep. I see now that they presented both a powerful deception and an image of loss. The dead people who had lived in those rooms had nowhere to go. Now, if you've got up from the cemetery and found your old street, a blocked doorway is nothing to you of

course; but what would they think when they melted through the facade and came out again immediately, evicted into the public space of the millyard?' Hilary Mantel, Hilary Mantel Papers, MN1496, The Huntington Library, San Marino, California.
72   Julian Wolfreys, *Victorian Hauntings: Spectrality, Gothic and the Uncanny* (London: Palgrave, 2002), p. xi.
73   Stephen Frosh, *Hauntings: Psychoanalysis and Ghostly Transmissions* (London: Palgrave Macmillan, 2013), p. 249.
74   Ibid., p. 250.
75   Hilary Mantel, 'The Woman in the Hall', in Hilary Mantel, *Every Day is Mother's Day* (London: Harper Perennial, 2006), pp. 10–13 (p. 10).
76   Lowe, *The Welfare State in Britain since 1945*, p. 349.
77   Both Muriel and Evelyn are at various times locked into or locked out of 2 Buckingham Avenue. While Muriel is immured by her mother in the back parlour Evelyn is forcibly ejected from the house as she stands on the doorstep: 'Suddenly she felt a terrific blow in the small of her back. She pitched forward, off the doorstep. One arm flailed in the air. With difficulty she regained her balance. She stood gasping, winded. The door clicked behind her. She was locked out' (*Every Day*, p. 88).
78   Anne Alvarez, *Live Company: Psychoanalytic Psychotherapy with Autistic, Borderline, Deprived and Abused Children* (London: Tavistock/Routledge, 1992), p. 9.
79   This lack of resources of all kinds in the sphere of social work in the 1970s and 1980s is usefully spoken to by Brid Featherstone who, in her essay 'I wouldn't do your job: Women, social work and child abuse', maintains that 'in their dealings with abusive mothers ... female social workers are hampered by poor theoretical tools and their location in organizational contexts which are often unhelpful', difficulties which are compounded by 'public sector contexts that are manifesting increased defensiveness and the inability to face both external and psychic reality'. Brid Featherstone, 'I wouldn't do your job: Women, social work and child abuse' in ed. by Wendy Holloway and Brid Featherstone, *Mothering and Ambivalence* (London: Routledge, 1997), p. 167.
80   Some of Isabel's early gothic predecessors include Princess Isabella who features in Horace Walpole's *The Castle of Otranto* (1764) and the character of Agnes, who is imprisoned in a sepulchre for the duration of Ann Radcliff's *The Mysteries of Udolpho* (1796).
81   Eve Kosofsky Sedgwick, *The Coherence of Gothic Conventions* (London: Methuen, 1986), p. 3.
82   The most notable example of this trope can be found in Clara Reeve's *The Old English Baron* (1778), a rewriting of Walpole's *Otranto*, which frames its narrative as containing various lacunae, including a four-year break in the tale and various elements of the manuscript made illegible by damp.

83 Lowe, *The Welfare State in Britain since 1945*, p. 350.
84 Ibid.
85 Mantel, 'The Woman in the Hall', p. 13.
86 Hilary Mantel, 'An Outsider's Eye: Louise Tucker Talks to Hilary Mantel', in *Every Day is Mother's Day* (London: Harper Perennial, 2006), p. 6.
87 Ibid.
88 Gordon, *Ghostly Matters*, p. 18.

Chapter 3

1 Hilary Mantel, *Giving up the Ghost: A Memoir* (London: Fourth Estate, 2010), p. 1.
2 Ibid.
3 Ibid., p. 5.
4 Hilary Mantel, *Eight Months on Ghazzah Street* (London: Harper Perennial, 2004). All further references to this edition are given in parenthesis in the text. From this point the novel will be referred to using the shortened form *Eight Months*.
5 David E. Long, *The Culture and Customs of Saudi Arabia* (London: Greenwood, 2005), p. 18.
6 Louis Althusser, *On Ideology* (London; New York: Verso, 2008), p. 36.
7 Ibid., p. 18.
8 Ibid., p. 40.
9 Hilary Mantel, MN1403, Hilary Mantel Papers, The Huntington Library, San Marino, California.
10 Esther Peeren, 'Spooky Mediums and the Redistribution of the Sensible: Sarah Waters's *Affinity* and Hilary Mantel's *Beyond Black*', in Esther Peeren, *The Spectral Metaphor: Living Ghosts and the Agency of Invisibility* (London: Palgrave, 2014), pp. 110–43.
11 As Peeren notes, 'travelling and visiting as foreigners' offers for Rancière the chance to encounter the 'unexpected spectacle of another humanity' (Jacques Rancière, *Short Voyages to the Land of the People*, trans. by James B. Swenson (Stanford: Stanford University Press, 2003), p. 1). This 'other humanity' is comprised of those who have been deemed to exceed the sensible order whose existence, and the demands for dissensus that existence provokes, can only be observed from the position of foreigner. Peeren, 'Spooky Mediums and the Redistribution of the Sensible', p. 134.
12 Robert Irwin, *Time Out*. This quotation has been featured on the book jacket of all editions of *Eight Months* to date. At the time of printing no bibliographic details for the original review could be found.
13 Indeed, the gothic quality of *Eight Months* was initially opaque even to its writer who states of the writing of the novel: 'the only thing I can say is that when I lived

through it I lived through it innocently. It wasn't until I had written the novel, indeed months afterwards, after it had been published and reviewed, that I thought "I've written a gothic novel!" and then it all fell perfectly into place'. Mantel, *Interview*, p. 284.

14 Hilary Mantel, 'A Kind of Alchemy: Sarah O'Reilly talks to Hilary Mantel', interview with Sarah O'Reilly, *Fludd* (London: Fourth Estate, 2010), p. 8.

15 Hilary Mantel, 'Hilary Mantel – The SRB Interview', *Scottish Review of Books*, 5 (2009) <http://www.scottishreviewofbooks.org/index.php/back-issues/volume-five/volume-five-issue-four/295-hilary-mantel-the-srb-interview> (accessed 10 September 2014).

16 Jacques Rancière, *The Politics of Aesthetics: The Distribution of the Sensible*, ed. and trans. by Gabriel Rockhill (London: Bloomsbury, 2013), p. 8.

17 Hilary Mantel, 'Veiled Threats', *The Guardian*, 11 September 2004, p. 31.

18 Ibid. Speaking in an interview in October 2015 Mantel described this 'avoidant gaze' as constituting a 'virtual veil which is accorded as a sign of respect to women who are not wearing [the veil] but are deemed in the context to be respectable women' before going on to state that 'this respect takes the form of looking through one'. 'Interview', p. 21. This 'respect' manifests itself again in Mantel's short story 'Sorry to Disturb' (Hilary Mantel, *The Assassination of Margaret Thatcher* (London: Fourth Estate, 2014)) which similarly gives an account of a Western woman living in Saudi Arabia, negotiating a fraught relationship with her neighbours: 'my male Saudi neighbour would come down from the first floor on his way out to his car and step over my brushstrokes without looking at me, his head averted. He was according me invisibility, as a mark of respect to another man's wife' (p. 11). This imposition of an apparitional veil illustrates clearly how what Rancière terms the 'apparently "natural logic"' of what is deemed visible and what is not is in fact wholly synthetic and fabricated. Jacques Rancière, *Dissensus: On Politics and Aesthetics*, ed. and trans. by Steven Corcoran (New York: London: Continuum, 2010), p. 139.

19 Rancière, *Dissensus*, p. 152.

20 Ibid., p. 37.

21 Ibid., p. 139.

22 Rancière, *The Politics of Aesthetics*, p. 8.

23 Ibid., p. 7.

24 See Aristotle's definition of the citizen as 'one who partakes in the fact of ruling and the fact of being ruled' discussed in Rancière, *Dissensus*, p. 27.

25 For the sake of clarity, it is important to state that the garment described as a veil in *Eight Months* is a *niqab*, a full face veil with a slit to allow the wearer to see. The slit is either permanently covered with a mesh which obscures the eyes or else has a detachable mesh panel which can be pulled down to conceal the eyes from view or raised to reveal them.

26 Rancière, *Politics of Aesthetics*, p. 8.
27 Rancière, *Dissensus*, p. 38.
28 Frances's inability to accurately pronounce Samira's maid's name is crucial as it not only co-opts Frances into the process by which domestic servants in the Kingdom are denied full personhood but also implicates the reader in this process as they are similarly forced to refer to the character through the mangled pronunciation provided by Samira. A similar scene of misnaming occurs during Frances's first visit to her neighbour Yasmin's home. Here her neighbour tries to assist Frances with the pronunciation of her maid's name: 'Shams' Yasmin said. 'As in Champs Elysées' (p. 68). In this exchange Mantel orchestrates a neat demonstration of the dominating potential of these discussions around naming. Yasmin's recourse to the phrase 'Champs Elysées' as a way of assisting Frances's pronunciation translates Shams' name into an alien cultural milieu and in so doing references a further cultural appropriation since the Champs Elysées itself takes its name from the Elysian Fields mentioned in classical Greek mythology. Meanwhile Frances's difficulty in grasping the name in the first place gestures towards the wider struggle to 'get hold of' unfamiliar cultures that drives the narrative of *Eight Months*.
29 Peeren, *The Spectral Metaphor*, p. 5.
30 This lack of private space for domestic servants in *Eight Months* is underlined by an incident in which Frances's neighbour forces her maid to sleep on the dining room floor despite hosting parties in the room that go on until three in the morning (p. 174).
31 Rancière, *Dissensus*, p. 139.
32 Ibid., p. 139.
33 Mantel, *Interview*, p. 284.
34 Althusser, *On Ideology*, p. 48.
35 Ibid., p. 52.
36 Jacques Lacan, *The Four Fundamental Concepts of Psychoanalysis* (London: Vintage, 1998), p. 129.
37 Slavoj Žižek, 'The Big Other Doesn't Exist', *The Journal of European Psychoanalysis*, 5 (1997), 2, <http://www.psychomedia.it/jep/number5/zizek.htm> (accessed 18 February 2016).
38 Lacan, *The Four Fundamental*, pp. 75–84.
39 Henry Krips, 'The Politics of the Gaze: Foucault, Lacan, Žižek', *Culture Unbound*, 2 (2010), 91–102 (p. 93).
40 Lacan, *The Four Fundamental*, p. 84.
41 Rodolphe Gasché, 'The Witch Meta-Psychology', trans. by Julian Patrick, in *Returns of the French Freud: Freud, Lacan and Beyond*, ed. by Todd Dufresne (New York: Routledge, 1997), pp. 169–208 (p. 172).
42 Wolfreys, *Victorian Hauntings*, p. 6.
43 Lacan, *Four Fundamental*, p. 83.

44 Wolfreys, *Victorian Hauntings*, p. 5.
45 Rancière, *Dissensus*, p. 37.
46 Ibid., p. 36.
47 Althusser, *On Ideology*, p. 11.
48 Rancière, *Dissensus*, p. 36
49 Avery F. Gordon, *Ghostly Matters: Haunting and the Sociological Imagination* (Minneapolis: University of Minnesota Press, 2008), p. 3.
50 Derek Ruez, 'Partitioning the Sensible at Park 51: Rancière, Islamophobia and Common Politics', *Antipode*, 45 (2013), 1128–47 (p. 1128).
51 Stephen Corcoran, 'Introduction', in Jacques Rancière, *Dissensus: On Politics and Aesthetics*, ed. and trans. by Steven Corcoran (New York: London: Continuum, 2010), pp. 1–34 (p. 9).
52 Rancière, *Dissensus*, p. 36.
53 Ibid., p. 38.
54 Wolfreys, *Victorian Hauntings*, p. 5.
55 Ibid.
56 Inferences of potentially supernatural interference in the domestic space can also be found within 'Sorry to Disturb', a short story whose premise closely maps that of *Eight Months*. On one occasion the protagonist rearranges her living room furniture only to find upon waking in the morning that 'the furniture had been trying to move itself back. An armchair was leaning to the left, as if executing some tipsy dance; at one side its base rested on the carpet, but the other side was a foot in the air, and balanced finely on the rim of a flimsy wastepaper basket' (p. 14). In another incident she returns to her spare room to find that 'the doors of the fitted wardrobes, which were large and solid like coffin lids, had been removed from their hinges; they had been replaced, but hung by the lower hinges only, so that their upper halves flapped like the wings of some ramshackle flying machine' (p. 18). These scenes, again reminiscent of poltergeist activity, serve to underline the instability of Mantel's Jeddah-based protagonists within the space of their own homes, intimating how little 'in possession of the ground' (*Eight Months*, p. 46) they really are.
57 An early draft of the novel makes this intrapsychic functioning of State control even more explicit: 'He had believed the streets were safe, now he knows different. But anyway, what is the use of safety in the streets when there's so much violence in the head.' Hilary Mantel, MN24, Hilary Mantel Papers, The Huntington Library, San Marino, California.
58 Peeren, *The Spectral Metaphor*, p. 3.
59 Slavoj Žižek, *The Sublime Object of Ideology* (London: Verso, 1989), p. 43.
60 The ambivalent approach to the trope of the ghost and the situation of haunting that characterizes *Eight Months* is perhaps most succinctly captured early on in the novel as Frances notices in passing a man 'bent over an ironing board'. 'The man swept a garment from the ironing board and held it aloft; it was a *thobe*, narrow, shirt-like,

startling white against the shadows of the walls and the night sky. She imagined she could see the laundryman's face, creased with the weariness of long standing; as they turned the corner he laid the garment down again, and began to arrange its limbs. ... She got out of the car. The laundryman seemed as clear and sharp and meaningless as a figure in a dream; she knew she would never forget him' (p. 60). Here the clichéd image of the 'ghost in a sheet' evoked by the empty white *thobe* silhouetted against the night sky gives way to the true spectre within the moment, the domestic worker whose face Frances does not encounter directly and can only imagine, but whose presence is pervasive and inescapable.

61 This is not the first instance in which Mantel embeds an enigmatic haunted enclave within a domestic space: see also the 'spare room' of 2 Buckingham Avenue in *Every Day* and *Vacant Possession* discussed in Chapter 2.
62 Rancière, *Dissensus*, p. 38.
63 See the passage concerning Saul and the witch of Endor, First Book of Samuel, 28:3-25.
64 Jane Idleman Smith and Yvonne Yazbeck Haddad, *The Islamic Understanding of Death and Resurrection* (Oxford: Oxford University Press, 2002), p. 32.
65 Koran 23:100.
66 Hamid Algar, *Wahhabism: A Critical Essay* (Oneonta: Islamic Publications, 2002), p. 34.
67 Idleman Smith and Haddad, *The Islamic Understanding of Death and Resurrection*, p. 7.
68 Marinovitch, 'The Discourse of the Other', p. 192. A key literary predecessor for Frances can be found in Emily St Aubert, the protagonist of Ann Radcliffe's *The Mysteries of Udolpho* (1794) and investigator of its titular mysteries.
69 Claire Kahane, 'The Gothic Mirror', in *The (M)other Tongue: Essays on Feminist Psychoanalytic Interpretation*, ed. by Shirley Nelson Garner, Claire Kahane and Madelon Sprengnether (Cornell: Cornell University Press, 1985), p. 335.
70 Mantel, *Interview*, p. 285.
71 Hilary Mantel, 'Last Morning in Al Hamra', *The Spectator*, 14 August 2012.
72 Rancière, *Dissensus*, p. 157.
73 Ibid. p. 141.
74 Corcoran, 'Introduction', p. 7.
75 Rancière, *Dissensus*, p. 143.
76 Mantel, *Interview*, p. 230.

Chapter 4

1 Mantel, *Beyond Black*, pp. 213–14. All subsequent references to this edition are given in parentheses in the body of the text.

2. Didier Anzieu, *The Skin Ego* (London: Yale University Press, 1989), p. 79.
3. Steven Connor, 'Integuments: The Scar, the Skin and the Screen', *New Formations*, 39 (1999), 32–54 (p. 52).
4. Gayatri Chakravorty Spivak in Avery F. Gordon, *Ghostly Matters: Haunting and the Sociological Imagination* (London: University of Minnesota Press, 1997), p. 16.
5. Peeren, *The Spectral Metaphor*, p. 111.
6. Leigh Wilson, 'The Cross-Correspondences, the Nature of Evidence and the Matter of Writing', in *The Ashgate Research Companion to Nineteenth Century Spiritualism and the Occult*, ed. by Sarah Wilburn and Tatiana Kontou (Surrey: Ashgate, 2012), pp. 97–122 (p. 100).
7. Ibid., p. 100.
8. Hilary Mantel, MN1184, Hilary Mantel Papers, The Huntington Library, San Marino, California.
9. Philip Larkin, 'Annus Mirablis', in *Collected Poems*, ed. by Anthony Thwaite (London: Faber and Faber, 2003), p. 146.
10. The literature on the connection between spiritualism and communications technology is vast. Sarah Willburn and Tatiana Kontou's *Companion to Nineteenth-Century Spiritualism and the Occult* (Surrey: Ashgate, 2012) dedicates its entire first section to this critical link. It is also important to note that this connection is not a contemporary critical gesture but was drawn contemporaneously to the rise in nineteenth-century spiritualism. As Jeffrey Sconce puts it, 'both spiritualists and their antagonists elaborated the electrical mysteries of the telegraph into a theory of woman as technology'. Jeffrey Sconce, *Haunted Media: Electronic Presence from Telegraphy to Television* (Durham: Duke University Press, 2002), p. 14.
11. Sconce, *Haunted Media*, p. 49.
12. Jill Galvan, 'The Victorian Post-Human: Transmission, Information and the Séance', in *The Ashgate Research Companion to Nineteenth-Century Spiritualism and the Occult*, ed. by Tatiana Kontou and Sarah Willburn (Surrey: Ashgate, 2012), pp. 79–96 (p. 79).
13. Ibid., p. 80.
14. Ibid.
15. Ibid.
16. Ibid., p. 84.
17. Ibid., p. 85.
18. Ibid., p. 80.
19. This model of the medium as passive technological object is common to much of the literature on nineteenth-century spiritualism. Sconce describes the voices of the dead 'flow[ing] through' the medium (p. 14) while Anthony Enns describes spirit mediums as 'primarily engaged in the act of taking dictation from disembodied spirits'. Anthony Enns, 'The Undead Author: Spiritualism, Technology and

Authorship', in *The Ashgate Research Companion to Spiritualism and the Occult*, ed. by Tatiana Kontou and Sarah Wilburn (Farnham: Ashgate, 2012), pp. 55–78 (p. 60).
20 Galvan, 'The Victorian Post-Human', p. 79.
21 Ibid., p. 85.
22 Ferdinand Tönnies quoted in Juliette Flower MacCannell, *The Regime of the Brother: After Patriarchy* (London: Routledge, 1991), p. 11.
23 McLuhan, *Understanding Media* (Cambridge: MIT, 1994), p. 47.
24 This is particularly true of the work of Bernard Stiegler and Alison Landsberg, both of whom are invoked below. Michel de Certeau's *The Practice of Everyday Life* (1984) also speaks fruitfully to the connection between memory and technology in the late-twentieth and early-twenty-first centuries.
25 Alison Landsberg, *Prosthetic Memory: The Transformation of American Remembrance in the Age of Mass Culture* (New York: Columbia University Press, 2004), p. 4.
26 Ibid., p. 10.
27 Hilary Mantel, MN1189, Hilary Mantel Papers, The Huntington Library, San Marino, California.
28 Landsberg, *Prosthetic Memory*, p. 18.
29 Hilary Mantel, MN4, Hilary Mantel Papers, The Huntington Library, San Marino, California.
30 Landsberg, *Prosthetic Memory*, p. 33.
31 Michel de Certeau in Landsberg, p. 1.
32 Jeffrey Richards, Scott Wilson and Linda Woodhead (eds), 'Introduction', in *Diana: The Making of a Media Saint* (London: I.B. Tauris, 1999), pp. 1–19 (p. 2).
33 Adrian Kear and Deborah Lynn Steinberg, 'Ghost Writing', in *Mourning Diana: Nation, Culture and the Performance of Grief*, ed. by Adrian Kear and Lynn Steinberg (London: Routledge, 1999), pp. 1–14 (p. 3).
34 Ibid., p. 2.
35 Ibid.
36 Earlier drafts of the novel emphasize a withdrawing from and scaling back of traditional funerary rituals by Alison's clientele, even as they seek the dead out for recreation. As Al puts it: 'Haven't they got enough bereavement in their own lives? When their mothers and fathers die they just tidy them away. When my mother was young they used to at least have a ham tea. But now they'd take them to the vet if they could and get them incinerated like a defunct terrier. They don't want to know, mourning, any of that. Well you've seen them, Coll, at the crem. They turn up in anoraks.' Hilary Mantel, MN4, Hilary Mantel Papers, The Huntington Library, San Marino, California.
37 The way in which Alison frames this assertion varies in the novel. During her platform work the dead are described as resembling their living selves but 'healthy

and in their prime' (p. 34). Privately Alison acknowledges the darker reality of this continuity between life and death stating that the dead 'don't become decent people because they're dead. .... If you get people who are bad in life – ..., cruel people, dangerous people – why do you think they are going to be any better after they're dead?' (pp. 193–4).

38 Diana's wedding dress as a symbol of pre-mortem spectrality brought about through mediatization is an image Mantel returns to in her 'Royal Bodies' essay for the *London Review of Books* in which she talks at length about the life, death and mediatization of Diana. Strikingly Mantel describes Diana Spencer's emergence from the royal coach on the morning of her televised wedding to Prince Charles as follows: 'The extraordinary dress came first, like a flow of liquid, like ectoplasm emerging from the orifices of a medium.' Hilary Mantel, 'Royal Bodies', *London Review of Books* 35 (2013), 3–7.

39 Nigel Fountain in Rosalind Brunt, 'Princess Diana: A Sign of the Times' in *Diana: The Making of a Media Saint*, ed. by Jeffrey Richards, Scott Wilson and Linda Woodhead (London: I.B.Tauris, 1999), pp. 20–39, (p. 20).

40 Valery Hey, 'New Labour, New Britain and the "Dianaization" of Politics', in *Mourning Diana: Nation, Culture and the Performance of Grief*, ed. by Adrian Kear and Deborah Lynn Steinberg (London: Routledge, 1999), pp. 60–107 (p. 71).

41 Adrian Kear, 'Diana between Two Deaths: Spectral Ethics and the Time of Mourning', in *Mourning Diana: Nation, Culture and the Performance of Grief*, ed. by Adrian Kear and Lynn Steinberg (London: Routledge, 1999), pp. 169–86 (p. 171).

42 Stiegler, *Technics and Time*, trans. by Richard Beardsworth and George Collins (Stanford: Stanford University Press, 2011), p. 276.

43 Ibid., p. 268.

44 Kristina Lebedeva, 'Review Article: Bernard Stiegler, *Technics and Time, 2: Disorientation* (Stanford University Press, 2008)', *Parrhesia*, 7 (2009), 81–5 (p. 83).

45 Interestingly, the ability of the dead to outstrip the communication networks of the living was a frequently recorded phenomenon when spiritualism was at its peak. This incident echoes the claim made by Reverend Ashahel H. Jervis in 1849 that 'spirits had notified him of the death of a friend's son just hours before the telegram had reached him'. Enns, 'The Undead Author', p. 60.

46 Jacques Derrida and Bernard Stiegler, *Echographies of Television: Filmed Interviews* (Cambridge: Polity Press, 2002), p. 88.

47 Alwyn W. Turner, *A Classless Society: Britain in the 1990s* (London: Aurum, 2013), p. 10.

48 Hey, 'New Labour, New Britain and the "Dianaization" of Politics', p. 172.

49 Richard Johnson, 'Exemplary Differences: Mourning (and Not Mourning) a Princess', in *Mourning Diana: Nation, Culture and the Performance of Grief* (London: Routledge, 1999), pp. 15–51 (p. 30).

50 Russ Castronovo, *Necro Citizenship: Death, Eroticism and the Public Sphere in the Nineteenth Century United States* (Durham and London: Duke University Press, 2001), p. xiii.
51 This is clearly demonstrated in Mantel's depiction of the psychiatric patients released from Fulmers Moor in *Vacant Possession* and the treatment of women within the Saudi Arabian context of *Eight Months on Ghazzah Street*.
52 This passage makes reference to a number of London's satellite towns, most notably Enfield, home of one of the most well-known narratives of suburban haunting, that of the Enfield Poltergeist.
53 Bill Brown, 'Thing Theory', *Critical Inquiry*, 28 (2001), 1–22 (p. 4).
54 Bill Brown, *A Sense of Things: The Object Matter of American Literature* (Chicago: Chicago University Press, 2003), p. 18.
55 Mantel, *Interview*, p. 292.
56 Castronovo, *Necro Citizenship*, p. xii.
57 Mantel, *Interview*, p. 292.
58 Johnson, 'Exemplary Differences', p. 26.
59 Christopher Morgan and David Smith, 'Coggan Brands Diana "A False Goddess with Loose Morals"', *Sunday Times*, 26 August 1998.
60 Richards, Wilson and Woodhead, 'Introduction', p. 6.
61 Knox, 'Giving Flesh to the "Wraiths of Violence"', p. 320.
62 Gordon, *Ghostly Matters*, p. 25.
63 James Joyce, 'The Universal Influence of the Literary Renaissance', in *James Joyce in Padua*, ed. and trans. by Louis Berron (London: Random House, 1977), p. 21.
64 Connor, 'Integuments', p. 32.
65 Fletcher, 'The Scenography of Trauma: A "Copernican" Reading of Sophocles', *Oedipus the King*', *Textual Practice*, 21(2007), 17–41 (p. 18).
66 Laplanche, 'A Short Treatise on the Unconscious', in *Essays on Otherness*, trans. by Luke Thurston, ed. by John Fletcher (London: Routledge, 1999), pp. 84–116 (p. 92).
67 Mike Davies, 'Gothic's Enigmatic Signifier: The Case of J. Sheridan Le Fanu's *Carmilla*', in *Seductions and Enigmas: Laplanche, Theory, Culture*, ed. by John Fletcher and Nicholas Ray (London: Lawrence and Wishart, 2014), pp. 159–75 (p. 172).
68 Connor, 'Integuments', p. 41.
69 Laplanche, 'Three Meanings of the Word "Unconscious" in the Framework of the General Theory of Seduction', in *Freud and the Sexual: Essays 2000-2006*, ed. by John Fletcher, trans. by John Fletcher, Jonathan House and Nick Ray (New York: International Psychoanalytic Books, 2011), pp. 203–22 (p. 208).
70 Anzieu, *The Skin Ego*, p. 40.
71 Ibid., p. 105.
72 Ibid.

73 Ibid., p. 11.
74 Ibid., p. 34.
75 Mantel's own conception of the Spirit world in operation in Beyond Black resonates powerfully with Alison's attempts to access her past and comprehend the communications of the ghosts who plague her. In preparatory notes for the novel she states: 'Spirit world is inside us, it is the territory of the collective unconscious and maybe of what is deeply repressed and denied. It is what we have forgotten – the things we don't remember even if we are prompted.' Hilary Mantel, MN1407, Hilary Mantel Papers, The Huntington Library, San Marino, California.
76 Anzieu, *The Skin Ego*, p. 40.
77 Ibid.
78 Fletcher, 'Scenography of Trauma', p. 36.
79 Sophocles, *Oedipus the King*, in *The Complete Greek Tragedies*, ed. by David Greene and Richmond Lattimore (Chicago: University of Chicago Press, 1991), pp. 9–77 (p. 55), l.1036.
80 For a more detailed exposition of this see Fletcher, 'The Scenography of Trauma', p. 36.
81 Mantel's approach to intertextuality evokes Alison's own mediumistic vocalization of the speech of others, stating that 'before I became utterly self-conscious about the process, other people's words were sliding into me and getting minced through my own psychic operations and now they are a natural mode for me and I don't put quotation marks around them in speech, I don't think of them as other'. Mantel, *Interview*, p. 266.
82 Anzieu, *The Skin Ego*, p. 40.
83 Catherine Belsey, 'The Death of the Reader', *Textual Practice*, 23 (2009), 201–14 (p. 202).

Chapter 5

1 Mantel, *Wolf Hall*, p. 649. All further references to this edition given in parentheses in the body of the text.
2 Hilary Mantel, interviewed by Sarah O'Reilly, 'Making It New', in *Wolf Hall* (London: Fourth Estate, 2010), pp. 2–9 (p. 6).
3 Tom Holland, 'Books of the Year', *Daily Telegraph*, 6 December 2009, <http://www.telegraph.co.uk/culture/books/6710158/Books-of-the-Year.html> (accessed 24 June 2015).
4 Christopher Taylor, '*Wolf Hall* by Hilary Mantel – Review', *Guardian*, 2 May 2009, <http://www.theguardian.com/books/2009/may/02/wolf-hall-hilary-mantel> (accessed 13 April 2015).

5   Byatt, 'Fathers', pp. 9–35 (p. 9).
6   B. D. Stoker, 'Bygonese: Is this Really the Authentic Language of Historical Fiction?' *New Writing*, 9 (2012), 308–18.
7   P. I. Kaufman, 'Dis-Manteling More', *Moreana*, 47 (2010), 164–93.
8   Byatt, 'Fathers', p. 10.
9   A. S. Byatt, 'Forefathers', in *On Histories and Stories: Selected Essays* (London: Chatto and Windus, 2000), pp. 36–64 (p. 38).
10 Byatt, 'Fathers', p. 9.
11 Ibid., p. 38. Here Byatt holds up Mantel as a writer of historical fiction (in this case *A Place of Greater Safety* (1992)) which appears at first 'innocently realist' but which in fact embodies 'an act of shocking rebellion against current orthodoxies'.
12 Jacques Derrida in Derrida and Stiegler, *Echographies*, p. 25.
13 I use 'translate' here not merely in its linguistic sense i.e 'To turn from one language into another'; 'to change into another language retaining the sense' (Johnson); 'to render'; also, 'to express in other words, to paraphrase', but also to invoke its other subordinate meanings which implicate a movement from one space and orientation to another. The term is also defined in the *Oxford English Dictionary* as 'to bear, convey, or remove from one person, place or condition to another; to transfer, transport' with a specific example of such usage being given as 'to remove the dead body or remains of a saint, or, by extension, a hero or great man, from one place to another'. Given the focus in *Wolf Hall* upon both the complexities of linguistic translation and the status of the dead and of saints, such a multifaceted understanding of 'translation' is appropriate.
14 Jerome de Groot, *Remaking History: The Past in Contemporary Historical Fiction* (London: Routledge, 2015), p. 21.
15 Ibid., p. 22.
16 Mantel, 'Making It New', p. 7.
17 Thomas Cromwell's 'Last Will and Testament' is transcribed in Roger Bigelow Merriman's *The Life and Letters of Thomas Cromwell* (Oxford: Oxford University Press, 2000), pp. 56–63. The version found in *Wolf Hall* clearly draws heavily on this document in terms of structure and content, often replicating the historical version. Yet, the fictive document contains a poignant reinstatement of a line which is crossed out in the original: 'And to my litill Doughters Anne and Grace'. Mantel's version includes 'marriage portions of [Cromwell's] daughter Anne, and his little daughter Grace' (p. 148) and thus brings together the acts of writing, dying, editing and remembering. As Merriman points out, these redacted references to Anne and Grace constitute all of the evidence we have that Cromwell had children other than his son Gregory.
18 Merriman, *The Life and Letters of Thomas Cromwell*, p. 60.
19 Stiegler, *Technics*, p. 177.

20 Ibid., p. 5.
21 Ibid., p. 140.
22 Jacques Derrida, 'The Art of Memoirs', trans. by Jonathan Culler, in *Memoirs for Paul de Man* (New York: Columbia University Press, 1989), pp. 45–88 (p. 59).
23 Ibid., p. 59.
24 Derrida and Stiegler, *Echographies*, p. 86.
25 Bernard Lamy quoted in Elizabeth Eisenstein, *Divine Art, Infernal Machine: The Reception of Printing in the West from First Impressions to the Sense of an Ending* (Oxford; Philadelphia: University of Pennsylvania Press, 2011), p. 47.
26 Ibid.
27 Derrida in Derrida and Stiegler, *Echographies*, p. 117.
28 Ibid. It is important to note that writing for Derrida does not only refer to physical inscription, though that is the manifestation I choose to focus on here. Rather, Derrida uses the term 'writing' or 'archi-writing', in tight collaboration with the terms 'trace', 'difference', and 'text', and considers that 'writing [names] properly the functioning of language in general'. Geoffrey Bennington in Geoffrey Bennington and Jacques Derrida, *Jacques Derrida*, trans. by Geoffrey Bennington (London; Chicago: University of Chicago Press, 1993), pp. 49–50.
29 Anthony Low, '*Hamlet* and the Ghost of Purgatory: Intimations of Killing the Father', *English Literary Renaissance*, 29 (1999), 443–67 (p. 450).
30 Stephen Greenblatt, *Hamlet in Purgatory* (Princeton; Oxford: Princeton University Press, 2001), p. 17.
31 Ibid., p. 152.
32 As Anthony Low puts it, 'after the English Reformers dispensed with Purgatory, however, it was no longer clear to anyone where ghosts came from. … Instead of doing away with ghosts the abolition caused them to flourish, at the same time that they became theologically inexplicable, vaguer', a statement that acknowledges both the persistence and unruly circulation of ghosts in the post-Purgatory period. Low, '*Hamlet* and the Ghost of Purgatory', p. 455.
33 King Henry himself acknowledges this permeability later in the novel, following the appearance to him in a dream of his dead brother King Arthur. When questioned as to the precise nature of the apparition, Henry asserts that 'during the twelve days, between Christmas Day and Epiphany, God permits the dead to walk. This is well known'. *Wolf Hall*, p. 274.
34 Two separate sources (P. Waterton, *Pietas Mariana Britannica* (London: Waterton, 1879) and E. Hoskins, *Horae Beatae Mariae Virginis* (London: Longmans, Green and Co, 1901)) attest that the scene Mantel depicts here is based on a real event, reporting that a visitor to Esher palace in 1529 did indeed discover Thomas Cromwell 'leaning in a window of the great chamber reading his hours'. John Harthan, *Books of Hours and their Owners* (London: Thames and Hudson, 1977), pp. 32–3.

35 Richard Rex, *Henry VIII and the English Reformation* (Basingstoke: Palgrave Macmillan, 2006), p. xvi.
36 The unique quality possessed by Books of Hours and their powerful connection to their owner is attested to in John Harthan's *Books of Hours and their Owners*. Harthan states that 'much of the charm of Books of Hours comes from the realization that each example was personally commissioned or bought, and decorated with greater or lesser elaboration according to the taste, status and wealth of the owner. Across the centuries they still preserve this connection, intimate and often revealing, with a specific individual'. p. 12.
37 Annotations and marginalia are widely found within medieval Books of Hours. For example, as Eamon Duffy notes 'almost half of the 300 Books of Hours in the Bibliothèque Nationale de France in Paris have manuscript annotations and additions of some sort, and it was very common indeed for English owners too to annotate their books'. Eamon Duffy, *Marking the Hours: English People and their Prayers, 1240-1570* (New Haven: Yale University Press, 2006), p. 38. While, as is apparent from Thomas More's prayer book, printed books too were subject to annotation by their owners, the annotations in Books of Hours most commonly detail history of ownership, family trees and heraldry etc, rather than reflecting on the contents of the book itself.
38 For a facsimile and transcription of More's heavily annotated Book of Hours and Latin Psalter see Louis L. Martz and Richard S. Sylvester's *Thomas More's Prayerbook: A Facsimile Reproduction of the Annotated Pages* (New Haven.: Yale University Press, 1969).
39 Jacques Derrida, 'Sarah Koffman (1934–94)', in *The Work of Mourning*, ed. by Pascale-Anne Brault and Michael Naas (London: University of Chicago Press, 2001), pp. 165–88 (p. 176).
40 At the opening of the passage Cromwell's interrogation of one of his fellow onlookers as to the nature of Joan Boughton's crime allows the religious convictions associated with the practice of Lollardy, for example the denial of transubstantiation and the refutation of the cult of saints, to be explicated: 'she is a Loller. That's one who says the God on the altar is a piece of bread. … She says the saints are but wooden posts' (p. 353).
41 For example, see Elizabeth Eisenstein's disavowal of the notion that, for the Protestant cause, print was merely an instrumental means to an end, in favour of an understanding of print as a 'pre-condition for the Protestant Reformation' for which 'the new medium was a precipitant'. Elizabeth L. Eisenstein, *The Printing Press as an Agent of Change* (Cambridge: Cambridge University Press, 1979), p. 310. Likewise, Alison Shell points out that the large body of printed counter-Reformation material has been 'unfairly marginalised' and argues that its presence points to a sustained Catholic engagement with print technology. Alison Shell, *Catholicism, Controversy*

    and the English Literary Imagination, 1558-1660 (Cambridge: Cambridge University Press, 1999), p. 13.
42. R. I. Moore, 'Literacy and the making of heresy c. 1000 - 1150', *Heresy and Literacy, 1000-1530,* ed.by Peter Biller and Anne Hudson, (Cambridge: Cambridge University Press, 1994), pp. 19–37 (p. 35).
43. Bob Scribner, 'Heterodoxy, Literacy and Print in the Early German Reformation', in *Heresy and Literacy, 1000-1530,* ed.by Peter Biller and Anne Hudson, (Cambridge: Cambridge University Press, 1994), pp. 255–78 (p. 257).
44. Cromwell's jealousy has an ironic quality here when considered alongside Eisenstein's point that 'The first ... campaign ever mounted by any government in any state in Europe to exploit fully the propaganda potential of the press was that conducted by Thomas Cromwell to back up the actions of Henry VIII'. Eisenstein, *The Printing Press,* p. 312.
45. Jesse M. Lander, *Inventing Polemic: Religion, Print and Literary Culture in Early Modern England* (Cambridge: Cambridge University Press, 2006), p. 15.
46. David Lowenstein, 'Writing and the Persecution of Heretics in Henry VIII's England: *The Examination of Anne Askew',* in *Heresy, Literature and Politics in Early Modern English Culture* (Cambridge: Cambridge University Press, 2006), pp. 11–39 (pp. 15–6).
47. Rex, *Henry VIII and the English Reformation,* p. 93.
48. Ibid. Not only were the products of the press subject to unregulated circulation, the press itself was often equally unstable since 'dissidents took advantage of the handpress whenever they could – installing it in secret places and moving it around'. Eisenstein, *Divine Art,* p. 33.
49. Harold Weber, *Paper Bullets: Print and Kingship under Charles II* (Lexington: University of Kentucky, 1996), pp. 137–9.
50. Joad Raymond, *Pamphlets and Pamphleteering in Early Modern Britain* (Cambridge: Cambridge University Press, 2003), pp. 204–5. Raymond argues here that early print productions, and pamphlets in particular, relied upon the 'summoning' (p. 27) of dead subjects to give their arguments weight, a technique which continued into the seventeenth century. 'Ghosts were revived to speak of the past and to incriminate or vindicate the present' and writers 'ventriloquized' ghosts to provide the voice for their own writing. I argue that Raymond's position should not just be understood in terms of a prosopopeic rhetorical device but hits upon a broader effect of print, that is its relationship with the supernatural and the phantasmal, its ability to conjure a multiplicity of ghosts.
51. The historic figure of Hugh Latimer was closely associated with Protestant martyr Robert Barnes whose work was reportedly recommended to Cromwell by his servant Stephen Vaughan. In a letter of 14 November 1531 Vaughan instructed Cromwell to 'look well upon Dr Barnes' book. It is such a piece of work that I

have not seen any like it. I think he shall seal it with his blood', reconfirming the very real linkages already demonstrated between the notion of corpse and corpus. Letter from Stephen Vaughan to Thomas Cromwell, *Letters and Papers, Foreign and Domestic, Henry VIII*, vol. 5, 1531–1532 (London: Her Majesties Stationary Office, 1880), p. 245.

52 It is particularly interesting that Mantel understands the text generally as disembodied and capable of permeating the self without recourse to material inscription, as this comment makes clear: 'You inhale texts, they're your atmosphere'. Hilary Mantel, *Email Interview - Answers*, in Lucy Arnold, 'Where the Ghosts of Meaning Are: Haunting and Spectrality in the Work of Hilary Mantel' (PhD Thesis, University of Leeds, 2016), p. 254.

53 The instability of a text, instituted either by the editing process or by the process of reading and interpretation, and the potentially stabilizing quality of print, is succinctly articulated in *Wolf Hall*'s sequel *Bring up the Bodies* in a discussion of Thomas Wyatt's poetry: '[Wyatt] jots a verse on some scrap of paper, and slips it to you, …. Then he slides a paper to some other person, and it is the same verse, but a word is different. Then that person says to you, did you see what Wyatt wrote? You say yes, but you are talking of different things. Another time you trap him and say, Wyatt, did you really do what you describe in this verse? He smiles and tells you, it is the story of some imaginary gentleman, no one we know; or he will say, this is not my story I write, it is yours, though you do not know it. … He will declare, you must believe everything and nothing of what you read' to which it is suggested that 'someone should take [Wyatt's] verses to the printer' on the basis that 'that would fix them'. Hilary Mantel, *Bring up the Bodies* (London: Fourth Estate, 2013), p. 413.

54 This understanding of the Mantelian ghost as, on one level, something that never happened, but could have, is perhaps where *Wolf Hall* most closely engages with the notion of haunting: 'beneath every history, another history' (p. 66). This conceptualization is fleshed out poignantly in *Giving up the Ghost*: 'When you turn and look back down the years, you glimpse the ghosts of other lives you might have led. All your houses are haunted by the person you might have been. … You think of the children you might have had but didn't. When the midwife says "It's a boy," where does the girl go? When you think you're pregnant, and you're not, what happens to the child that has already formed in your mind? You keep it filed in a drawer of your consciousness, like a short story that wouldn't work after the opening lines' (p. 20).

55 The issue of translation and the vernacular Bible as a text associated with Protestantism is ironically alluded to in *Fludd*, strikingly with reference to the idea of the 'unmarked quotation' as Father Angwin admits that 'he thought it on the whole dangerous to disabuse his flock of the notion that the Bible is a Protestant book, and had tended to leave his quotations unattributed' (*Fludd*, p. 75).

56 When it is considered that the passage continues 'suppose the human skull were to become capacious, spaces opening inside it, chambers humming like bee hives', a striking still-life is created from the objects of skull, books and desk that recalls the contents of Holbein the Younger's famous painting 'The Ambassadors'. The significance of Holbein's work for Mantel's intertextual strategy is explored fully below but it is useful to note that this reference alludes to a painting which is profoundly intertextual in its own right, including as it does images of Martin Luther's translation of a hymn book alongside a book of mathematics by Peter Apian.

57 In her book *Intertextuality: Debates and Contexts*, Mary Orr usefully identifies how the term intertextuality has come to obscure the myriad of techniques which produce it. Mary Orr, *Intertextuality: Debates and Contexts* (Cambridge: Polity Press, 2003), p. 14.

58 Julia Kristeva, *Desire in Language: A Semiotic Approach to Literature and Art*, ed. by Leon S. Roudiez (New York: Colombia University Press, 1980), p. 36, p. 66.

59 Mantel, *Email Interview*, p. 254. It is pertinent for our understanding of Mantel as both legatee and legator that she goes on to state that, among other functions, her use of intertexts 'allows [her] to acknowledge the unseen influence of (mostly) dead writers'. This formulation leads to a positioning of Mantel's literary influences as both mainly deceased but also, perhaps, only 'mostly' dead, suggesting their post-mortem persistence.

60 A passage conjecturing the response of King Henry's deceased brother, Arthur, to the progress of Henry's divorce includes the sentence: 'But are [Arthur's] small bones stirring in their tomb at Worcester saying that was not it? That was not it at all?', an allusion to the phrase 'That is not what I meant at all, that is not it at all' present in Eliot's 'Prufrock' poem. Hilary Mantel, MN1836, Hilary Mantel Papers, The Huntington Library, San Marino, California.

61 Lander, *Inventing Polemic*, p. 29.

62 The earliest known use of quotation marks can be found in a copy of Flavius Philostratus's *De Vitis Sophistarum*, printed in 1516, in Strasburg. Unlike in contemporary usage, these early quotation marks were set in the margins of printed texts in order to indicate a line which contained a quotation. Douglas McMurtrie, *Concerning Quotation Marks* (New York: Privately Published, 1934), p. 4.

63 Scribner, 'Heterodoxy, Literacy and Print in the Early German Reformation', p. 256.

64 Ibid., p. 276.

65 The significance of this historical and literary context for the exploration of textuality as unavoidably intertextual is underlined by Mary Orr's assessment that 'commentary, translation, exegesis, all return pre-modern views on interpretation and interpreting reference texts, including the bible, to the post-modern world of texts and intertextuality'. Orr, *Intertextuality*, p. 17.

66 Orr, *Intertextuality*, p. 148.
67 'translation, n.' OED Online. Oxford University Press, June 2015. Web. 6 July 2015.
68 This passage resonates with Mantel's own description of her approach to her writing process of which she says 'the remnants linger … bob back into another story, or intrude themselves into another medium … Nothing's wasted. Nothing's gone. Nothing's lost'. Hilary Mantel, *Email Interview – Answers*, in Lucy Arnold, 'Where the Ghosts of Meaning Are: Haunting and Spectrality in the Work of Hilary Mantel' (PhD Thesis, University of Leeds, 2016), p. 259.
69 Roland Barthes, *The Pleasure of the Text*, trans. by Richard Millar (New York: Hill and Wang, 1975), p. 64.
70 Orr, *Intertextuality*, p. 130.
71 Ibid., p. 135.
72 Patricia O'Connor, 'Holy Terrors', *The New York Times*, 2 July 2000, <https://www.nytimes.com/books/00/07/02/reviews/000702.02oconnt.html> (accessed 24 June 2015).
73 For a biography of the historical Robert Fludd see Tita French Baumlin, 'Robert Fludd', *The Dictionary of Literary Biography, Volume 281: British Rhetoricians and Logicians, 1500–1660*, Second Series (Detroit: Gale, 2003), pp. 85–99.
74 Derrida and Stiegler, *Echographies*, p. 24.
75 Book of Tobit, 5.5–6.
76 It is interesting to note that this use of visual intertexts reappears in *Wolf Hall* as Mantel describes several renowned paintings by Hans Holbein the Younger, including the famous depiction of Cromwell himself and Holbein's most prominent work, 'The Ambassadors' (p. 370), an oblique reference to which was noted earlier. In a gesture which mirrors her reinstatement of Anne and Grace Cromwell in Thomas Cromwell's fictionalized will, Mantel includes a lengthy passage describing a group portrait of Thomas More and family which is now lost, its existence only indicated by preparatory sketches and copies by other artists. The description includes the narrator's observation that 'the painter has grouped them so skilfully that there's no space between the figures for anyone new. The outsider can only soak himself into the scene, as an unintended blot or stain' (p. 230). This construction recalls strikingly the anamorphic skull present in 'The Ambassadors'. For more on Mantel's treatment of the More family portrait see de Groot, *Remaking History*, p. 24.
77 T. S. Eliot, 'The Love Song of J. Alfred Prufrock', in *Collected Poems, 1909-1962* ed. Thomas Stearns Eliot, (London: Faber and Faber, 1963), p. 13.
78 Ardis Butterfield, 'Introduction', in *Citation, Intertextuality and Memory in the Middle Ages and Renaissance*, ed. by Yolanda Plumley, Giuliano Di Bacco and Stefano Jossa, 2 vols (Exeter: University of Exeter Press, 2011), p. ii, pp. 1–5 (p. xiii).
79 de Groot, *Remaking History*, p. 31.

Afterword

1. Hilary Mantel, MN1244, Hilary Mantel Papers, The Huntington Library, San Marino, California.
2. Janice Radway, 'Foreword', in Avery F. Gordon, *Ghostly Matters: Haunting and the Sociological Imagination* (Minneapolis: University of Minnesota Press, 2008), pp. vii–xii (p. xi).
3. Colin Davis, '*Etats Present*: Hauntology, Spectres and Phantoms', in *The Spectralities Reader: Ghosts and Haunting in Contemporary Culture,* ed. by Maria del Pilar Blanco and Esther Peeren, (London: Bloomsbury, 2013), pp. 57–8.
4. Avery F. Gordon, *Ghostly Matters: Haunting and the Sociological Imagination* (University of Minneapolis: Minnesota Press, 1996), p. 22.
5. Mantel, *Interview*, Appendix 4, p. 276.
6. Ibid.
7. Hilary Mantel, 'Terminus', in *The Assassination of Margaret Thatcher* (London: Fourth Estate, 2014), pp. 193–202.
8. Hilary Mantel, MN43, Hilary Mantel Papers, The Huntington Library, San Marino, California.

Bibliography

Primary sources

Mantel, Hilary, *Beyond Black* (London: Fourth Estate, 2005).
Mantel, Hilary, 'Destroyed', in *Learning to Talk* (London: Harper Perennial, 2006), pp. 21–44.
Mantel, Hilary, *Every Day is Mother's Day* (London: Fourth Estate, 2006).
Mantel, Hilary, *Eight Months on Ghazzah Street* (London: Harper Perennial, 2004).
Mantel, Hilary, *Fludd* (London: Fourth Estate, 2010).
Mantel, Hilary, *Giving up the Ghost: A Memoir* (London: Fourth Estate, 2010).
Mantel, Hilary, *Ink in the Blood: A Hospital Diary* (London: Fourth Estate, 2010).
Mantel, Hilary, 'King Billy is a Gentleman', in *Learning to Talk* (London: Harper Perennial, 2006), pp. 1–20.
Mantel, Hilary, 'Sorry to Disturb', in *The Assassination of Margaret Thatcher* (London: Fourth Estate, 2014), pp. 1–36.
Mantel, Hilary, *Vacant Possession* (London: Fourth Estate, 2006).
Mantel, Hilary, *Wolf Hall* (London: Fourth Estate, 2010).

Secondary sources

'The Devil's Work: Hilary Mantel's Ghosts', *The New Yorker*, Monday 25 July 2005, <www.newyorker.com/magazine/2005/07/25/devils-work> (accessed 3 September 2015).
'Giving up the Ghost: A Memoir', *Publisher's Weekly*, 14 July 2003, <www.publishersweekly.com/978-0-8050-7472-7> (accessed 3 September 2015).
'The Man Booker Prize: Facts and Figures', <themanbookerprize.com/facts-figures> (accessed 18 June 2016).
Addley, Esther, 'So Bad It's Good', *The Guardian*, 15 June 2007, <www.theguardian.com/society/2007/jun/15/childrensservices.biography> (accessed 15 January 2016).
Algar, Hamid, *Wahhabism: A Critical Essay* (Oneonta, NY: Islamic Publications, 2002).
Althusser, Louis, *On Ideology*, trans. by Ben Brewster (London: Verso, 2008).
Alvarez, Anne, *Live Company: Psychoanalytic Psychotherapy with Autistic, Borderline, Deprived and Abused Children* (London: Tavistock/Routledge, 1992).

Anderson, Hephzibah, 'Hilary Mantel: On the Path from Pain to Prizes', *The Observer*, 19 April 2009, <www.theguardian.com/books/2009/apr/19/hilary-mantel-man-booker> (accessed 15 December 2015).

Anderson, Linda, 'At the Threshold of the Self: Women and Autobiography', in *Women's Writing: A Challenge to Theory*, ed. by Moira Monteith (Brighton: Harvester, 1986), pp. 54–71.

Anzieu, Didier, *The Skin Ego* (London: Yale University Press, 1989).

Arnold, Lucy, 'Where the Ghosts of Meaning Are: Haunting and Spectrality in the Work of Hilary Mantel' (PhD Thesis: University of Leeds, 2016).

Baker, Charley, *Madness in Post-1945 British and American Fiction* (London: Palgrave, 2010).

Baron-Cohen, Simon and John E. Harrison (eds), *Synaesthesia: Classic and Contemporary Readings* (Oxford: Blackwell, 1997).

Barthes, Roland, *The Pleasure of the Text*, trans. by Richard Millar (New York: Hill and Wang, 1975).

Bartlett, Peter and David Wright, 'Community Care and Its Antecedents', in *Outside the Walls of the Asylum: The History of Care in the Community 1750–2000*, ed. by Peter Bartlett and David Wright (London: Athlone Press, 1999), pp. 1–18.

Baumlin, Tita F., 'Robert Fludd', in *The Dictionary of Literary Biography, Volume 281: British Rhetoricians and Logicians, 1500–1660*, 2 (Detroit: Gale, 2003).

Belsey, Catherine, 'The Death of the Reader', *Textual Practice*, 23 (2009), 201–14.

Benstock, Shari, *The Private Self: Theory and Practice of Women's Autobiographical Writings* (Chapel Hill: University of North Carolina Press, 1988).

Bigelow Merriman, Roger, *The Life and Letters of Thomas Cromwell* (Oxford: Oxford University Press, 2000).

Biller, Peter, 'Heresy and Literacy: Earlier History of the Theme', in *Heresy and Literacy, 1000–1530*, ed. by Peter Biller and Anne Hudson (Cambridge: Cambridge University Press, 1994), pp. 1–18.

Bloom, Clive, *Gothic Horror* (London: Macmillan, 1988).

Botting, Fred, 'In Gothic Darkly: Heterotopia, History, Culture', in *A Companion to the Gothic*, ed. by David Punter (London: Blackwell, 2000), pp. 3–14.

Brace, Marianne, 'Hilary Mantel: The Exorcist', *Telegraph*, 10 May 2003, <www.independent.co.uk/artsentertainment/books/features/hilary-mantel-the-exorcist-590258.html> (accessed 3 September 2015).

Briggs, Julia, 'The Ghost Story', in *A Companion to the Gothic*, ed. by David Punter (Oxford: Blackwell, 2000), pp. 122–31.

Brooke, Rupert, *The Complete Poems of Rupert Brooke* (London: Sidgwick & Jackson, Ltd, 1934).

Brotchie, Jane, 'Do We Care Who Cares? – The Neglect of those Who Look after the Ill at Home', *The Guardian*, 7 September 1988.

Brown, Bill, *A Sense of Things: The Object Matter of American Literature* (Chicago: Chicago University Press, 2003).

Brown, Bill, 'Thing Theory', *Critical Inquiry*, 28 (2001), 1–22.
Butler Yeats, William, 'The Lake Isle of Innisfree', in *The Collected Works of W.B Yeats*, ed. by Richard J. Finneran and George Mills Harper, 3 vols (Basingstoke: Macmillan, 1991).
Butterfield, Ardis, 'Introduction', in *Citation, Intertextuality and Memory in the Middle Ages and Renaissance*, ed. by Yolanda Plumley, Giuliano Di Bacco and Stefano Jossa, 2 vols (Exeter: University of Exeter Press, 2011), ii (2011), pp. 1–5.
Byatt, Antonia Susan, 'Fathers', in *On Histories and Stories: Selected Essays* (London: Chatto and Windus, 2000), pp. 9–35.
Byatt, Antonia Susan, 'Forefathers', in *On Histories and Stories: Selected Essays* (London: Chatto and Windus, 2000), pp. 36–64.
Carpenter, Siri, 'Everyday Fantasia: The World of Synaesthesia', *Monitor on Psychology* 32 (2001) <www.apa.org/monitor/mar01/synesthesia.aspx> (accessed 14 September 2015).
Castronovo, Russ, *Necro Citizenship: Death, Eroticism and the Public Sphere in the Nineteenth Century United States* (Durham and London: Duke University Press, 2001).
Clendinnen, Inga, *Tiger's Eye: A Memoir* (Melbourne: Text Publishing, 2000).
Clendinnen, Inga, 'Unsuited to Everything', The New York Times, 5 October 2003, <www.nytimes.com/2003/10/05/books/unsuited-to-everything.html?pagewanted=all> (accessed 16 November 2012).
Connor, Steven, 'Integuments: The Scar, the Skin and the Screen', *New Formations*, 39 (1999), 32–54.
Corcoran, Stephen, 'Introduction', in Jacques Rancière, *Dissensus: On Politics and Aesthetics* (London: Continuum, 2010), pp. 1–26.
Coward, Ros, 'The Heaven and Hell of Mothering: Mothering and Ambivalence in the Mass Media', in *Mothering and Ambivalence*, ed. by Wendy Holloway and Brid Featherstone (London: Routledge, 1997), pp. 111–18.
Cytowic, Richard E., *The Man Who Tasted Shapes* (Cambridge: MIT Press, 2003).
Cytowic, Richard E. and David M. Eagleman, *Wednesday Is Indigo Blue: Discovering the Brain of Synaesthesia* (Cambridge: MIT Press, 2011).
Davies, Mike, 'Gothic's Enigmatic Signifier: The Case of J. Sheridan Le Fanu's *Carmilla*', in *Seductions and Enigmas: Laplanche, Theory, Culture*, ed. by John Fletcher and Nicholas Ray (London: Lawrence and Wishart, 2014), pp. 159–75.
Davis, Colin, 'Etats Present: Hauntology, Spectres and Phantoms', in *The Spectralities Reader: Ghosts and Haunting in Contemporary Culture*, ed. by Esther Peeren and Maria del Pilar Blanco (London: Bloomsbury, 2013), pp. 57–8.
Davis, Colin, *Haunted Subjects: Deconstruction, Psychoanalysis and the Return of the Dead* (Basingstoke: Palgrave, 2007).
De Groot, Jerome, *Remaking History: The Past in Contemporary Historical Fictions* (London: Routledge, 2015).

Derrida, Jacques, 'The Art of Memoirs', in *Memoirs for Paul de Man*, trans. by Jonathan Culler (New York: Columbia University Press, 1989), pp. 45–88.

Derrida, Jacques, *Demeure: Fiction and Testimony*, trans. by Elizabeth Rottenberg (Stanford: Stanford University Press, 2000).

Derrida, Jacques, 'Passions: 'An Oblique Offering', in *Derrida: A Critical Reader*, ed. by David Wood (Oxford: Blackwell, 1992), pp. 5–35.

Derrida, Jacques, *Resistances of Psychoanalysis*, trans. by Peggy Kamuf, Pascale-Anne Brault and Michael Naas (Stanford: Stanford University Press, 1998).

Derrida, Jacques, 'Sarah Koffman (1934–1994)', in *The Work of Mourning*, ed. by Pascale-Anne Brault and Michael Naas (London: University of Chicago Press, 2001), pp. 165–88.

Derrida, Jacques, *Spectres of Marx: The State of Debt, the Work of Mourning and the New International* (London: Routledge, 2006).

Derrida, Jacques and Bernard Stiegler, *Echographies of Television: Filmed Interviews*, trans. by Jennifer Bajorek (Cambridge: Polity Press, 2002).

Duffy, Eamon, *Marking the Hours: English People and their Prayers, 1240–1570* (New Haven: Yale University Press, 2006).

Eisenstein, Elizabeth, *Divine Art, Infernal Machine: The Reception of Printing in the West from First Impressions to the Sense of an Ending* (Oxford and Philadelphia: University of Pennsylvania Press, 2011).

Eisenstein, Elizabeth, *The Printing Press as an Agent of Change* (Cambridge: Cambridge University Press, 1979).

Eliot, Thomas Stearns, 'The Love Song of J. Alfred Prufrock', in *Collected Poems, 1909–1962* (London: Faber and Faber, 1963), pp. 13–17.

Ellis, Kate Ferguson, *The Contested Castle: Gothic Novels and the Subversion of Domestic Ideology* (Urbana: University of Illinois Press, 1989).

Enns, Anthony, 'The Undead Author: Spiritualism, Technology and Authorship', in *The Ashgate Research Companion to Spiritualism and the Occult*, ed. by Tatiana Kontou and Sarah Wilburn (Farnham: Ashgate, 2012), pp. 55–78.

Featherstone, Brid, 'I wouldn't do your Job: Women, Social Work and Child Abuse', in *Mothering and Ambivalence*, ed. by Wendy Holloway and Brid Featherstone (London: Routledge, 1997), pp. 167–92.

Featherstone, Brid, 'The Scenography of Trauma: A "Copernican' Reading of Sophocles" *Oedipus the King*', *Textual Practice*, 21 (2007), 17–41.

Flower MacCannell, Juliette, *The Regime of the Brother: After Patriarchy* (London: Routledge, 1991).

Frosh, Stephen, 'Haunting: Psychoanalysis and Ghostly Transmissions', *American Imago*, 69 (2012), 241–64.

Fry, Geoffrey K., *The Politics of the Thatcher Revolution: An Interpretation of British Politics, 1979–1990* (London: Palgrave Macmillan, 2008).

Galvan, Jill, 'The Victorian Post-Human: Transmission, Information and the Séance', in *The Ashgate Research Companion to Nineteenth-Century Spiritualism and the*

Occult, ed. by Tatiana Kontou and Sarah Willburn (Surrey: Ashgate, 2012), pp. 79–96.

Gardiner, James, *Letters and Papers, Foreign and Domestic, Henry VIII, Vol. 5, 1531–1532* (London: Her Majesties Stationary Office, 1880).

Gasché, Rodolph, 'The Witch Meta-Psychology', in *Returns of the French Freud: Freud, Lacan and Beyond*, ed. by Todd Dufresne, trans. by Julian Patrick (New York: Routledge, 1997).

Goffman, Erving, *Asylums: Essays on the Social Situation of Mental Patients and Other Inmates* (New Brunswick: Aldine Transactions, 2007).

Gordon, Avery F., *Ghostly Matters: Haunting and the Social Imagination* (Minneapolis: University of Minnesota Press, 1997).

Gordon, Avery F., *Ghostly Matters: Haunting and the Social Imagination* (Minneapolis: University of Minnesota Press, 2008).

Greenblatt, Stephen, *Hamlet in Purgatory* (Princeton and Oxford: Princeton University Press, 2001).

Kaufman, Peter Iver, 'Dis-Manteling More', *Moreana*, 47 (2010), 164–93.

Krips, Henry, 'The Politics of the Gaze: Foucault, Lacan, Žižek', *Culture Unbound*, 2 (2010), 91–102.

Harthan, John, *Books of Hours and their Owners* (London: Thames and Hudson, 1977).

Hastings, Chris, 'Thatcher "murder" is BBC's Book at Bedtime', *Daily Mail*, 13 December 2014, <www.dailymail.co.uk/news/article-2873006/Thatcher-murder-BBC-s-Book-Bedtime-Radio-4-ignores-protests-author-s-sick-perverted-fantasy-coveted-broadcast-slot.html> (accessed 29 February 2016).

Hay, Simon, *A History of the Modern British Ghost Story* (Basingstoke: Palgrave Macmillan, 2011).

Henke, David, 'Suicide Claim Leads to Social Security Debate', *The Guardian*, 21 June 1985.

Hey, Valery, 'New Labour, New Britain and the "Dianaization" of Politics', in *Mourning Diana: Nation, Culture and the Performance of Grief*, ed. by Adrian Kear and Deborah Lynn Steinberg (London: Routledge, 1999), pp. 60–107.

Hill, Michael, *The Welfare State in Britain: A Political History Since 1945* (Aldershot: Edward Elgar, 1993).

Hillman, James, 'The Bad Mother, An Archetypal Approach', in *Fathers and Mothers*, ed. by P. Berry (Dallas: Spring Publications, 1990).

Holland, Tom, 'Books of the Year', *Daily Telegraph*, 6 December 2009, <www.telegraph.co.uk/culture/books/6710158/Books-of-the-Year.html> (accessed 24 June 2015).

Hoskins, Edgar, *Horae Beatae Mariae Virginis* (London: Longmans, Green and Co, 1901).

Howes, Marjory, 'Introduction', in *The Cambridge Companion to W.B. Yeats*, ed. by Marjorie Howes and John Kelly (Cambridge: Cambridge University Press, 2007), pp. 1–18.

Hughes, Kathryn, 'Ghost Stories', *The Guardian*, 10 May 2003, <www.theguardian.com/books/2003/may/10/featuresreviews.guardianreview18> (accessed 3 September 2015).

Hughes, Sarah, 'Out with Vampires, in with Haunted Houses: The Ghost Story is Back', *The Guardian*, 24 October 2015, <www.theguardian.com/books/2015/oct/24/out-with-vampires-in-with-haunted-houses-ghost-stories-are-back> (accessed 08 July 2016).

Hunsaker Hawkins, Anne, *Reconstructing Illness: Studies in Pathography*, 2nd edn (West Lafayette: Purdue University Press, 1999).

Idleman Smith, Jane and Yvonne Yazbeck Haddad, *The Islamic Understanding of Death and Resurrection* (Oxford: Oxford University Press, 2002).

Irwin, Robert, 'Review of Eight Months on Ghazzah Street, by Hilary Mantel' *Time Out* (London: Time Out Group, 1988).

Jacobus, Mary, *First Things: The Maternal Imaginary in Literature, Art and Psychoanalysis* (New York: Routledge, 1995).

Jenkins, Peter, 'How the Policies of Decay May Stir Britain Towards a New Beginning', *The Guardian*, 28 December 1984.

Johnson, Richard, 'Exemplary Differences: Mourning (and Not Mourning) a Princess', in *Mourning Diana: Nation, Culture and the Performance of Grief*, ed. by Adrian Kear and Lynn Steinberg (London: Routledge, 1999), pp. 15–39.

Kahane, Claire, 'The Gothic Mirror', in *The (M)other Tongue: Essays on Feminist Psychoanalytic Interpretation*, ed. by Shirley Nelson Garner, Claire Kahane and Madelon Sprengnether (Cornell: Cornell University Press, 1985).

Kear, Adrian, 'Diana between Two Deaths: Spectral Ethics and the Time of Mourning', in *Mourning Diana: Nation, Culture and the Performance of Grief*, ed. by Adrian Kear and Lynn Steinberg (London: Routledge, 1999), pp. 169–86.

Kear, Adrian and Deborah Lynn Steinberg, 'Ghost Writing', in *Mourning Diana: Nation, Culture and the Performance of Grief*, ed. by Adrian Kear and Lynn Steinberg (London: Routledge, 1999), pp. 1–14.

Knox, Sara, 'Giving Flesh to the 'Wraiths of Violence': Super Realism in the Work of Hilary Mantel', *Australian Feminist Studies*, 25 (2010), 313–23.

Lacan, Jacques, *The Four Fundamental Concepts of Psychoanalysis*, ed. by Jacques Alain Miller, trans. by Alan Sheridan (London: Vintage, 1998).

Lander, Jesse M., *Inventing Polemic: Religion, Print and Literary Culture in Early Modern England* (Cambridge: Cambridge University Press, 2006).

Landsberg, Alison, *Prosthetic Memory: The Transformation of American Remembrance in the Age of Mass Culture* (New York: Columbia University Press, 2004).

Laplanche, Jean, 'A Short Treatise on the Unconscious', in *Essays on Otherness*, trans. by Luke Thurston, ed. by John Fletcher (London: Routledge, 1999), pp. 84–116.

Laplanche, Jean, 'Three Meanings of the Word "Unconscious" in the Framework of the General Theory of Seduction', in *Freud and the Sexual: Essays 2000–2006*, ed. by John Fletcher, trans. by John Fletcher, Jonathan House and Nick Ray (New York: International Psychoanalytic Books, 2011), pp. 203–22.

Larkin, Philip, *Collected Poems* (London: Faber and Faber, 2003).
Lebedeva, Kristina, 'Review Article: Bernard Stiegler, *Technics and Time, 2: Disorientation* (Stanford University Press, 2008)', *Parrhesia*, 7 (2009), 81–5.
Long, David E., *The Culture and Customs of Saudi Arabia* (Westport: Greenwood, 2005).
Low, Anthony, '*Hamlet* and the Ghost of Purgatory: Intimations of Killing the Father', *English Literary Renaissance*, 29 (1999), 443–67.
Lowe, Rodney, *The Welfare State in Britain* (London: Palgrave Macmillan, 2005).
Lowenstein, David, 'Writing and the Persecution of Heretics in Henry VIII's England: *The Examination of Anne Askew*', in *Heresy, Literature and Politics in Early Modern English Culture*, ed. by David Lowenstein and John Marshal (Cambridge: Cambridge University Press, 2006).
Luckhurst, Roger, 'The Contemporary London Gothic and the Limits of the Spectral Turn', *Textual Practice*, 16 (2002), 527–46.
Mantel, Hilary, 'Author, Author', *The Guardian*, 24 May 2008, <www.theguardian.com/books/2008/may/24/1> (accessed 11 April 2016).
Mantel, Hilary, 'In Conversation', interview with Eileen Pollard, 'What Is Done and What Is Declared: Origin and Ellipsis in the Writing of Hilary Mantel' (Unpublished Doctoral Thesis: Manchester Metropolitan University, 2013).
Mantel, Hilary, 'An Evening with Hilary Mantel', Manchester Metropolitan University, Manchester, 30 September 2015.
Mantel, Hilary, 'Hilary Mantel – The SRB Interview', interview by Colin Waters, *Scottish Review of Books* 5 (2009) <www.scottishreviewofbooks.org/index.php/back-issues/volume-five/volume-five-issue-four/295-hilary-mantel-the-srb-interview> (accessed 10 September 2014).
Mantel, Hilary, 'A Kind of Alchemy: Sarah O'Reilly talks to Hilary Mantel', interview by Sarah O'Reilly, in *Fludd* (London: Fourth Estate, 2010), pp. 2–11.
Mantel, Hilary, 'Last Morning in Al Hamra', *Spectator*, 14 August 2012, <http://blogs.spectator.co.uk/2012/08/lastmorning-in-al-hamra-shiva-naipaul-prize-1987> (accessed 03 May 2015).
Mantel, Hilary, 'Making It New', interview by Sarah O'Reilly, in Hilary Mantel, *Wolf Hall* (London: Fourth Estate, 2010), pp. 2–9.
Mantel, Hilary, 'P.S. Ideas, Interviews, Features', interview with Fanny Blake, in Hilary Mantel, *Giving up the Ghost: A Memoir* (London: Harper Perennial, 2004).
Mantel, Hilary, 'Royal Bodies', *London Review of Books*, 35 (2013), 3–7.
Mantel, Hilary, 'Veiled Threats', *The Guardian*, 11 September 2004, <www.theguardian.com/books/2004/sep/11/featuresreviews.guardianreview23> (accessed 3 May 2015).
Mantel, Hilary, 'The Woman in the Hall', in Hilary Mantel, *Every Day is Mother's Day* (London: Harper Perennial, 2006), pp. 10–13.
Marinovich, Sarolta, 'The Discourse of the Other: Female Gothic in Contemporary Women's Writing', *Neohelicon*, 21 (1994), 189–205.
Martz, Louis L. and Richard S. Sylvester, *Thomas More's Prayerbook: A Facsimile Reproduction of the Annotated Pages* (New Haven: Yale University Press, 1969).
McLuhan, Marshal, *Understanding Media* (Cambridge: MIT, 1994).

McMurtrie, Douglas, *Concerning Quotation Marks* (New York: Privately Published, 1934).
Michaud, Ginette, 'Literature in Secret: Crossing Derrida and Blanchot', *Angelaki: Journal of Theoretical Humanities*, 7 (2002), 69–89.
Miller, Alisa, 'Rupert Brooke and the Growth of Commercial Patriotism in Great Britain 1914–1918', *Twentieth Century British History*, 21 (2010), 141–62.
Miller, Nancy K., 'The Entangled Self: Genre Bondage in the Age of Memoir', *PMLA*, 122 (2007), 237–48.
Moore, R. I, 'Literacy and the making of heresy *c*. 1000 – 1150' in *Heresy and Literacy, 1000–1530*, eds Peter Biller and Anne Hudson, (Cambridge: Cambridge University Press, 1994), pp. 19–37.
Morgan, Christopher and David Smith, 'Coggan Brands Diana "A False Goddess with Loose Morals"', *Sunday Times*, 26 August 1998.
Nelson, Ben, '"Inadequate" Community Care Attacked: House of Lords, Parliament', *Times (London)*, 8 December 1988.
Nikolić, Danko, 'Is Synaesthesia Actually "Ideasthesia": An Investigation into the phenomenon', in *Proceedings of the Third International Congress on Synaesthesia, Science and Art* (Granada, Spain, 2009) <www.danko-nikolic.com/wp-content/uploads/2011/09/Synesthesia2009-Nikolic-Ideaesthesia.pdf> (accessed 14 September 2015).
Noll, Richard, *Vampires, Werewolves and Demons: Twentieth Century Reports in the Psychiatric Literature* (New York: Bruner/Mazel, 1992).
O'Connor, Patricia, 'Holy Terrors', *The New York Times*, 2 July 2000, <www.nytimes.com/books/00/07/02/reviews/000702.02oconnt.html> (accessed 24 June 2015).
Orr, Mary, *Intertextuality: Debates and Contexts* (Cambridge: Polity Press, 2003).
Parker, Roszika, *Torn in Two: The Experience of Maternal Ambivalence* (London: Virago, 1995).
Payne, Sarah, 'Outside the Walls of the Asylum? Psychiatric Treatment in the 1980s and 1990s', in *Outside the Walls of the Asylum: The History of Care in the Community 1750–2000*, ed. by Peter Bartlett and David Wright (London: Athlone Press, 1999), pp. 244–65.
Peeren, Esther, *The Spectral Metaphor: Living Ghosts and the Agency of Invisibility* (London: Palgrave, Macmillan, 2014).
Peeren, Esther and Maria del Pilar Blanco (eds), *The Spectralities Reader: Ghosts and Haunting in Contemporary Cultural Theory* (London: Bloomsbury, 2013).
Pollard, Eileen, '"But at Second Sight the Words Seemed Not So Simple" (Virginia Woolf, 1929): Thickening and Rotting Hysteria in the Writing of Hilary Mantel and Virginia Woolf', *The Virginia Woolf Miscellany*, 80 (2011), 24–6.
Pollard, Eileen, 'What Is Done and What Is Declared: Origin and Ellipsis in the Writing of Hilary Mantel' (Unpublished Doctoral Thesis, Manchester Metropolitan University, 2013).
Prodromou, Amy, 'Writing the Self into Being: Illness and Identity in Inga Clendinnen's *Tiger's Eye* and Hilary Mantel's *Giving up the Ghost*', in *Identity*

and Form in Contemporary Literature, ed. by Ana Maria Sánchez-Arce (London: Routledge, 2014), pp. 195–209.
Rancière, Jacques, *Dissensus: On Politics and Aesthetics*, trans. by Stephen Corcoran (London: Continuum, 2010).
Rancière, Jacques, *The Politics of Aesthetics: The Distribution of the Sensible*, ed. and trans. by Gabriel Rockhill (London: Bloomsbury, 2013).
Rancière, Jacques, *Short Voyages to the Land of the People*, trans. by James B. Swenson (Stanford: Stanford University Press, 2003).
Raymond, Joad, *Pamphlets and Pamphleteering in Early Modern Britain* (Cambridge: Cambridge University Press, 2003).
Rex, Richard, *Henry VIII and the English Reformation* (Basingstoke: Palgrave Macmillan, 2006).
Richards, Jeffrey, Scott Wilson and Linda Woodhead, 'Introduction', in *Diana: The Making of a Media Saint* (London: I.B. Tauris, 1999), pp. 1–19.
Riddell, Peter, *The Thatcher Decade: How Britain Has Changed in the 1980s* (Oxford: Basil Blackwell, 1989).
Ruez, Derek, 'Partitioning the Sensible at Park 51: Rancière, Islamophobia and Common Politics', *Antipode*, 2 (2013), 1128–47.
Saunders, Max, *Self-Impression: Life-Writing, Autobiografiction and the Forms of Modern Literature* (Oxford: Oxford University Press, 2013).
Sconce, Jeffrey, *Haunted Media: Electronic Presence from Telegraphy to Television* (Durham: Duke University Press, 2002).
Scribner, Bob, 'Heterodoxy, Literacy and Print in the Early German Reformation', in *Heresy and Literacy, 1000–1530*, ed. by Peter Biller and Anne Hudson (Cambridge: Cambridge University Press, 1994), pp. 255–78.
Sedgwick, Eve Kosofsky, *The Coherence of Gothic Conventions* (London: Methuen, 1980).
Shakespeare, William, *Hamlet, Norton Critical Edition*, ed. by Robert S. Miola (London: W.W. Norton, 2011).
Shell, Alison, *Catholicism, Controversy and the English Literary Imagination, 1558–1660* (Cambridge: Cambridge University Press, 1999).
Shengold, Leonard, *Soul Murder: The Effects of Childhood Abuse and Deprivation* (London: Yale University Press, 1989).
Sherman, Jill, 'Fears for Former Patients / Mental Health Association Calls for Greater Supervision of People Discharged from Psychiatric Hospitals', *The Times (London)*, 11 August 1986.
Sophocles, 'Oedipus the King', in *The Complete Greek Tragedies*, ed. by David Greene and Richard Lattimore (Chicago: University of Chicago Press, 1991), pp. 9–77.
Stiegler, Bernard, *Technics and Time*, trans. by Richard Beardsworth and George Collins (Stanford: Stanford University Press, 2011).
Stoker, Bryony D., 'Bygonese: Is this Really the Authentic Language of Historical Fiction?' *New Writing*, 9 (2012), 308–18.

Taylor, Christopher, 'Wolf Hall by Hilary Mantel – Review', *The Guardian*, 2 May 2009, <www.theguardian.com/books/2009/may/02/wolf-hall-hilary-mantel> (accessed 13 April 2015).

Thatcher, Margaret, 'Speech at Conservative Party Conference (plus address to overflow meeting)', <www.margaretthatcher.org/document/104717> (accessed 27 May 2016).

Thatcher, Margaret, 'Speech to the Conservative Political Centre Summer School', 6 July 1979, <www.margaretthatcher.org/document/104107> (accessed 16 January 2016).

Thatcher, Margaret, 'Speech to the Conservative Women's Conference', 25 May 1988, <www.margaretthatcher.org/document/107248> (accessed 27 May 2016).

Thatcher, Margaret, 'Speech to the Canadian and Empire Clubs in Toronto', 27 September 1983, <www.margaretthatcher.org/document/105443> (accessed 27 May 2016).

Thatcher, Margaret, 'Speech to the National Society for the Prevention of Cruelty to Children', 16 May 1984, < www.margaretthatcher.org/document/105682> (accessed 27 May 2016).

Thatcher, Margaret, 'Press Conference for American correspondents in London', 25 June 1980, <www.margaretthatcher.org/Speeches/displaydocument.asp?docid=104389&doctype=1> (accessed 16 January 2016).

Thatcher, Margaret, 'Remarks on Becoming Prime Minister (St Francis's Prayer)', 4 May 1979, <www.margaretthatcher.org/document/104078> (accessed 21 April 2016).

Thatcher, Margaret, 'TV Interview for HTV George Thomas *in Conversation*', 13 September 1983, <www.margaretthatcher.org/document/105188> (accessed 27 May 2016).

Thatcher, Margaret, 'TV Interview for *The Weekend World* ('Victorian Values')', 19 January 1983, <www.margaretthatcher.org/document/105087> (accessed 16 January 2016).

Toynbee, Polly, 'There is No Hiding Place. I Feel I am Losing my Mind. There is Nowhere else for him to go, Even for a few Days – Just One Cry for Help / Focus on the Association of Carers', *The Guardian*, 10 December 1984.

Tsur, Reuven, 'Issues in Literary Synaesthesia', *Style*, 47 (2007), 30–51.

Turner, Alwyn W., *A Classless Society: Britain in the 1990s* (London: Aurum, 2013).

Waterton, P., *Pietas Mariana Britannica* (London: Waterton, 1879).

Weber, Harold, *Paper Bullets: Print and Kingship under Charles II* (Lexington: University of Kentucky, 1996).

Welshman, John, 'Rhetoric and Reality: Community Care in England and Wales, 1948–1974', in *Outside the Walls of the Asylum: The History of Care in the Community 1750–2000*, ed. by Peter Bartlett and David Wright (London: Athlone Press, 1999), pp. 204–26.

Wilson, Leigh, 'The Cross-Correspondences, the Nature of Evidence and the Matter of Writing', in *The Ashgate Research Companion to Nineteenth Century Spiritualism and the Occult*, ed. by Tatiana Kontou and Sarah Wilburn (Surrey: Ashgate, 2012), pp. 97–122.

Winnicott, Donald W., 'Hate in Countertransference', *International Journal of Psychotherapy*, 30 (1949), 69–74.

Wolfreys, Julian, *Victorian Hauntings: Spectrality, Gothic and the Uncanny* (London: Palgrave, 2002).

Woolf, Virginia, *A Room of One's Own and Three Guineas* (London: Chatto and Windus, 1984).

Yagoda, Ben, *Memoir: A History* (New York: Riverhead, 2009).

Žižek, Slavoj, 'The Big Other Doesn't Exist', *The Journal of European Psychoanalysis*, 5 (1997) <www.psychomedia.it/jep/number5/zizek.htm> (accessed 18 December 2015).

Žižek, Slavoj, *The Sublime Object of Ideology* (London: Verso, 1989).

Index

Althusser, Louis 84, 92–4
Anzieu, Didier 110, 136–7, 139, 142
asylum 64, 67, 196 n.57. *See also* psychiatric care
autobiography 13–14, 22, 24, 40–1, 188 n.22, 188 n.29. *See also* memoir
   Derrida 29, 31–2, 188 n.23
   Eight Months on Ghazzah Street 84, 107
   Giving up the Ghost 2, 9, 13, 16–19, 31–2, 187 n.2

Bible 25, 50–1, 159, 162–3
   and intertextuality 165, 213 n.55, 214 n.65
Books of Hours 152–4, 210 n.34, 211 nn.36–38
Bronte, Emily 172
   Wuthering Heights 172–3

care in the community 46, 68–9, 73, 77, 80
Cromwell, Anne 171, 178, 183, 209 n.17, 215 n.76
Cromwell, Elizabeth 152–4, 160, 166, 168, 171
Cromwell, Grace 152–3, 171, 176, 183, 209 n.17, 215 n.76
Cromwell, Thomas 151–5, 166–7, 177, 181, 212 n.51, 215 n.76
   and Last Will and Testament 148–50, 170–1, 209 n.17
   and print culture 157–60, 162–3, 212 n.44

Derrida, Jacques 6, 147, 171
   and autobiography 9, 17, 22, 29–31, 180, 188 n.23, 210 n.28
   and textuality 150–1, 156

Eliot, T. S.
   The Lovesong of J. Alfred Prufrock 165, 172–3, 214 n.60
endometriosis 16, 19, 34

gothic 47, 49, 80, 85, 107, 185 n.8
   heroine 76–8, 101, 103–4, 196 n.80
   history of 45–6, 49, 67, 192 n.2, 193 n.3, 196 n.6
   and Mantel 5, 10–11, 43–5, 62–4, 71, 180, 185 n.14, 192 n.3, 199 n.13
grief 52–3, 59, 123

Henrician Reformation. *See* Protestant Reformation
historical fiction/novel 8, 145–8, 179, 181, 209 n.11
history 7, 11, 108, 110, 119, 121–2, 145–8, 176–7, 213 n.54
Hodgson Burnett, Frances
   The Secret Garden 28, 30–3

inheritance 119, 147–51, 156, 164, 171, 175–7, 181
intertextuality 140, 143, 173–4
   history of 165–6, 214 n.57, 214 n.65
   and life writing 20–2, 24, 31
   and Mantel 4, 208 n.81
   Wolf Hall 145–6, 165–8, 176
Irishness 22–4, 31, 189 n.36

Lacan, Jacques 9, 18, 92–3
Laplanche, Jean 135–6
Larkin, Phillip 114, 140, 142
life writing. *See* autobiography; memoir
Lollardy 157–8, 211 n.40

Mantel, Hilary
   Beyond Black 3, 11, 109–11, 179, 180, 182–3
   and the dead 197 n.71, 208 n.75

and Diana Spencer 109, 123, 125
and history 106, 119–22
and intertextuality 141–2
and mediumship 51–2, 85, 111, 115–17
and social death 129, 131, 133–4
and trauma 136–7, 139
Bring up the Bodies 1, 11, 213 n.53
Eight Months on Ghazzah Street 8, 10–11, 83, 109, 180
 and gothic 85–6, 100, 104, 199 n.13
 and politics 87–9, 92–3, 95, 99, 101, 107, 202 n.57
 and social death 90–1, 181, 201 n.28, 201 n.30, 207 n.51
 and spectrality 84, 86, 93–4, 99, 202 n.56
Every Day is Mother's Day 1, 43–7, 64, 81, 84
 and changelings 79–80
 and feeding/eating 57–8
 and houses 47–8, 50, 194 n.23, 194 n.30, 198 n.77, 203 n.61
 and mediumship 51–2
 and motherhood 54–6, 59–63, 195 n.47
 and psychiatric care 64–6
 and social care 73, 78, 195 nn.51, 52
Fludd 21, 25, 147, 150, 165, 168–76, 182, 185 n.14, 213 n.55
Giving up the Ghost 2, 9, 12–14, 40–2, 179–80, 183
 and ghosts 17–18, 21, 26–7, 30, 84, 190 n.47, 213 n.54
 and illness 16, 20, 31, 34, 188 n.17
 and intertextuality 22–5, 31, 140, 143, 189 n.36, 189 n.44
 and *The Secret Garden* 28, 31–3
 and synaesthesia 35–9, 191 n.66
Learning to Talk 9, 22–4, 143
 'Clean Slate' 41
 'Destroyed' 21, 26–7
 'King Billy is a Gentleman' 21–4, 26–7
 'Terminus' 182
A Place of Greater Safety 1, 147, 209 n.11

Vacant Possession 1, 43–4, 46–8, 81
 and Care in the Community 68–72
 and changelings 79–80
 and feeding/eating 56–7
 and ghosts 27, 50–1, 53, 83–4, 197 n.67, 203 n.61
 and motherhood 49, 54, 60
 and psychiatric care 64–7, 207 n.51
 and social care 73–8, 195 n.51, 197 n.68
Wolf Hall 1, 11, 178, 181–2
 and ghosts 3, 147, 176, 210 n.33, 213 n.54, 215 n.76
 and historical fiction 145–6, 148, 176–7
 and intertextuality 21, 143, 147, 164–6, 168–71, 174
 and print 146, 148–51, 155–6, 158–64
 and Purgatory 151–2
media 4, 109–12, 118–22
 and Diana Spencer 123–9, 131–2, 206 n.38
 and Mantel 44, 206 n.38
medium 11, 51–3, 109–20, 122, 125–7, 129, 132–3, 143
memoir 13–27, 180, 187 n.3, 188 n.22, 189 n.32
 and *Giving up the Ghost* 1, 3, 9, 29–37, 39–42, 84–5
 and *Learning to Talk* 189 n.36, 191 n.70
memory 14, 17, 81, 110, 125, 181
 and history 149, 158
 prosthetic 119–20, 122–3, 126, 205 n.24
 and trauma 134, 137–8
Moor, Thomas 154–6, 162–3, 167, 170, 211 nn.37, 38, 215 n.76
motherhood 41–5, 47, 54–5, 60–1, 194 n.25, 195 n.47
 and feeding/eating 56–9
 and gothic 45, 50, 53, 55, 76, 79, 193 n.10
 and pregnancy 49
mourning 125, 181, 205 n.36

Oedipus 141–2

poltergeist   59, 63, 88, 96, 98, 202 n.56, 207 n.52
Princess Diana. *See* Diana Spencer
print   152–3, 155–9, 162–4, 213 n.53
   and Books of Hours   154–5, 211 n.37
   and intertextuality   165–7, 214 n.62
   print culture   125, 146, 150, 159–61, 176, 181, 212 n.50
   and Protestant Reformation   211 n.41, 212 n.44
printing press   146, 160–2, 211 n.41, 212 n.44
prosthetic memory. *See* memory
Protestant Reformation   11, 125, 146–7, 150–6, 159–69, 173, 176, 211 n.41
psychiatric care   10, 46, 54, 64–8, 196 n.57, 197 n.68
Purgatory   11, 146, 151–3, 163, 210 n.32

Rancière, Jacques   8–10, 85–9, 95, 101, 107, 199 n.11

Sadler, Rafe   148–50
Saudi Arabia   34, 83–92, 94–5, 98–9, 104–5, 108, 200 n.18
séance   51–3, 59–61, 115–17, 134–5
Shakespeare, William
   Hamlet   142, 172–3
   Richard II   142
   Richard III   71–2

skin   11, 109–11, 119–22, 134–43, 155
social care   10, 44, 46–7, 71–3, 76–7
social death   129, 131, 133, 140
Spencer, Diana   109, 123–9, 131–3, 135, 206 n.38
spirit medium. *See* medium
spiritualism   51, 53, 109, 127
   and technology   110–12, 115–16, 204 n.10, 204 n.19, 206 n.45
Stiegler, Bernard   8–9, 125–6, 149–50, 205 n.24
synaesthesia   33, 35–9, 191 nn.64–66

technics   9, 125, 150
tele-technologies   11, 109–11, 115–17, 119–27, 143, 180
textiles   160, 164, 166–8, 176
Thatcher, Margaret   44–8, 60, 68, 71–3, 76, 193 n.13, 195 n.47, 196 nn.60, 61
translation   148–51, 159, 162–6, 176–7, 209 n.13, 213 n.55, 214 n.65
trauma   27–31, 39, 51–3, 60–4, 134–8, 141, 195 n.51
Tyndale, William   149, 159–64, 176

Wahhabi Islam   10, 83, 89, 102, 103
Wolsey, Thomas (Cardinal)   155–6, 167, 170
Wyatt, Thomas   11, 213 n.53

www.ingramcontent.com/pod-product-compliance
Lightning Source LLC
Chambersburg PA
CBHW052036300426
44117CB00012B/1841